Painting Landscapes

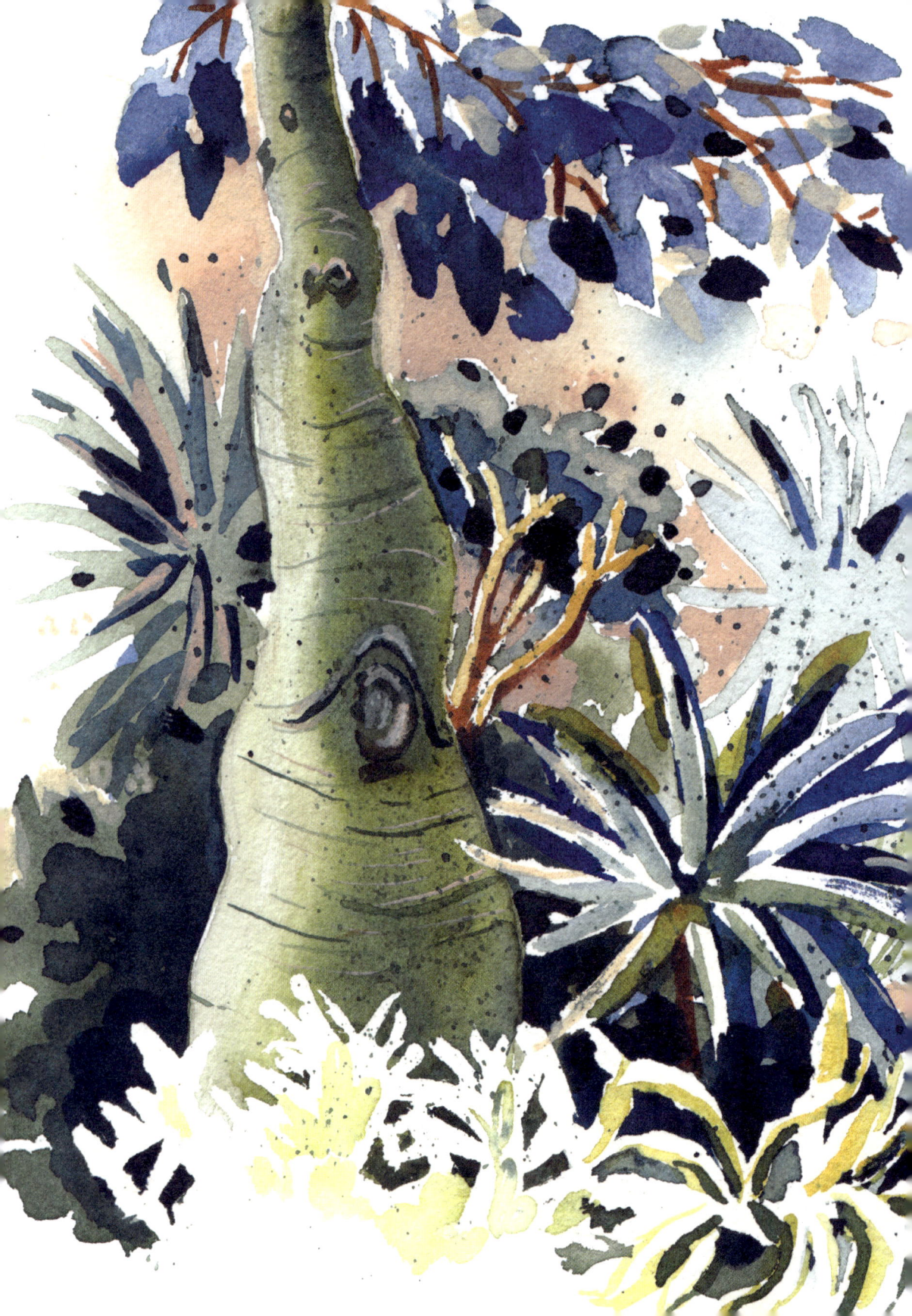

Painting Landscapes

CONNECT TO CALM THROUGH THE BEAUTY OF WATERCOLOUR

Inga Buividavice

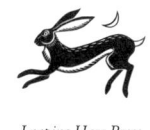

Leaping Hare Press

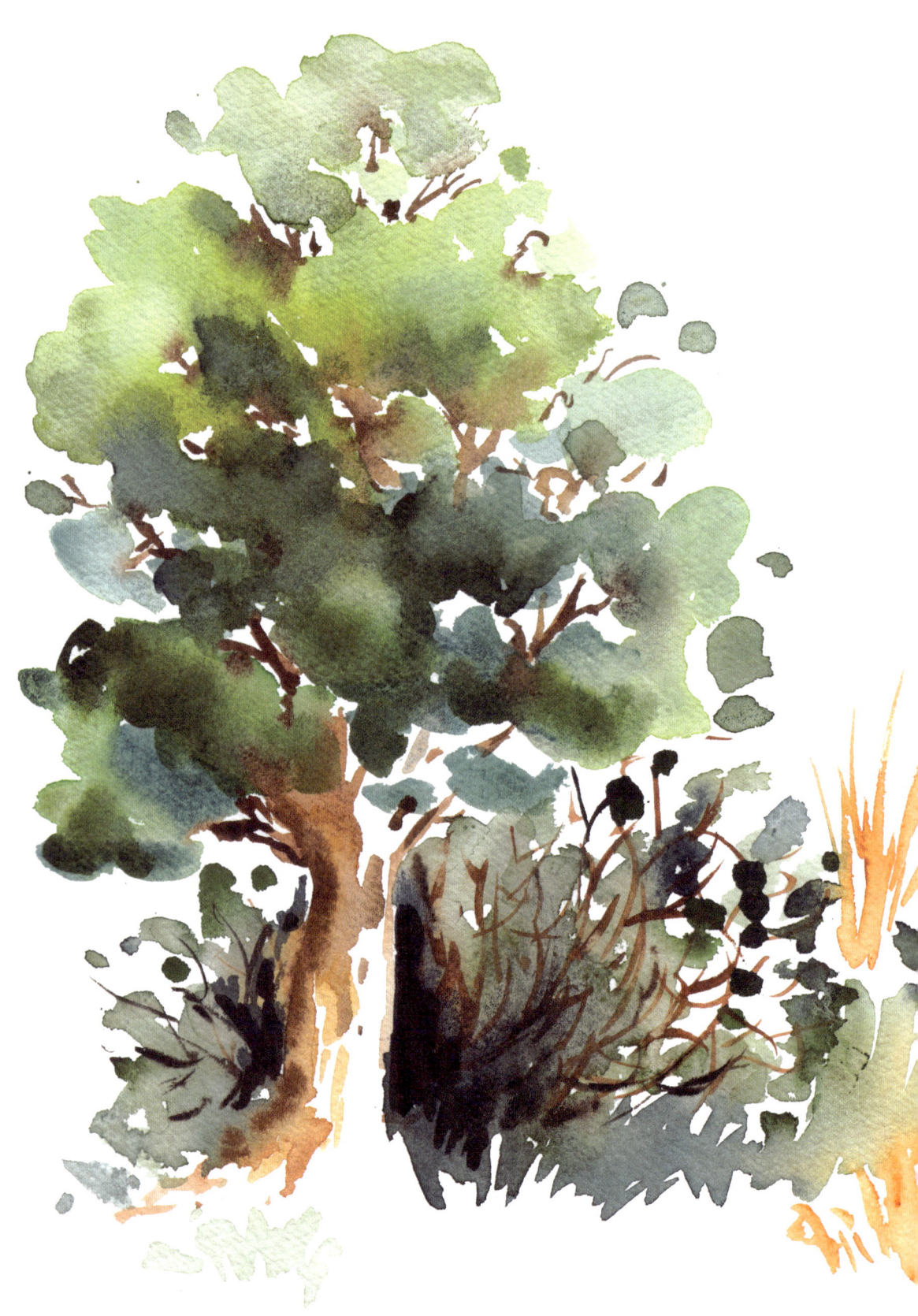

Contents

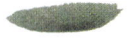

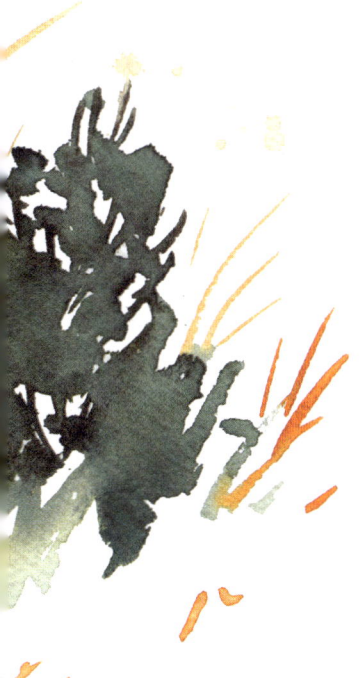

Introduction

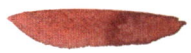

Painting watercolour landscapes is a blend of learnt technique, spontaneous artistic impulse, problem-solving, happy accident, and the unique behaviour of the medium itself. Needless to say, results can vary in quality, even for an experienced artist. In this book, I will teach you practical tips and techniques, but you will bring the other elements yourself.

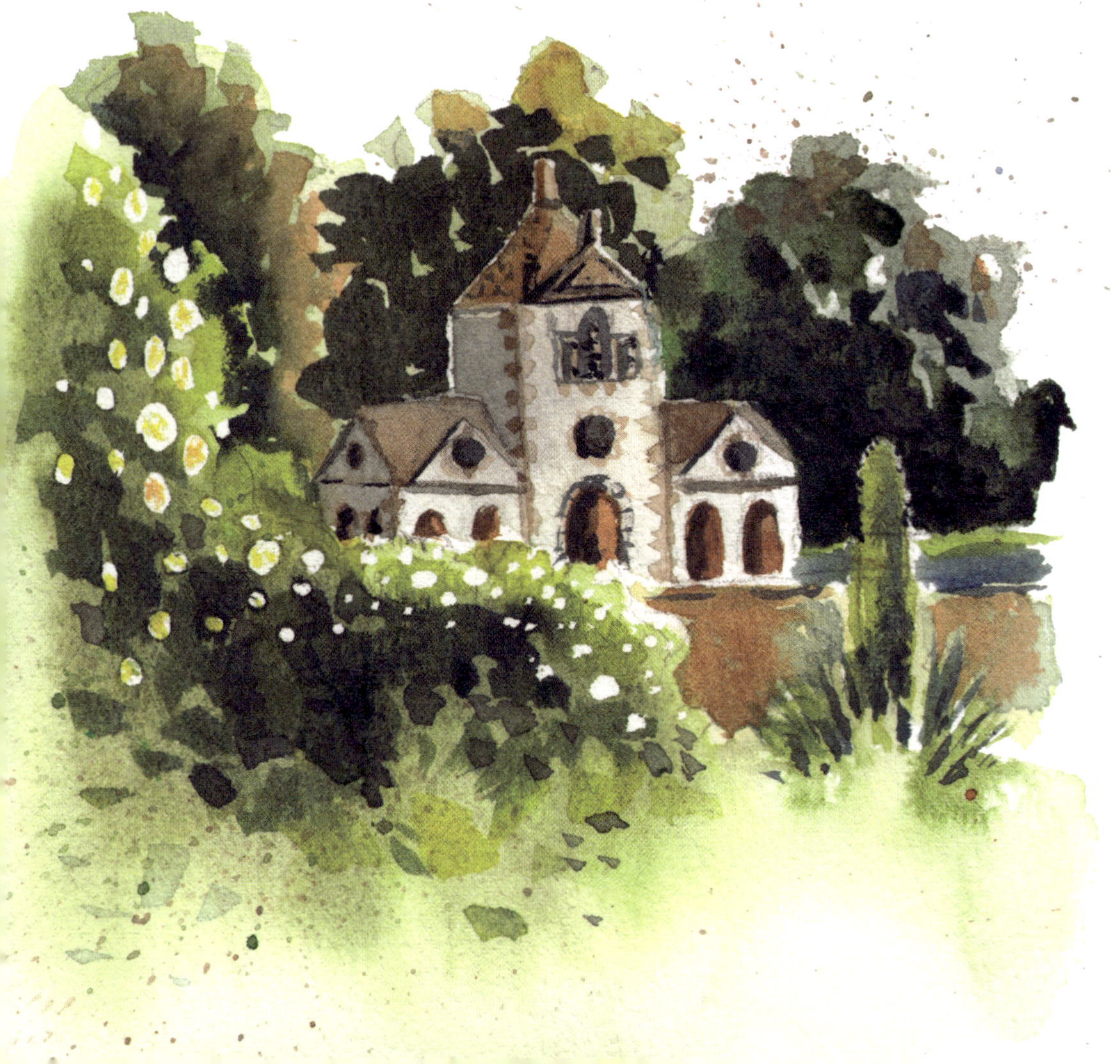

Besides teaching watercolour techniques and artistic principles, my mission is to inspire people to start painting with watercolour, and then to stick to it. I especially want to address beginners who may not feel confident and believe that being an artist requires some sort of special talent. I flinch when someone says, 'You are so talented', as this is not really what it's about; in all the work I've produced, I've been through so many ups and downs – and just when I think I've finally got it all figured out, I go downhill again. This has happened to me enough times now to know that the process is never linear; however, it does take less time and effort to bounce back up, which in turn inspires me with the confidence not to give up. I suggest looking at painting not as something you need to perfect, but as a practice for you to enjoy (even in times of frustration). Come to this place with no expectations and watch the magic happen. Most importantly, learn to love the process, because at the end of the day, what really matters is the enjoyment you get from painting.

When I first started painting watercolour landscapes, I was tasked with figuring out a new topic and how to approach it from different angles using this medium. Whilst my discoveries are fresh, I have put them together in this book for anyone who wants to follow the same path into landscape painting.

This is not a book about building a career as an artist and illustrator – though that still might happen regardless! It is a book that will help you to understand some basic techniques, and to encourage you to be happy with your work and feel inspired to carry on developing your style and building creative habits.

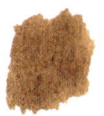 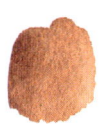 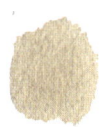   

Why landscapes?

Painting landscapes naturally leads to spending more time outside. And being outside offers so many benefits, including improved mental and physical health. Even without scientific data to back this up, we can feel the positive effects on ourselves: the boost in mood from sunlight, or the simple pleasure of breathing fresh air in a quiet forest, far from carbon-polluted cities. We are all a part of the natural world, and spending time outdoors makes us feel calmer and at peace.

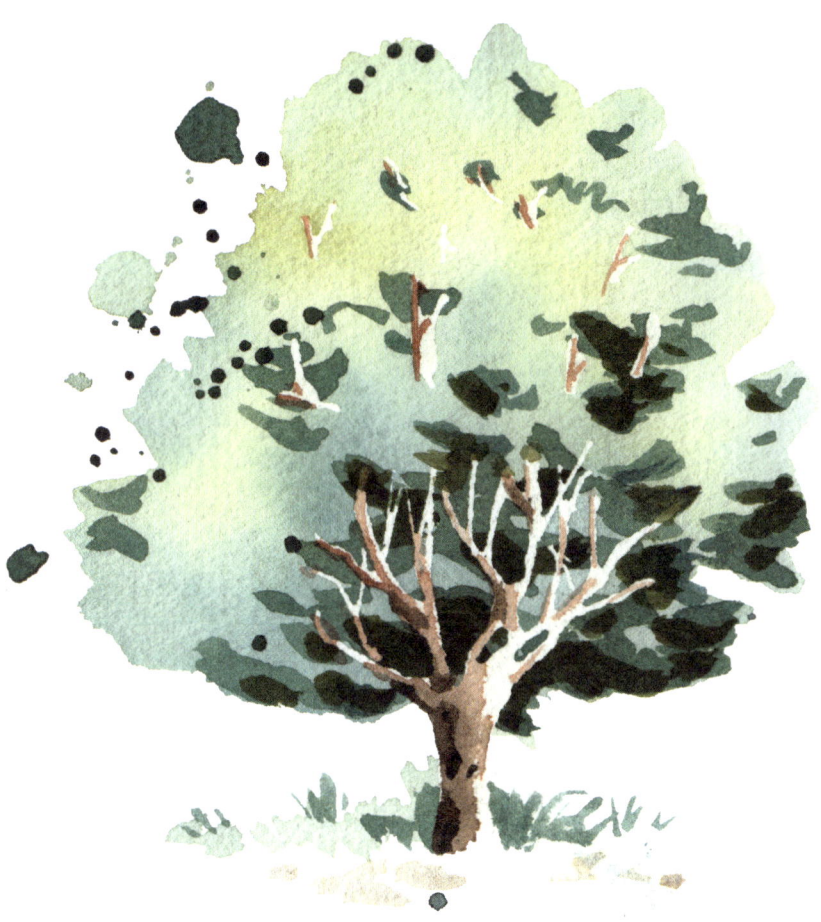

This realization came to me through painting. I didn't start painting nature because I was constantly outside and couldn't help noticing all the beautiful things around me. It was quite the opposite: I started spending more time in nature looking for inspiration, and ultimately created a deep connection with it.

Painting landscapes is a brilliant way of cultivating creativity whilst also embracing and benefitting from the natural world around you. It requires you to understand how to paint the different elements and combine them all together in a harmonious composition. And luckily you can practise this skill easily, because landscapes are everywhere!

When you begin to paint, you develop an eye for interesting compositions, colours and moods, which you carry with you wherever you go. You have a sharper attention to detail, and will notice subtle differences between various trees and flowers, and can then take this experience and transfer it to paper.

We don't all see the world the same way, so it's only natural that you paint what interests you most. With every brushstroke you put on paper, you are capturing the state of your mind at that moment, the mood you were in while observing the scenery. Even your brushwork may shift from day to day which brings us to something profound: you are painting not only shapes and colours, but deeply personal memories and emotions. In this way, your paintings become a very personal diary of your feelings.

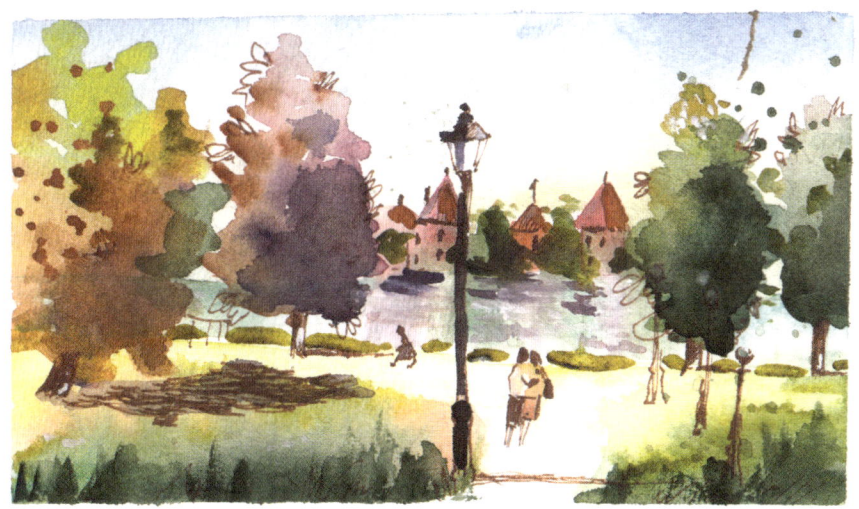

Starting with watercolours

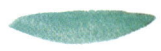

Watercolour as a medium has become increasingly popular over recent years, especially amongst beginners who want to try their hand at painting. Whilst being highly accessible, it is quite a complex media that allows very little room for mistakes. Once your paint is down on paper, it's hard to remove, and most of the time the best course of action is to start a new painting.

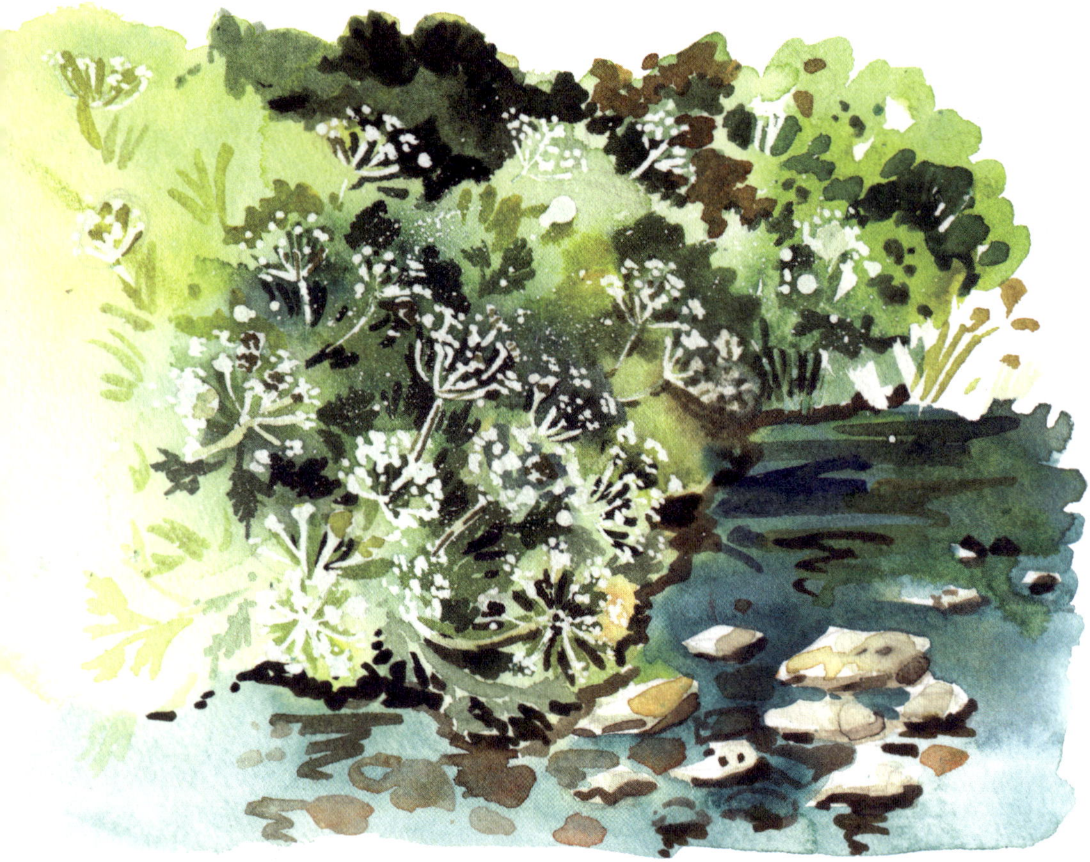

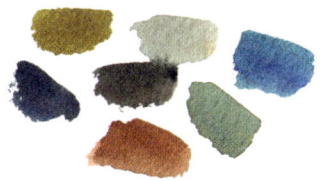

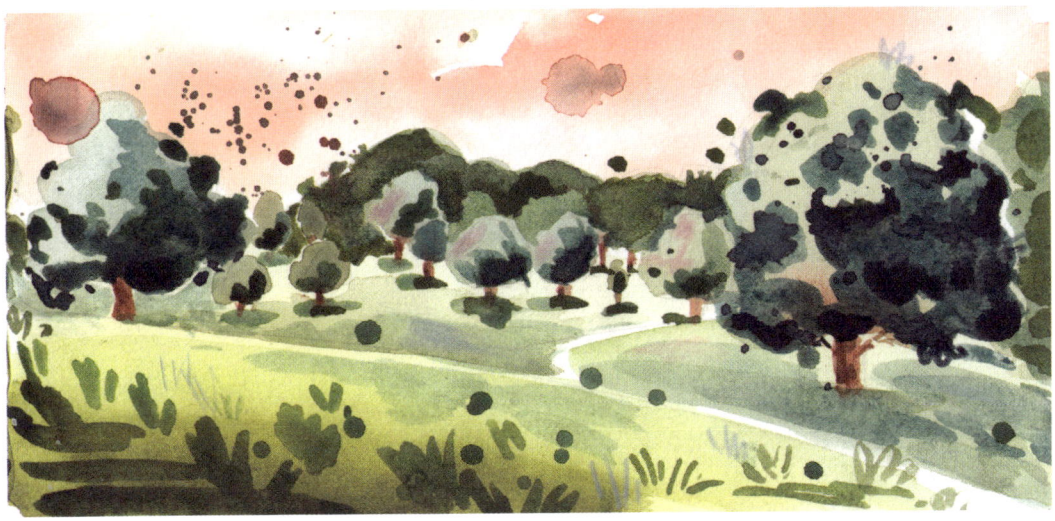

Watercolour painting requires planning. Most paintings are done in layers, working from lightest to darkest and using the white of the paper as highlight. So how do you approach a media that is hard to control, edit, and requires lots of thinking before you even start?

Don't let it scare you. Watercolour is also unpredictably beautiful, and often creates amazing washes on its own. The planning part you will get the hang of pretty quickly, as you start to try a few projects, whilst the hard-to-edit part, in my opinion, is what works to your advantage.

Have you ever seen street artists that spray paint so precisely and get the perfect result from their first attempt? This is because they have done it so many times that it becomes second nature. I am not saying that you have to practise the same painting over and over again, but repeating certain steps does make it easier to get things 'right' more often than not. And please note that when I say 'right', I only mean a desired result, because there is no right or wrong in art.

Supplies

Choosing art supplies is a highly personal matter and it depends on your preferences and habits around creating art. If you are always on the go, a good sketchbook and small painting palette would be the best option, along with travel brushes with lids. If you like painting at home, larger watercolour sets would be more convenient.

Regardless of the format, your painting will be a lot easier if your supplies are of the best quality. Here is an overview of the various supplies you will need.

Essentials

PAINT

Watercolour paints come in both tubes and pans. Tubes are my favourite, as the colours are more saturated and you can buy large amounts of a single colour. When you buy individual tubes, you will need a separate empty watercolour tin or plastic case with pans to squeeze paint into them. For the beginner, as you may still be deciding which colours you're leaning towards, it is best to start with a pan, containing a smaller amount of a range of colours. Later, you can start creating your own colour palette by only buying the colours you like and use the most.

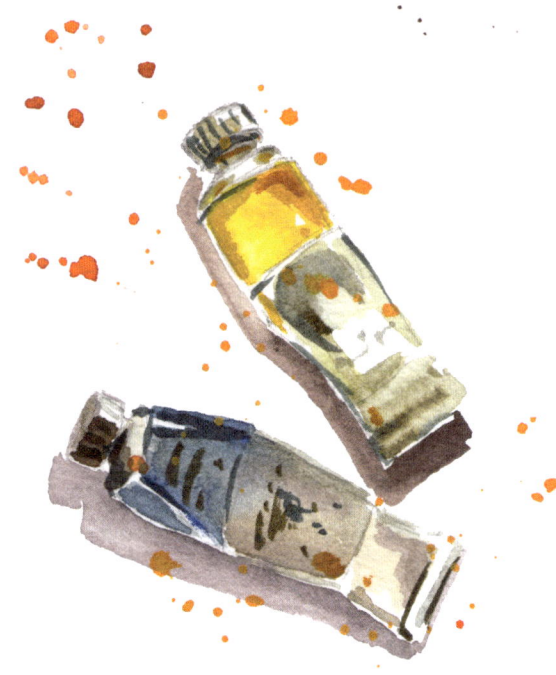

PAPER

Over the years I have discovered many different types of watercolour paper. I have learned that the biggest improvement to my painting comes when I use good-quality artist-grade paper. While I stand by this, I also find that for some types of painting I can get away with student-grade paper (or even mixed media paper), which also makes experimenting with different ideas a lot cheaper.

As a standard choice for artists, the ideal weight of watercolour paper is 300 gsm (140 lb); anything less will buckle, although a little buckling in a sketchbook is fine.

Paper should be 100 per cent cotton (as opposed to cellulose), which slows colour drying and allows maximum pigment manipulation.

Watercolour paper comes in three different textures: hot-pressed (smooth), cold-pressed (textured) and rough (rough textured). Cold-pressed is an optimal choice, while rough can allow for more interesting textures.

Hot-pressed paper is rapid drying, giving you less time to manipulate pigment, but it can be good for mixed media, especially watercolour and ink pens.

PALETTE

I usually mix colours directly in my watercolour case of watercolours, so I don't keep a lot of extra supplies around me while painting. Occasionally, when I need additional mixing space, I prefer a ceramic palette over a plastic one – it's much easier to mix colours on the ceramic surface.

WATER

Two water jars work best if you don't want to change the water often. One for cool colours (blues, purples, greens) and another for warm colours (reds, yellows, oranges).

Use paper towel or cloth to absorb excess water from a brush.

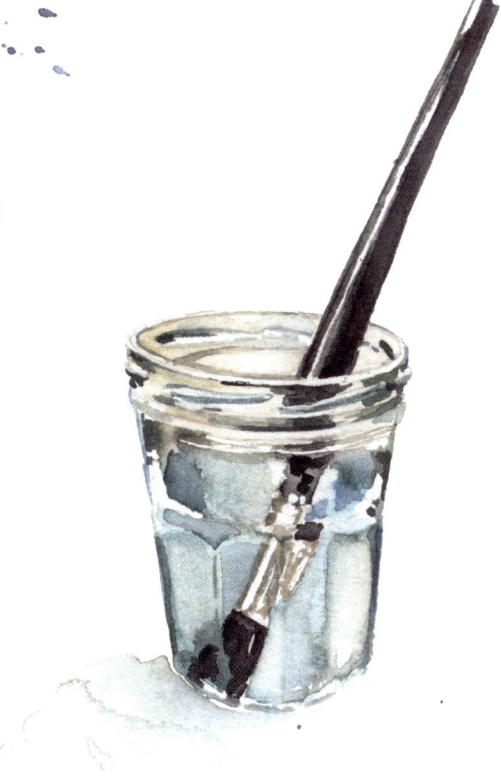

BRUSHES

For painting landscapes, I always use the same selection of brushes. The size will depend on the size of the artwork that you're creating; the following work best for paintings on A5 and A4 paper.

A size 2 mop brush is used for laying large washes. This brush could be used in place of everything else – it holds lots of water, making it great for large washes, and has a pointed tip for smaller details.

A size 8 flat brush is great for painting straight lines and angles, or for covering large, flat areas. It is useful for painting buildings and areas of calm water.

A size 3 round brush is good for painting smaller elements.

A size 4 liner brush is useful for painting long lines, such as cables, fences, blades of grass and tree branches.

Note:

Unfortunately there is no universal numbering system for brushes, and each different type of brush, as well as the different manufacturers, have a different size style of numbering. For example, a mop brush of size 2 is medium-size, while a round brush of size 3 is a lot smaller than the mop.

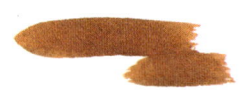

PENCIL AND ERASER

For sketching before painting, it is better to use a hard pencil: HB or 2H. A kneadable eraser is gentler on paper than a regular one, and can be used to press against the sketch to lighten it before starting to lay watercolour washes. You can also use a hard eraser if you want, which is also useful for removing masking fluid.

MASKING TAPE

Masking tape fixes paper to the table and can also create a sharp edge between paint and paper.

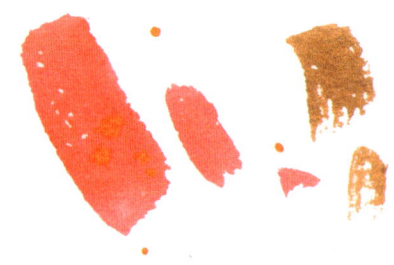

RESIST

When painting landscapes, using a resist medium can be especially helpful. There are several types of water-resistant materials available, such as masking fluid, wax crayons and gum arabic. I have used only masking fluid in the exercises in this book. For more details on how this is applied, see page 24.

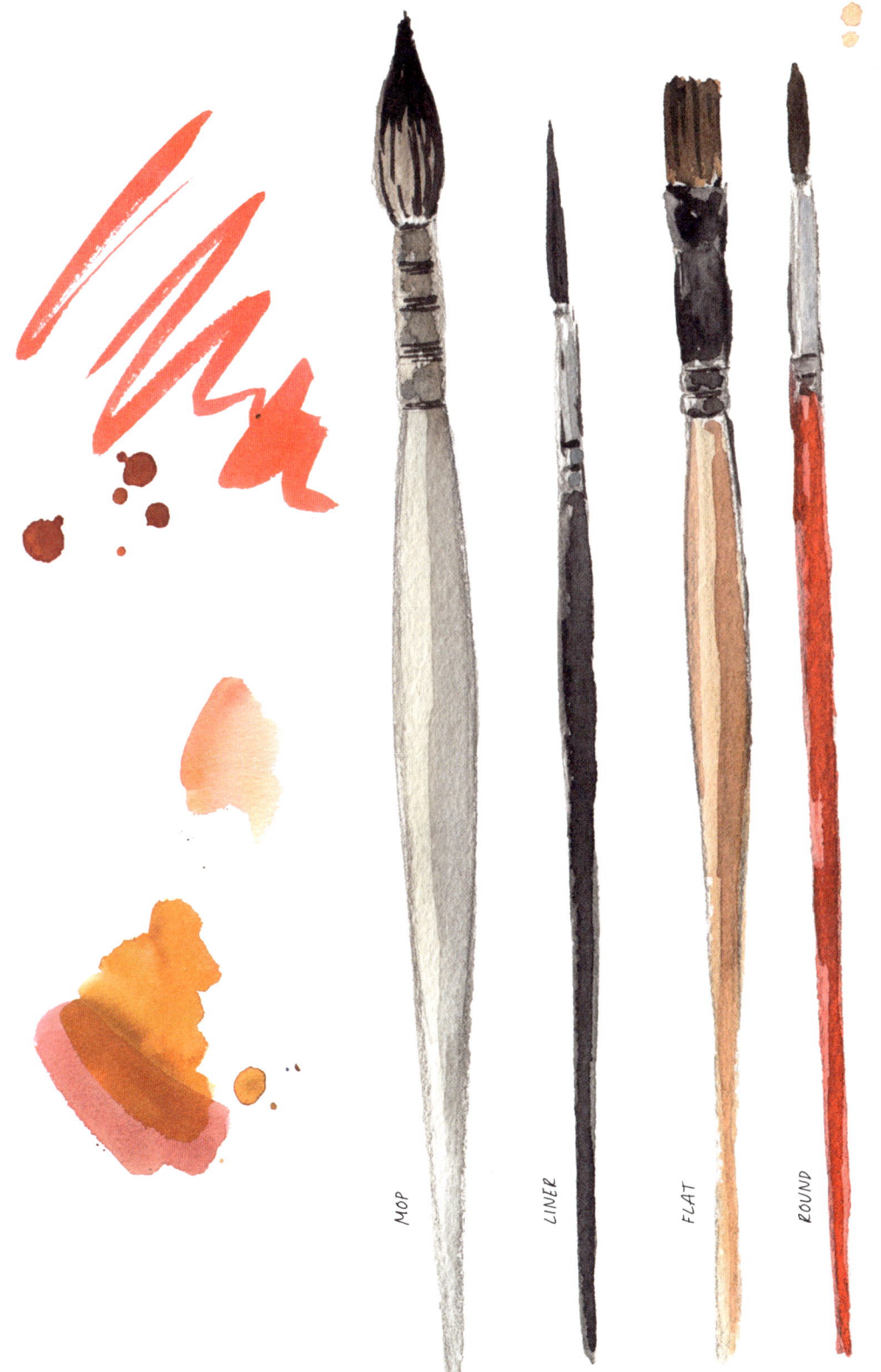

MOP

LINER

FLAT

ROUND

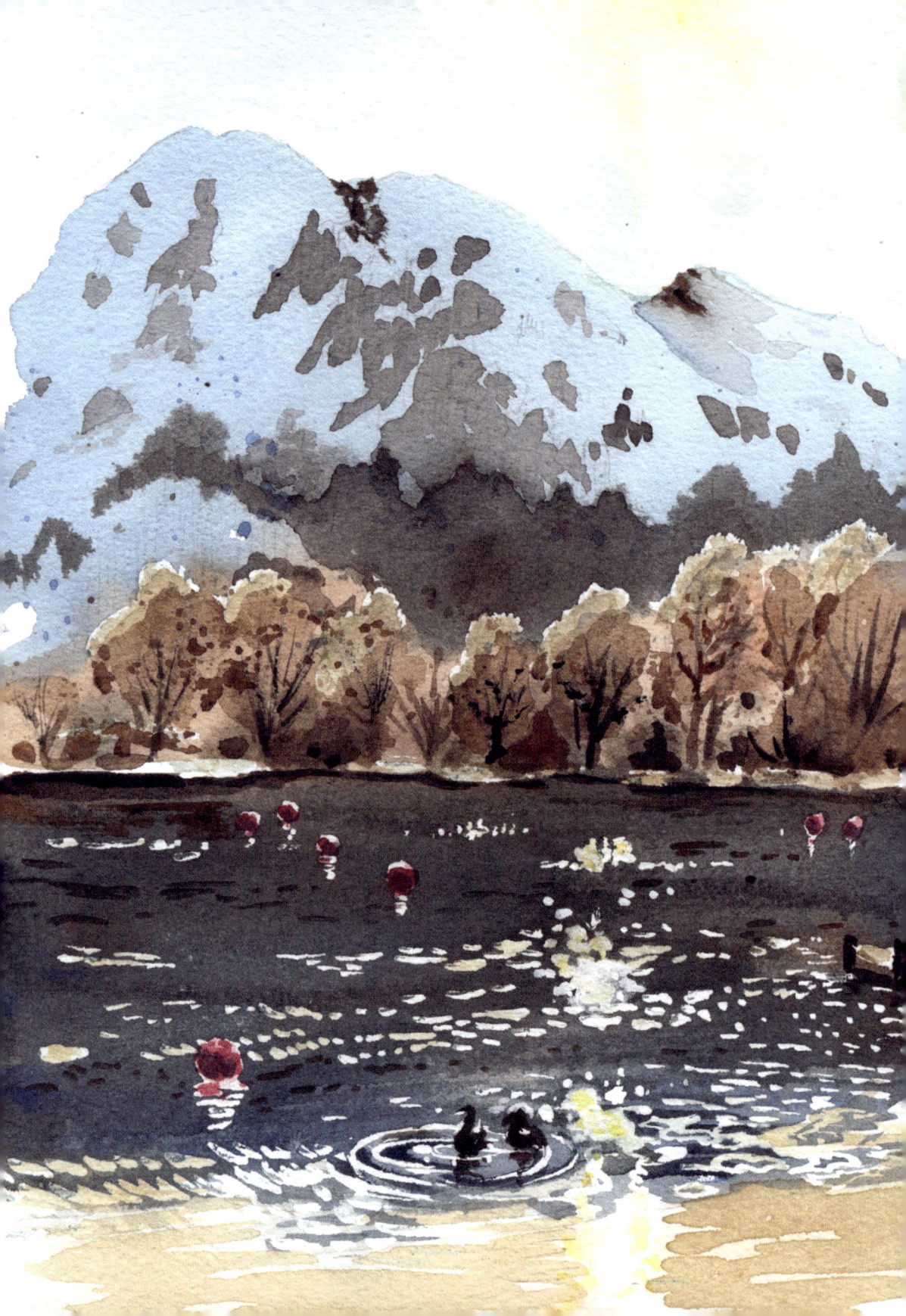

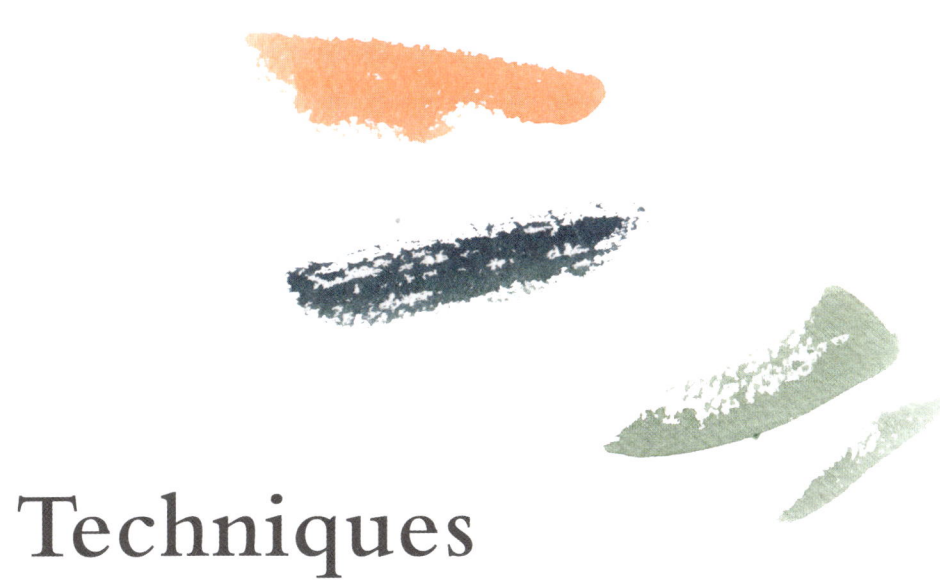

Techniques

There is something very satisfying in experimenting with watercolour techniques. Playing with washes and colours can create beautiful, unplanned effects, and this is how watercolour painting can be summed up: part planning and applying what you know, and part letting go and allowing watercolour to surprise you with its unpredictability.

When practising the techniques outlined, it's all about conscious play. Start by following the instructions, then explore variations just to see what happens. Learn the techniques, practise by creating art, but always give yourself space to play.

Flat wash

The process of painting with watercolours is all about creating washes. The most basic is a flat wash, when you apply paint very evenly, keeping colour tones the same. To create a flat wash, always keep the same amount of water on your brush. The end result should look just as the name suggests: flat.

Graded wash

As opposed to a flat wash, a graded wash involves using varying amounts of water to gradually dilute the watercolour, creating a smooth, fading effect. To create an even, graded wash, start by applying a strong mix of colour to the paper, then gradually add more water to your brush as you move downwards, softening the colour and creating a smooth transition.

Hold your paper at a slight angle, with the stronger colour at the top and the water flowing downwards toward the bottom. Your colour will slowly bleed into the water, creating an even gradient. This effect is useful when painting skies.

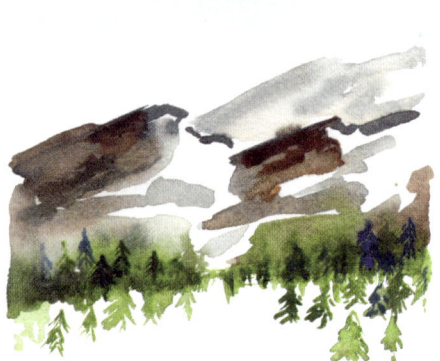

Wet-on-wet

Wet-on-wet is the process of adding wet paint to previously wetted paper or colour wash. Colours will mix directly on the paper, often creating beautiful and unexpected results.

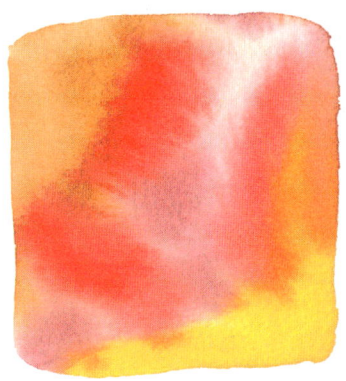

Wet-on-dry

The wet-on-dry technique involves applying wet paint to dry paper or a dry colour layer. Let's compare it with wet-on-wet by looking at the same bush painted using the two different techniques.

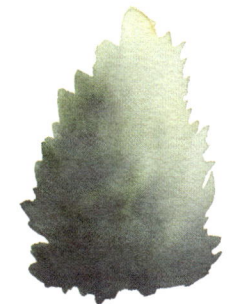

Using the wet-on-wet technique, shadows were created by adding more pigment while the paint was still wet. The shadows are very soft on this bush.

In the example below, the specific wet-on-dry technique used is called 'glazing', which involves layering wet-on-dry layers on top of each other to create shadows. The first wash is usually very light and watery.

When that is dry, the next layer is applied, using more pigment and less water. Then the same process is repeated for another layer. You can see more texture and harsher edges on this bush compared to the one created with wet-on-wet.

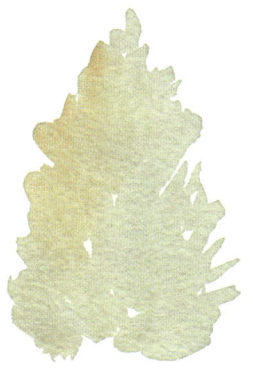 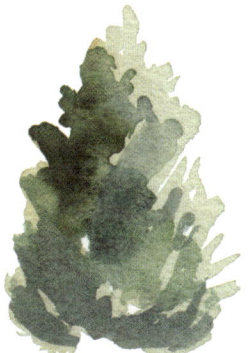 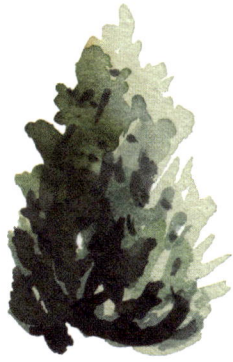

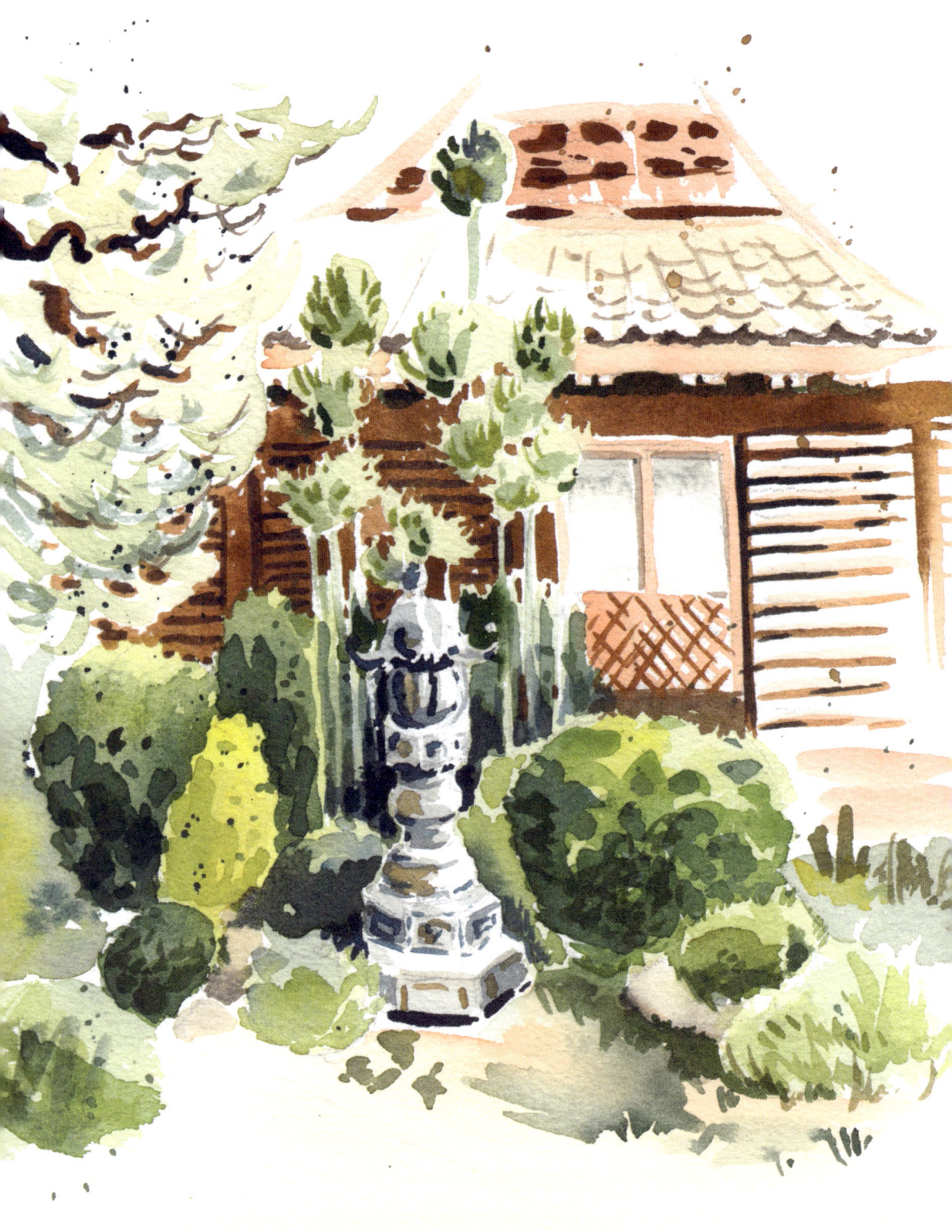

Negative painting

With watercolour, you cannot add light colours on top of dark. Well, you can, but they will not make the painting lighter, as they would if you were painting with oil or acrylic. When painting light objects on a dark background with watercolour, you almost have to paint backwards – instead of painting the object itself, you paint shadows around it to make it stand out.

Let's break this down: to paint bushes, start with an even light wash in the shape of a silhouette of a group of bushes. Once this layer is dry, add a layer of shadows, leaving the shape of the front bush unpainted. With each additional layer, deepen the shadows to help separate one bush from another and create a sense of depth.

 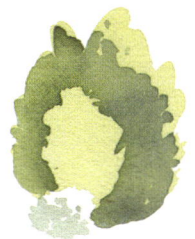 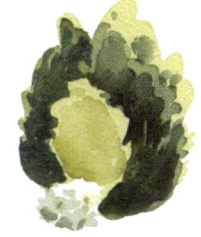 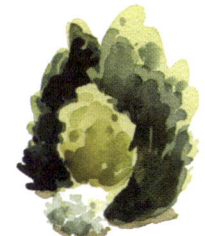

A very similar technique is used when painting these plants with a wall behind them. Firstly, the overall silhouette is defined without trying to separate one plant from another.

Next, a few details are added to enhance the shape, and lastly the background around the plants is added in a different colour.

 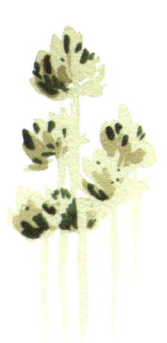 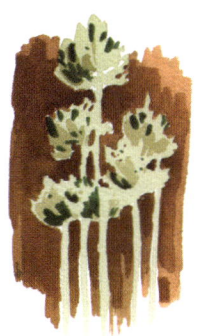 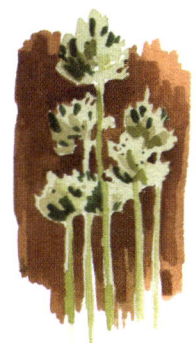

Dry brush

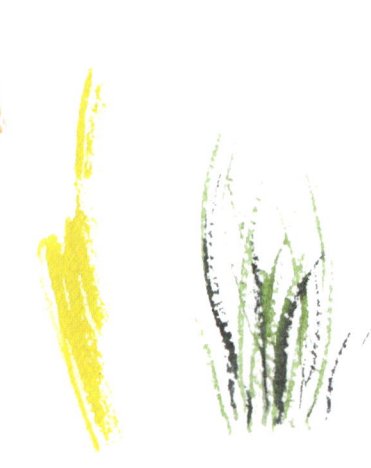

As the name suggests, dry brush is painting with a minimum amount of water. Load your brush with water, then load it with paint and use paper towel to absorb any excess water by gently pressing the bristles against it, leaving it on the 'dryer' side. Drag your brush against rough paper to create a textured effect. This is great for depicting grass, tree trunks and reflections in water.

Pulling

The pulling technique involves using a brush loaded with clean water to pull pigment from a wet area of paint on paper, creating a softer edge or gentle transition.

In this example, a stroke of medium-wet watercolour was first applied to the paper. Then, using a clean, wet brush, the rest of the roof was painted by pulling the pigment outward from the initial stroke.

In the next example, a thick layer of paint was used to paint the head, and then clean water was used to pull the colour down to form the rest of the person's silhouette. Pulling is somewhat similar to a graded wash, but it's typically used for smaller objects or details.

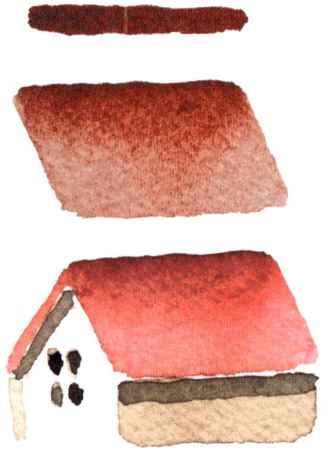

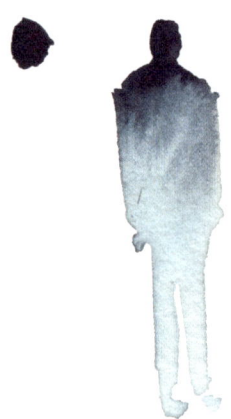

Softening

When you want to avoid harsh edges, use the softening technique, by painting with clean water next to wet paint to soften its edge.

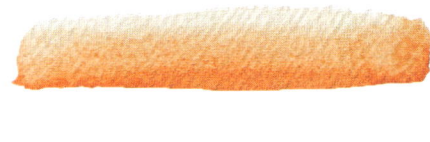
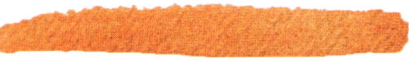

Effects

Another cool way to create texture with watercolour is to sprinkle salt crystals over it. Salt will absorb the pigment, creating star-like shapes and an uneven texture. Brush any excess grains off when the paint is dry.

Similarly, you can add water splashes to create a blooming effect. The effect will be more visible if you do this as your paint starts to dry; if you add water to a very wet wash, the water will just mix with the already very wet surface, barely creating any blooms.

WATER

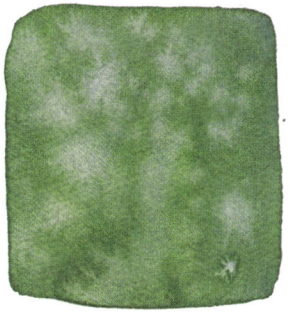

SALT

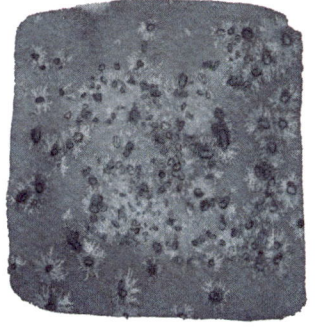

Masking fluid

Masking fluid is a resist medium that acts like a quick-drying adhesive and is used to cover areas of paper to prevent them from being painted. When painting landscapes, for me masking fluid is invaluable, making it easier to create different textures and avoid unpainted parts when painting around something is too difficult.

It works in a very simple way: you apply it to the area that you want to protect from paint, and later rub it off. The main challenge comes at application. Because it is very similar to glue, sometimes it's hard to apply it precisely. You can buy masking fluid with a tiny precision nozzle for easier application, but it still won't be exactly precise, though I find it's good enough for most sketches.

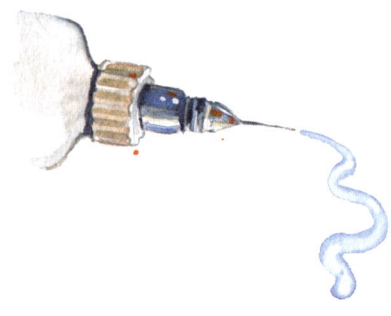

Alternatively, you can buy masking fluid in a bottle and then use various application tools. Keep in mind that masking fluid will ruin your brushes, so it's better to use old ones and rinse them with soapy water after each use.

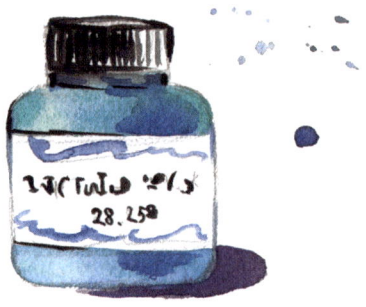

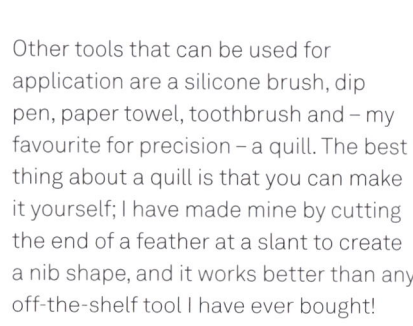

Other tools that can be used for application are a silicone brush, dip pen, paper towel, toothbrush and – my favourite for precision – a quill. The best thing about a quill is that you can make it yourself; I have made mine by cutting the end of a feather at a slant to create a nib shape, and it works better than any off-the-shelf tool I have ever bought!

APPLICATION

One way of using masking fluid is to apply it to unpainted paper.

1. Apply masking fluid in the shape you want to protect from paint and leave it to dry fully.

2. Paint over this shape with watercolour and leave it to dry.

3. Remove the masking fluid by either rubbing it with a hard eraser or using your fingers.

4. Lastly, add details to the unpainted area.

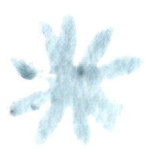 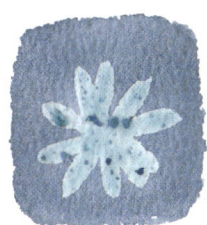  

You can also apply masking fluid to painted paper. Repeat the same steps as above, but use the fluid to protect the first layer of colour.

 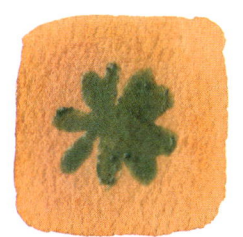

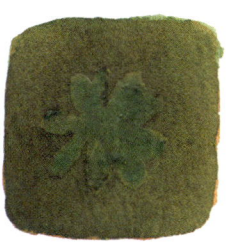 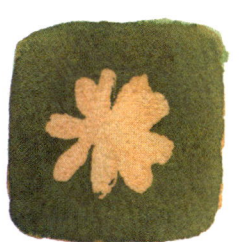 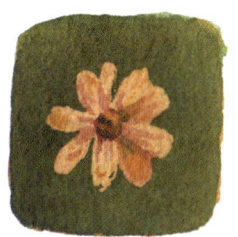

GRASS TEXTURE

Creating the texture of grass, where the blades in the foreground are lighter than those in the background, can be hard if you attempt to paint around each blade. Using masking fluid is a perfect solution for creating long, slim blades.

1. Apply masking fluid in the shape of grass blades overlapping each other.

2. Apply a few layers of darker green to represent blades of grass at the back, letting each layer dry before moving onto the next.

3. Peel off the masking fluid.

4. Paint over the white blades with a light yellow colour to unify with the rest of the painting, while still keeping them light.

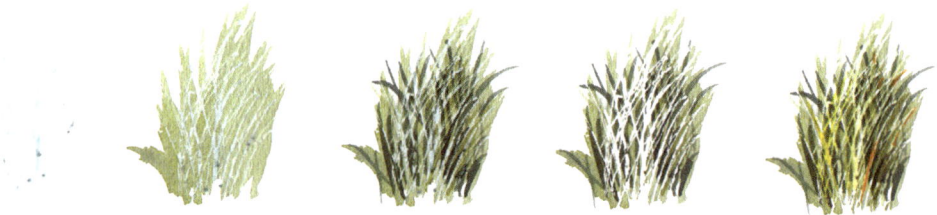

TREE TRUNK TEXTURE

In this example, masking fluid has been used to create a detailed tree trunk texture using exactly the same method as above.

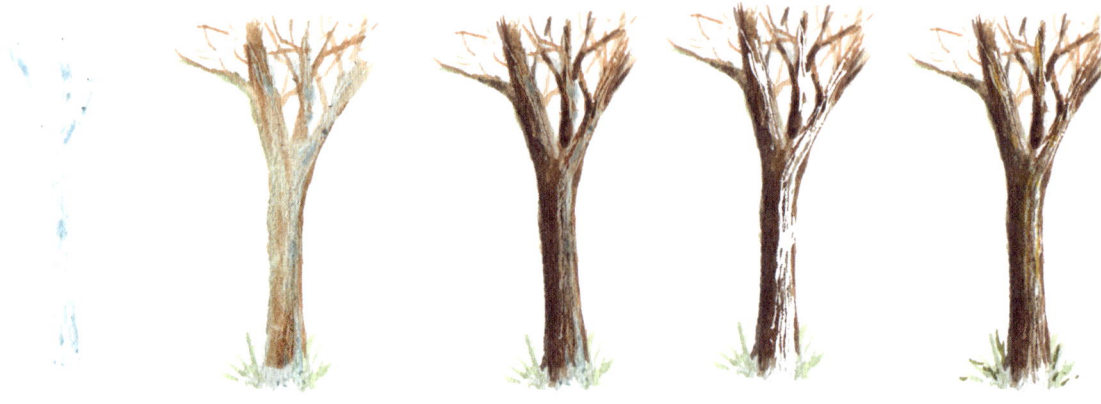

MEADOW

Here, I have used masking fluid to protect white daisy blooms in a very detailed meadow full of greenery. Keeping my flowers blocked out, I can concentrate on painting stems and leaves without worrying about having to paint around the blooms.

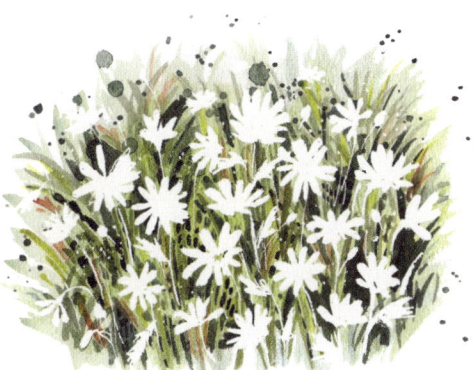

After peeling off the masking fluid I added a few shadows and details to the flower blooms.

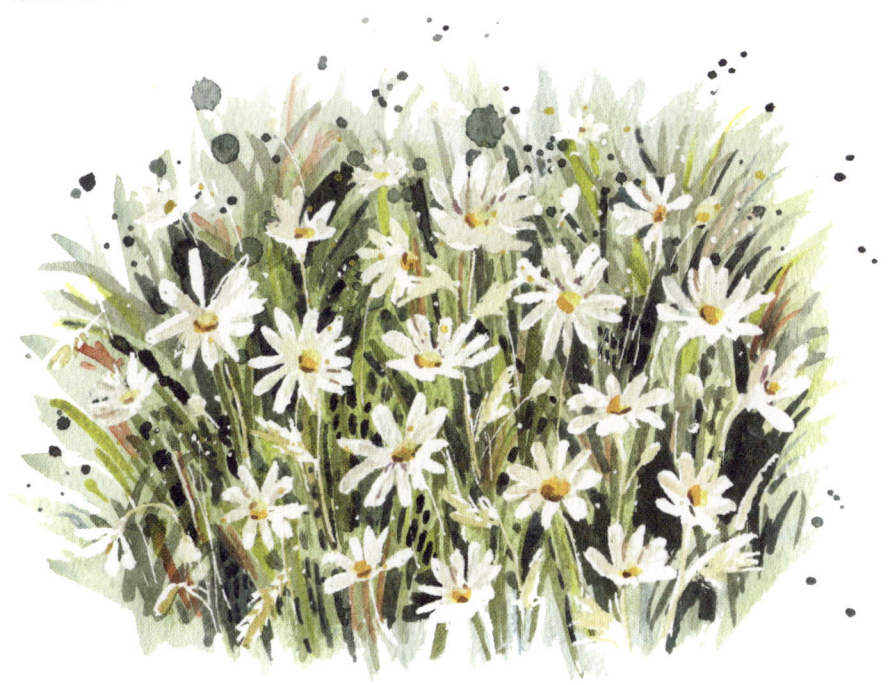

Drawing

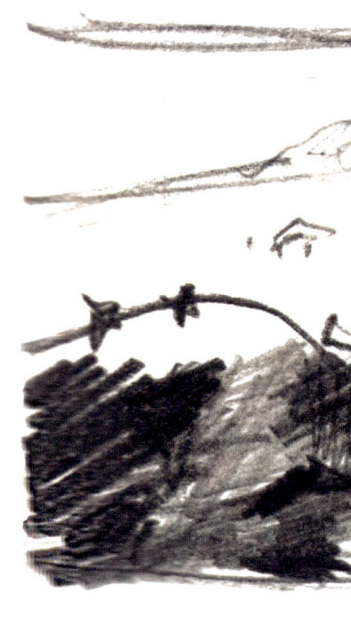

Drawing is the mother of all arts. Whether you are good at it and have decided to take watercolour as the next step, or just jumped straight into painting, it is worth always having drawing as a separate skill. There are many books on drawing, and a few are mentioned in the Resources section at the back of the book (see page 156).

The best part of sketching first with a pencil is that because you don't have any colours distracting you, you can focus on the composition in its purest form, crafting your image by utilizing shapes and values. It's also useful when you want to make a quick sketch on location. I find painting from my sketches is usually more successful than painting from a photograph, because a lot of the thinking about composition and values has been done at the sketching stage, so you're already halfway there, while the photo is just a form of raw inspiration.

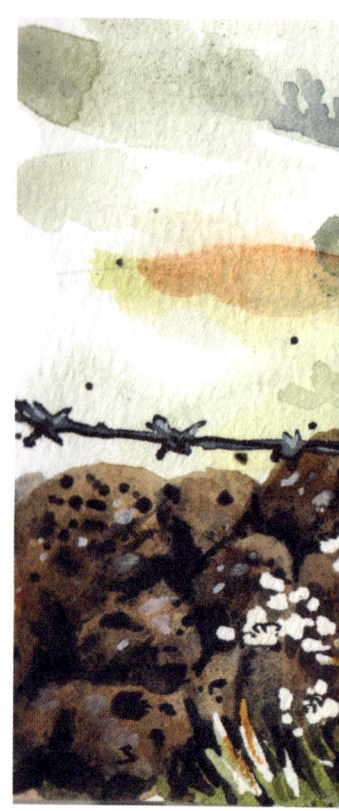

Whether you decide to do a pencil drawing before painting over it with watercolour is ultimately a matter of personal preference. I like to lightly sketch a few of the larger shapes or key elements of a painting first. There's no need to add any details – just enough to create a basic guide to provide structure and make the painting process feel more approachable.

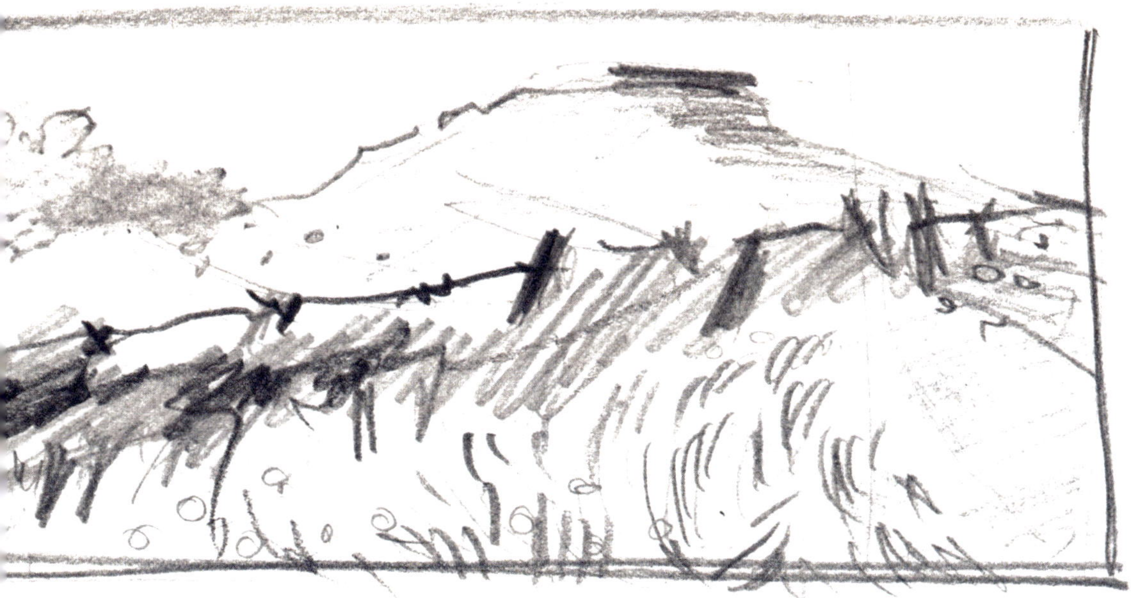

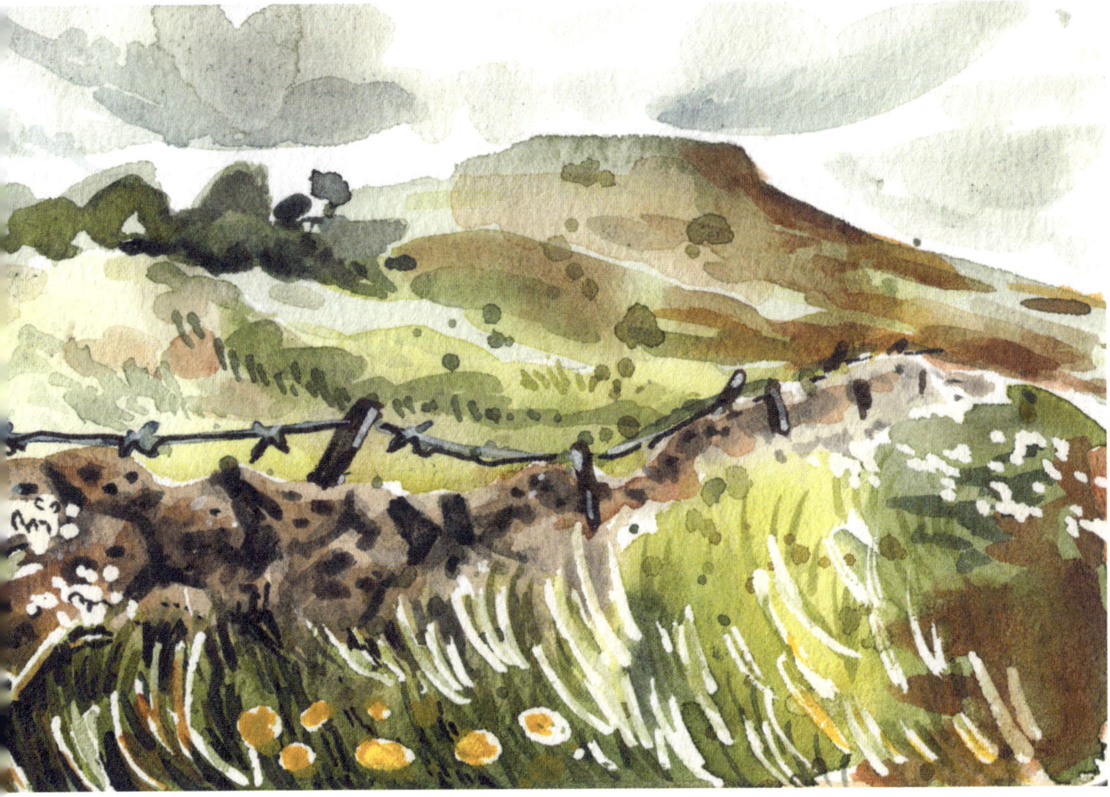

Pencils for drawing

When drawing small thumbnail sketches for use as a reference, the main purpose is to determine the proportion of different objects and value masses; in other words, how much of the image will be in light, midtone or dark shades, and where those darker areas will be placed. For this, use soft 2B and 4B pencils, which will achieve a decent dark tone. For a pencil drawing to be used under watercolour, a hard pencil is best: HB and 2HB.

Note:

The main mistake I see beginners make is pressing too hard on the pencil. Try to consciously handle the pencil as lightly as you can in the beginning, and build up your tones gradually. Only press harder at the final stages of drawing.

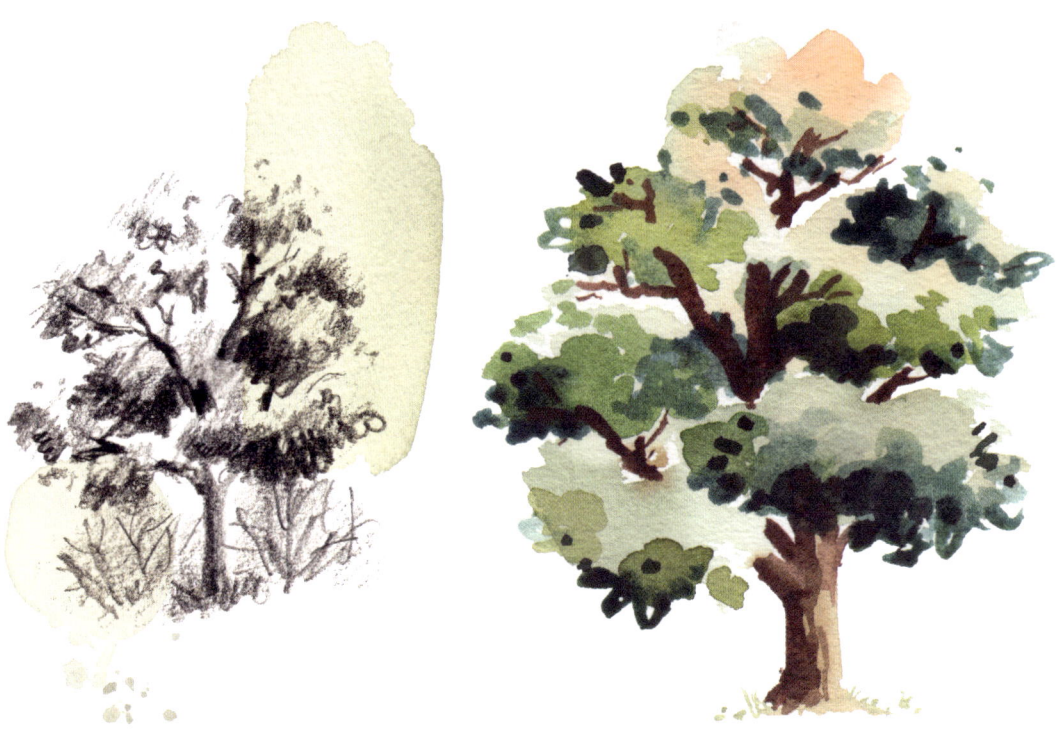

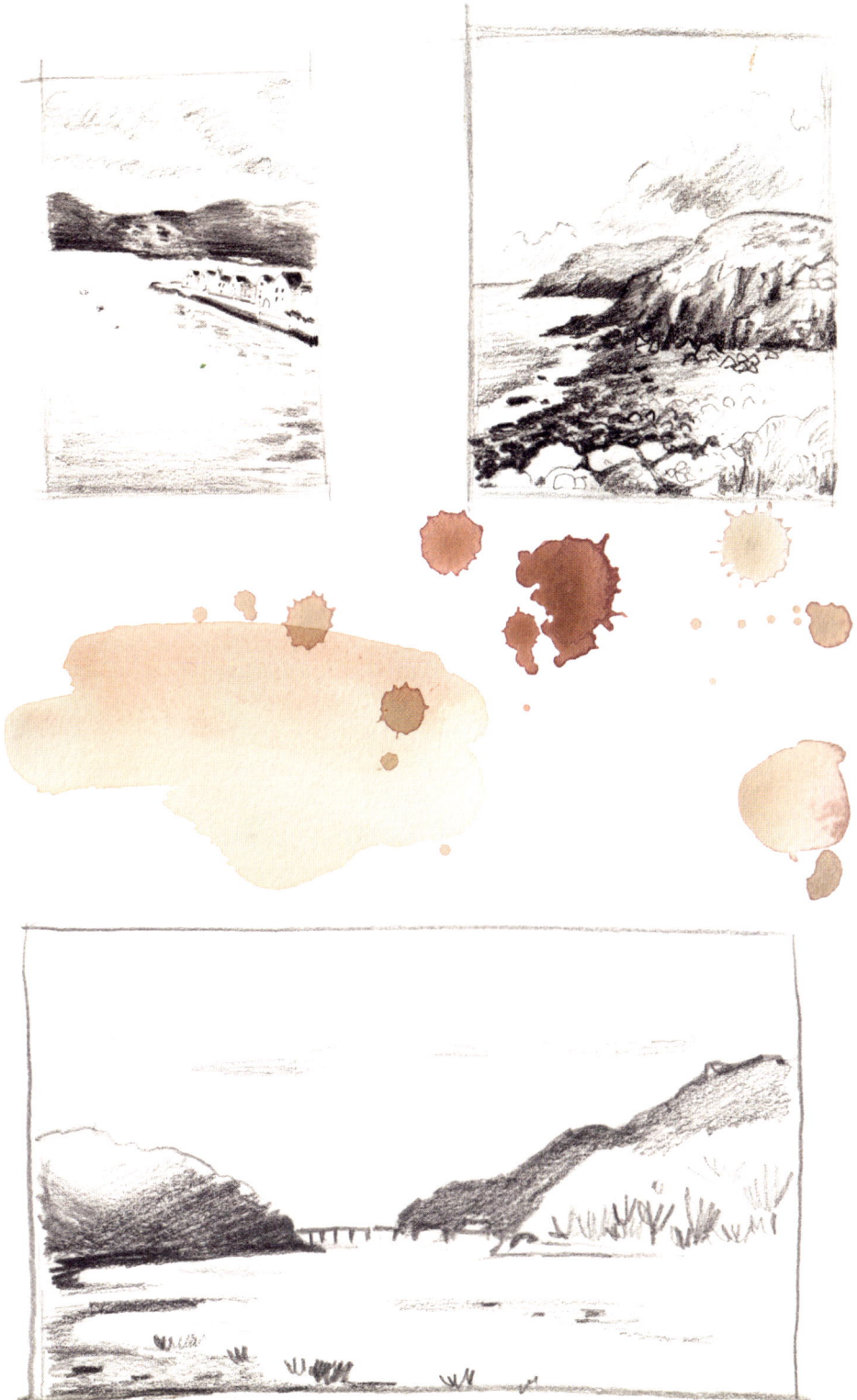

Colour

Colour is probably my favourite mode of expression in painting. It can create a mood or emphasize the hero subject. Here is an overview of the basics of working with colour.

Colour values

Watercolour is a very translucent media, and it gets lighter and more transparent as you add more water. Every colour will have its darkest and lightest state, and every shade in-between, depending on the amount of water added. The different shades are referred to as colour values.

To get to know your watercolours better, a simple exercise you can do is to gradually mix colours with water to get a feel for how to achieve different values.

Colour wheel

A colour wheel is a circular arrangement of colours organised in a way that nearby colours have the closest relation. If you've been painting for a while, you most likely know the colour wheel inside out and don't even have to think about it. For beginners, the important thing to know is how the colour wheel is made and how it works for colour mixing.

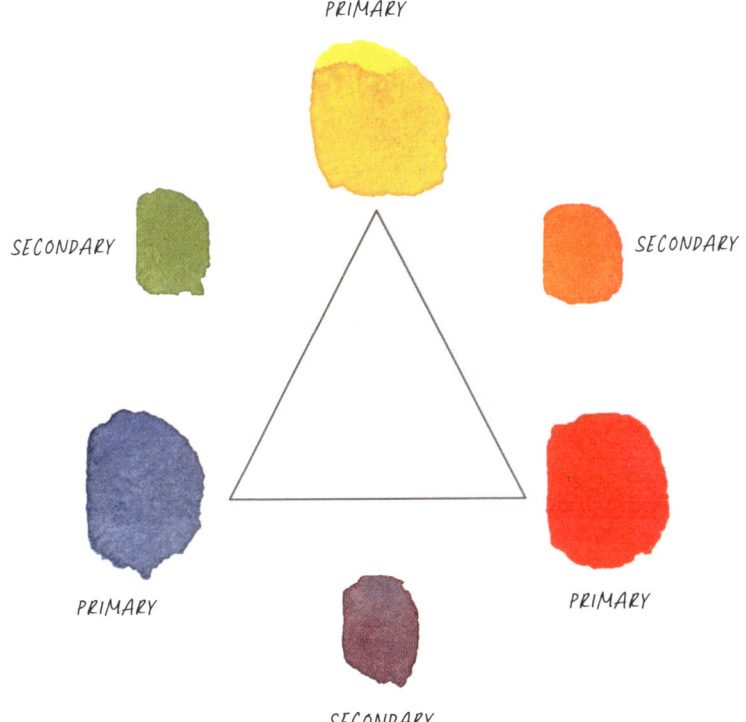

PRIMARY

SECONDARY

SECONDARY

PRIMARY

PRIMARY

SECONDARY

The first thing you need to know is that the three primary colours – yellow, blue and red – cannot be created, so it is best to have them in your watercolour set. Colours created by mixing two primary colours are called secondary colours: blue and yellow make green; red and yellow make orange; blue and red make purple. These appear between the relevant primary colours on the wheel.

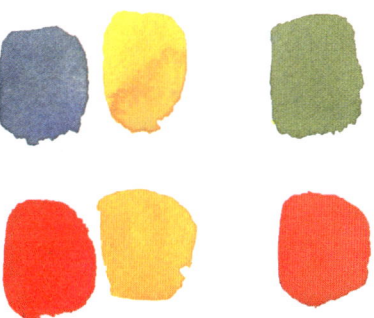

Mixing colours

To go deeper into colour mixing, experiment by mixing primary and secondary colours together. Similar to colour values (see page 32), if you mix two different colours together you will get different shades dependent on the proportions of each colour you use.

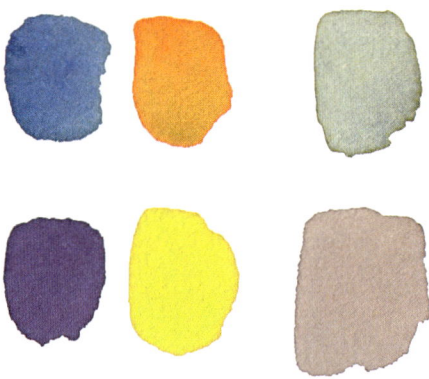

Try this exercise. Take a yellow colour on your palette and gradually add green to it, a little at a time, until you get to pure green. See all the different shades you can get as you mix the two colours.

You can also mix the same two colours directly on paper by creating a graded wash (see page 18).

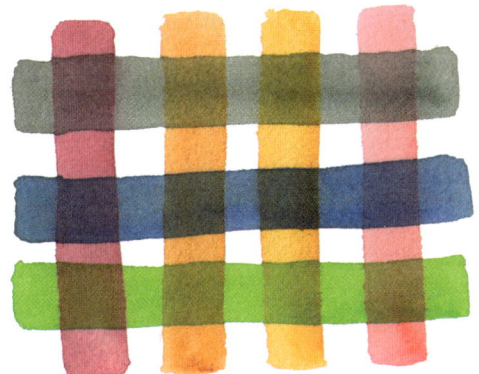

A less-used way of mixing colours is by overlaying two or more colour washes when the layer below is dry. The colours will not mix completely, but the new shade will have both colours and will create an illusion of new colour, especially if observed from a distance.

GREYS AND NEUTRALS

To create the most clean and saturated colours, you should mix colours that sit closely together on the colour wheel. Mixing colours sat opposite each other will create a range of greys and neutrals. Opposite colours are yellow and purple, orange and blue, green and red. Your greys will have different undertones depending on the two colours you mix and the proportion of each.

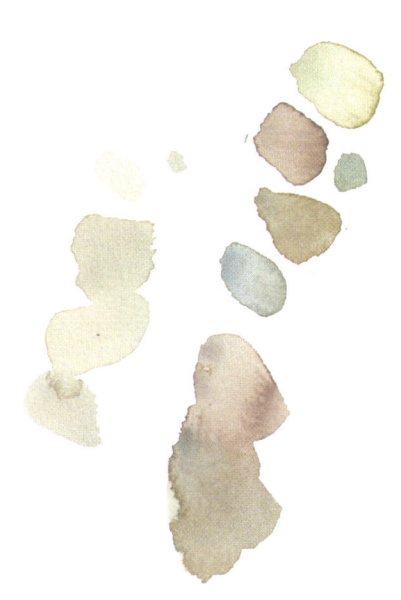

GRANULATING COLOURS

It's worth mentioning granulating colour. This is the property of certain watercolours, normally earthy tones and some blues, in which the pigments separate as they dry, creating a grainy texture. Granulating colours add texture to your painting and are particularly useful when painting rough surfaces. Textured paper (cold pressed and rough) will enhance granulations as well as a higher water to paint ratio. You will recognize granulating colours by the texture on the sample swatches in the shop.

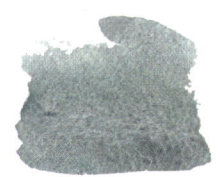

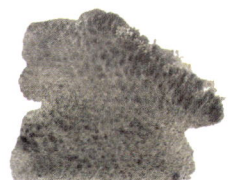

COLOUR STUDIES

Thumbnail paintings

Creating a harmonious colour palette requires experimentation. I suggest making a few colour study thumbnails before starting a larger painting, or simply as an exercise to explore how different colour combinations create different moods.

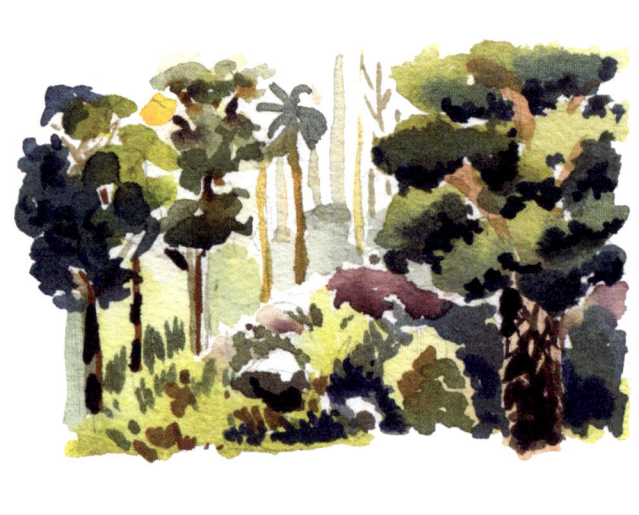
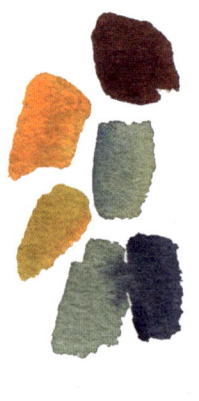

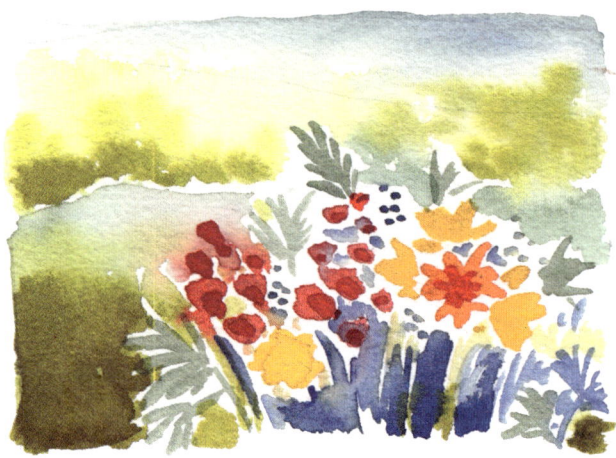
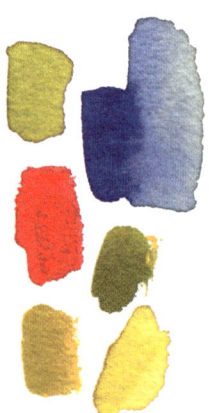

Mood

Colour creates mood, and conveying this is more important than trying to replicate the exact colours you see. Let's look at some examples. The painting opposite is a cool landscape of a remote island in Scotland. The colours are mostly earthy and neutral, creating the impression of a colder climate.

In the painting below, the colours are much more saturated, and while a red tree and purple shadow is not what was in the original landscape, it creates a colourful, tropical mood as the colours in warm climates always feel more saturated.

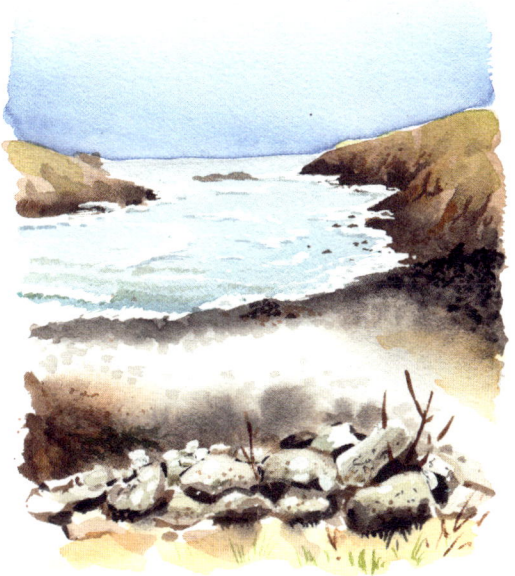

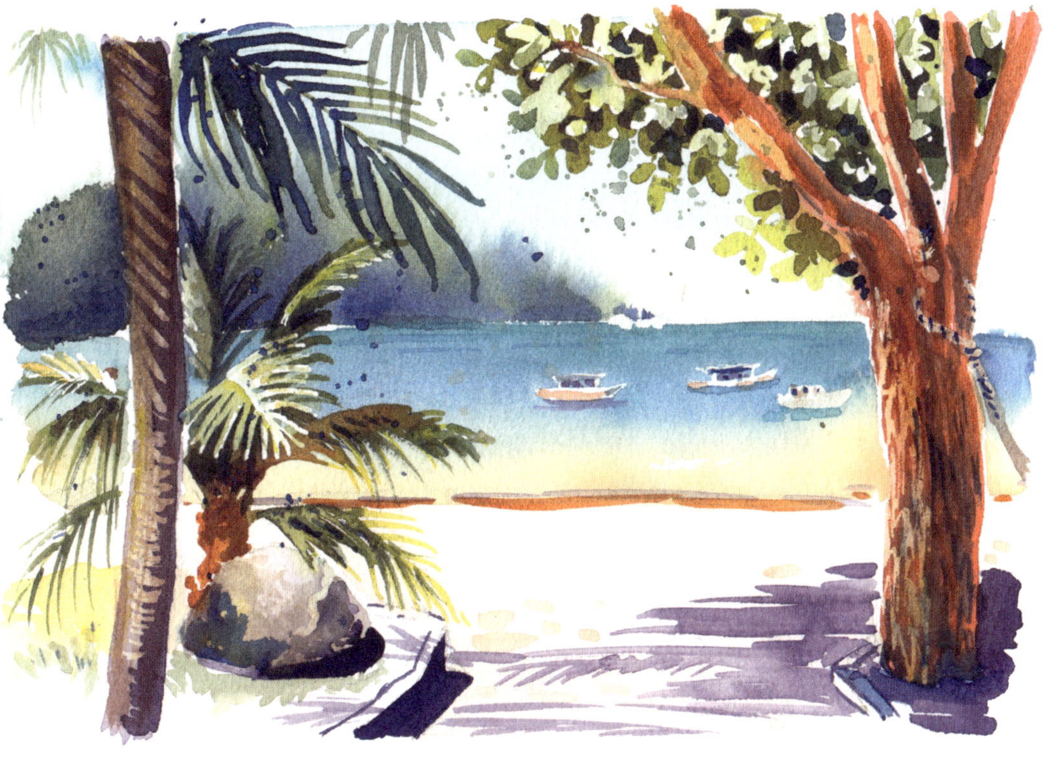

Composition

Composition in painting refers to the arrangement of objects on paper. Attractive paintings will always have a point of interest and objects that are in harmony with each other. This is achieved through the colour tones, hues, shapes and scales of objects.

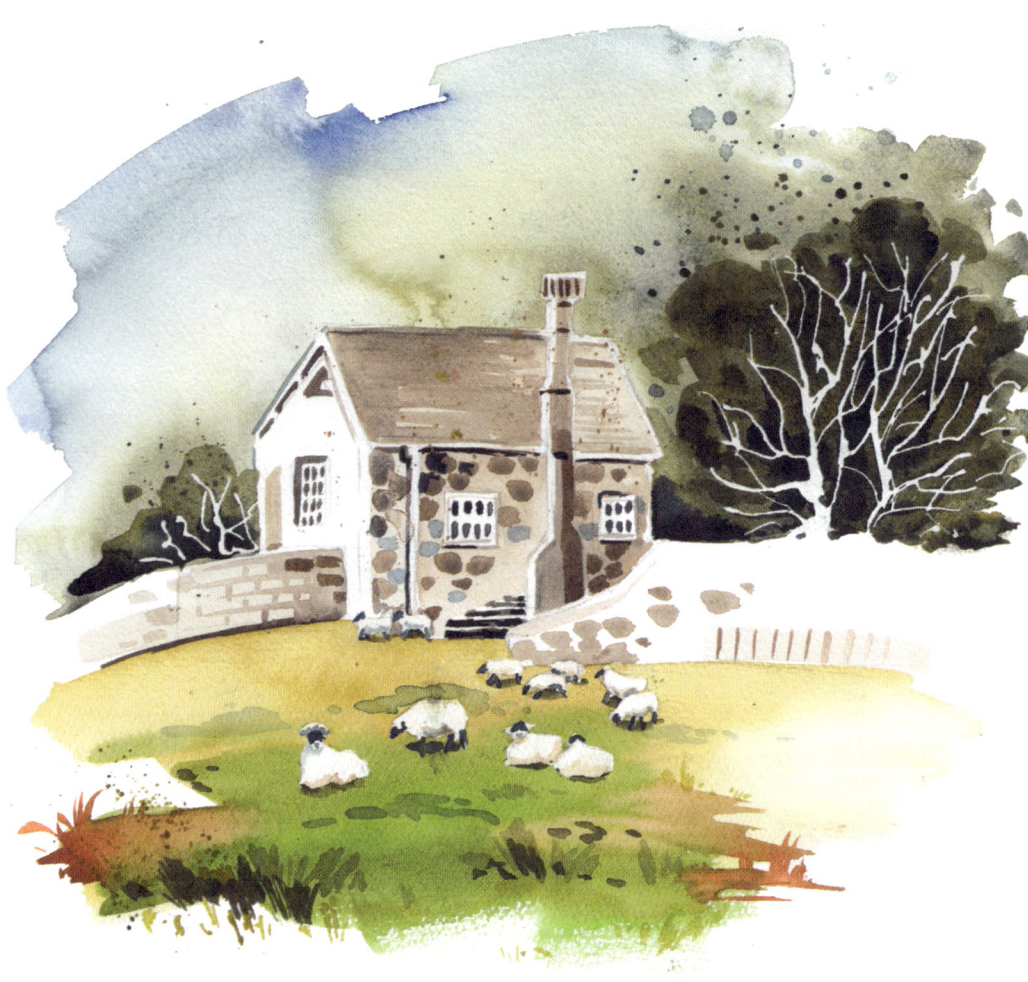

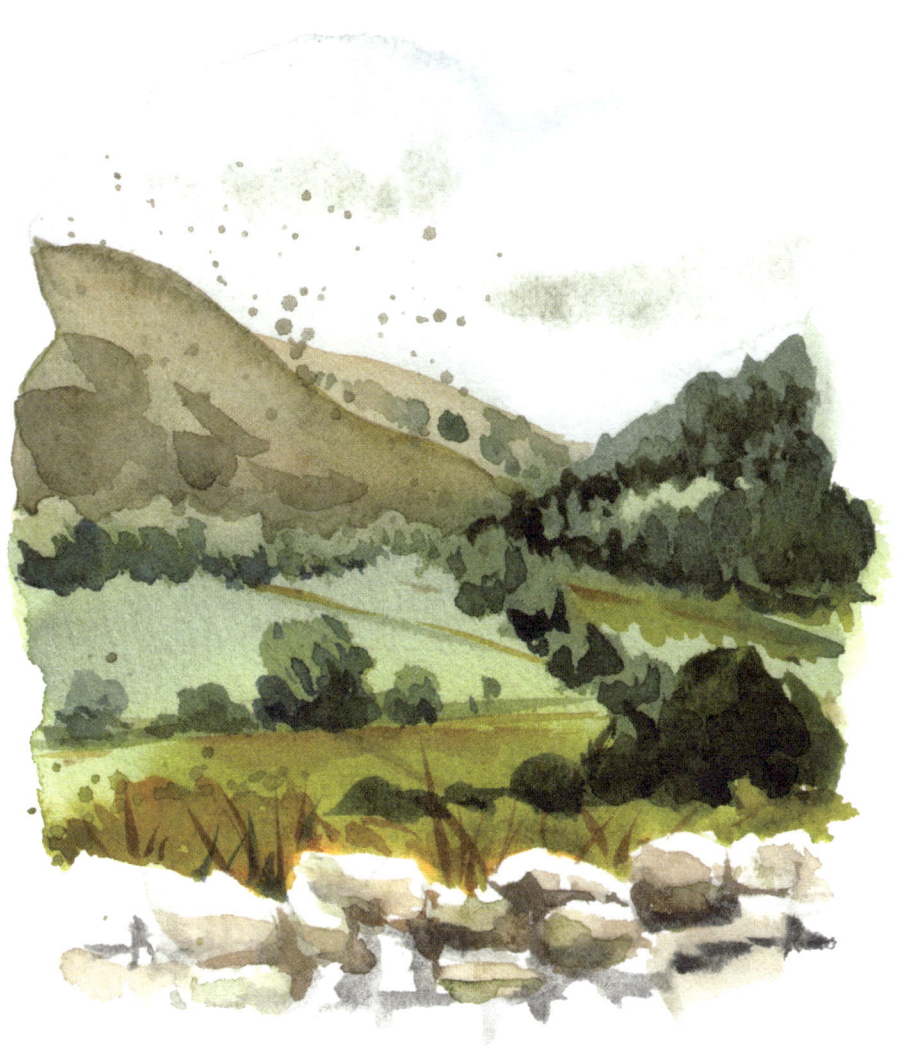

Seeing in shapes

Think of everything you want to paint as an abstract shape rather than a tree, a bush, a hill … Once you start seeing your objects as shapes it becomes easier to arrange them without concentrating on details. Nature can be very generous and provide harmonious postcard-worthy compositions, but occasionally you need to use creative licence and adjust the contrast to enhance your main subject.

Beauty in contrast

Have you ever snapped a photo of the most breathtaking scenery to show to your friend, only to find a dull, lifeless image on your phone? The scale is lost and all the greenery blurs together, with the shapes suddenly vanishing. This is because the camera flattens the image, and sometimes when we paint we do the same.

This will never happen if you use the proper contrast of hue, tone, texture and scale. It's the first rule of a good composition.

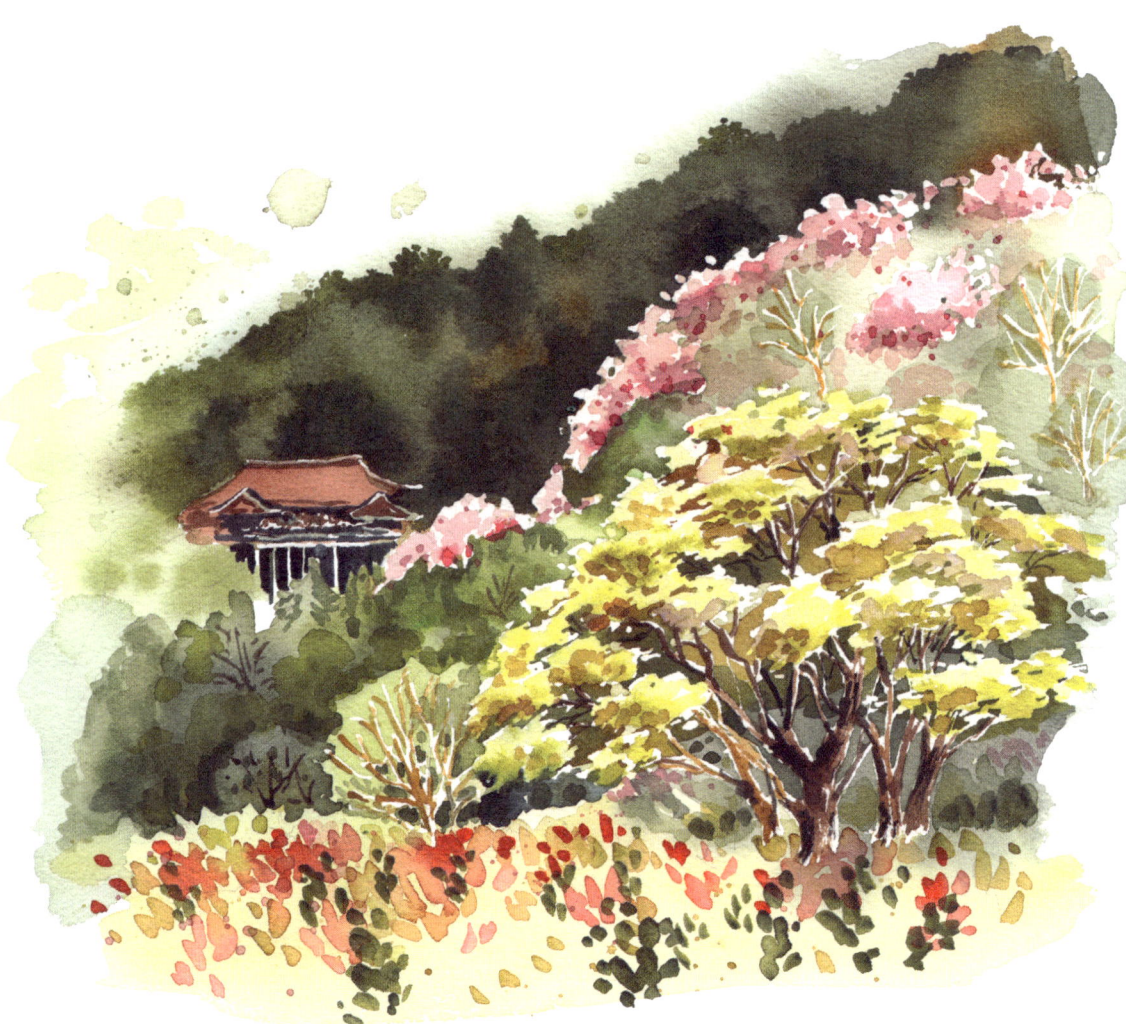

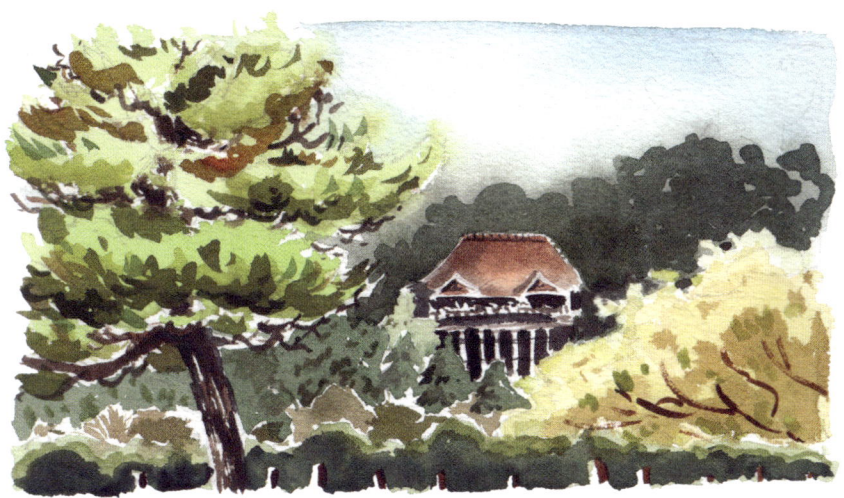

HUE

Let's look at the example above. Where does your eye go first? Whilst it's not the largest object in the painting, your gaze is immediately drawn to the temple because it stands out in the green scenery. This method uses contrasting hues to highlight the main subject.

TONE

Tonal, or value, contrast is especially important when it comes to two objects overlapping. If the tonal contrast is poor, the painting will look flat, just like a phone camera image. Take a look at this example below: two objects are painted in different hues, one with strong tonal contrast, the other with very similar values. Whilst different hues are used, the contrast is so soft that it is hard to make out one shape from the other.

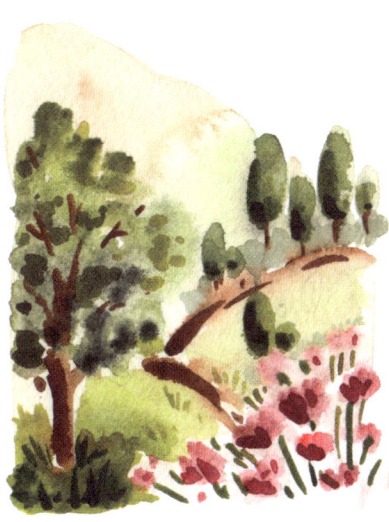

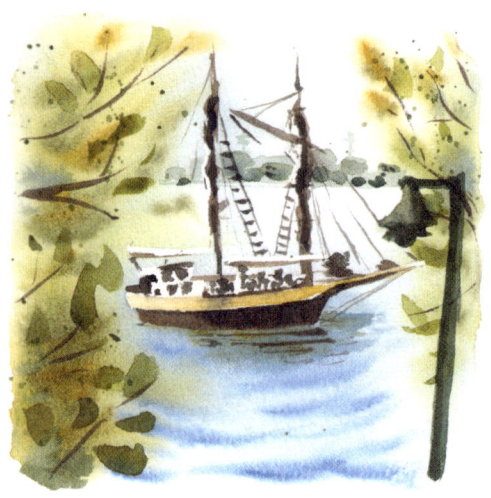

TEXTURE

In this example you can see a mixture of wet-on-wet and wet-on-dry techniques (see page 19). Whilst the object arrangement is pretty straightforward, what makes this sketch interesting is the contrast between the soft waves and blurry greenery in the foreground and the sharp edges of the boats and branches.

SCALE

Contrast of scale does not necessarily mean having a large and a small object in the painting. It also refers to value masses – large shapes or areas of similar lightness or darkness.

Contrast can be achieved by having a scale difference between light and dark parts of the painting – perhaps a large shadow, or dark tree in the foreground, or dark greenery in the background.

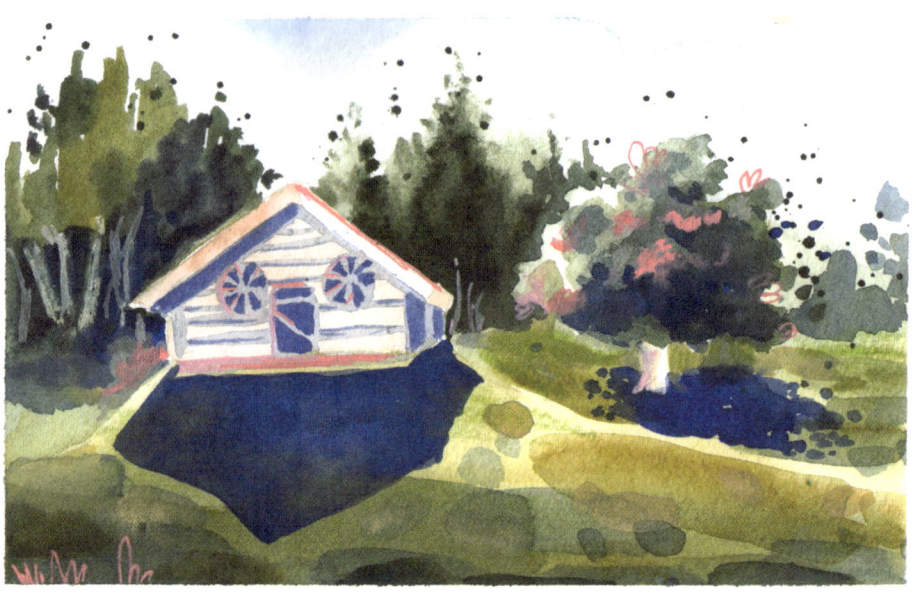

Focal point

Look at these two variations of a very simple sketch. In the painting on the left the mountain road has no cars, and your eye doesn't know where to look first.

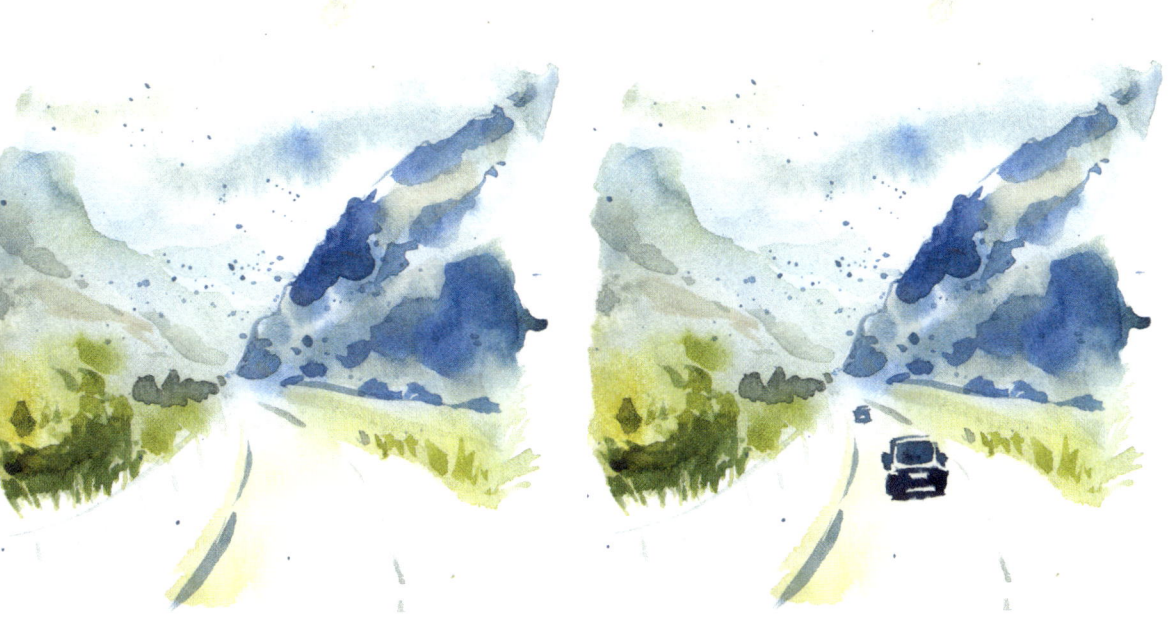

When you add a car in the foreground, which is a lot darker than the surroundings, it becomes your focal point. Also, the viewer can imagine themselves being on a road trip, following the car. What was once just a landscape now tells a story.

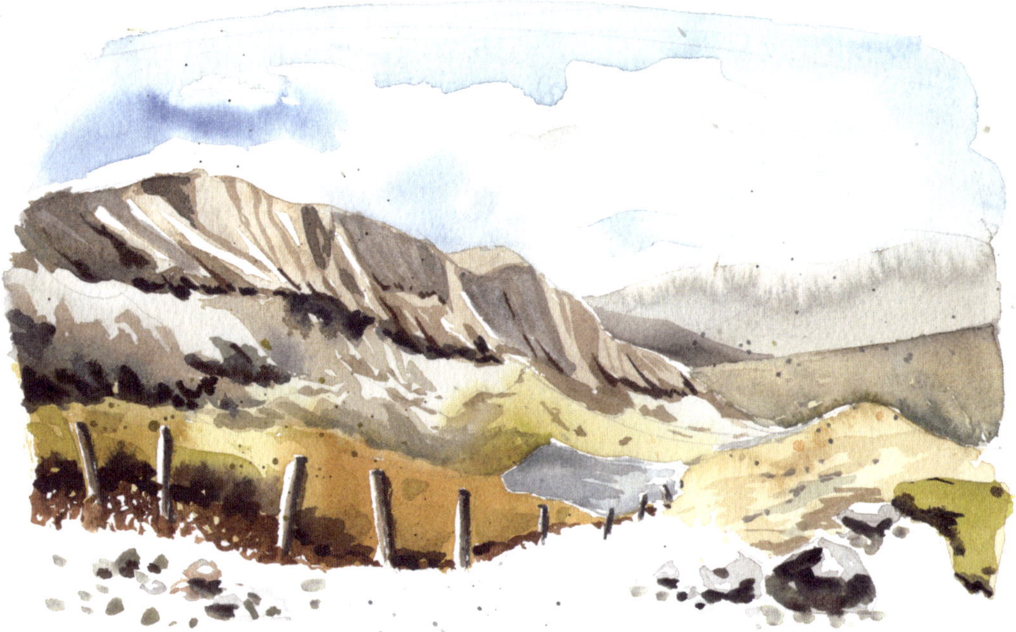

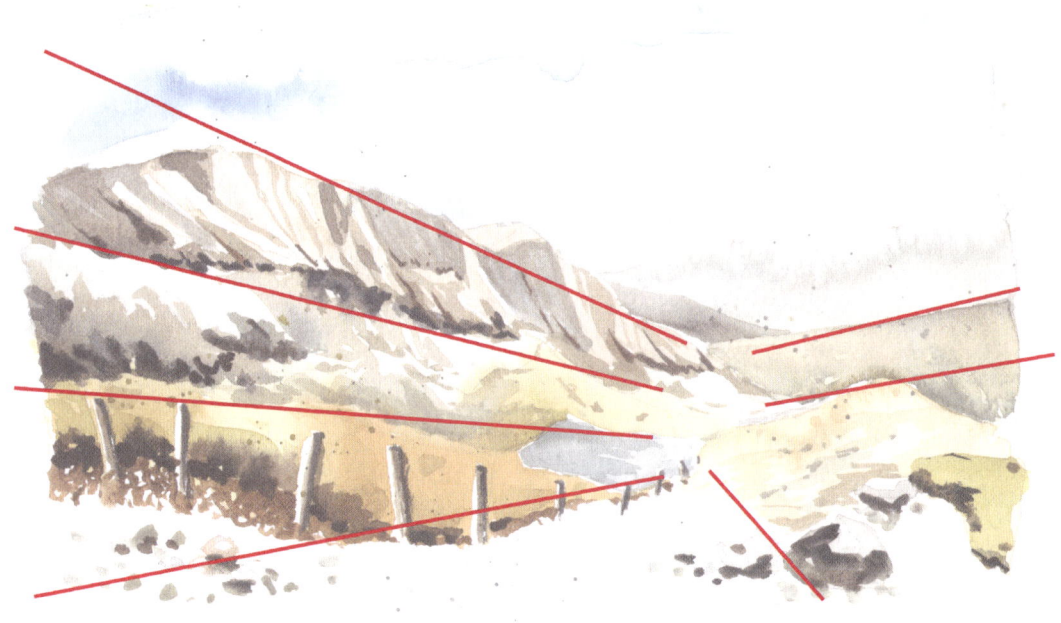

Leading lines

RADIATING LINES

Lines that lead the eye feel inviting and give a direction to follow. You cannot go wrong with this type of composition, though to make it more interesting you could have smaller lines going in a different direction, such as this fence.

DIRECTION

Intersecting lines create intrigue in a composition. In the painting below, the blades of grass go in a completely different direction to the other lines in the painting, making it feel more dynamic.

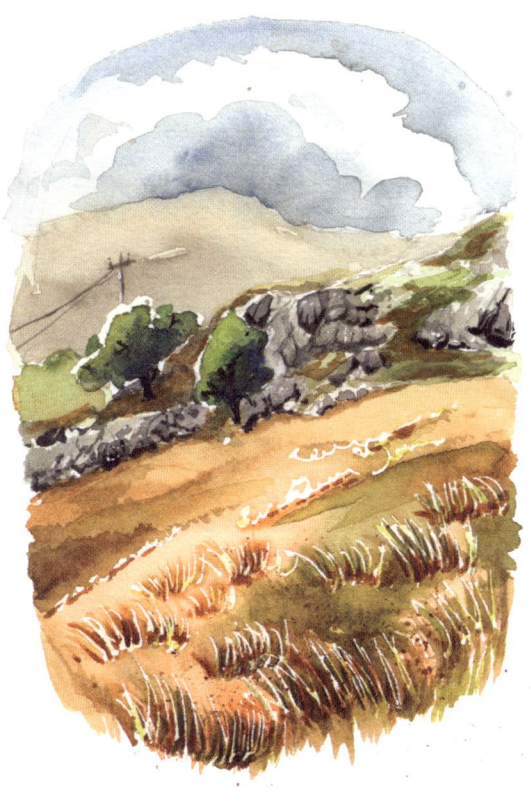

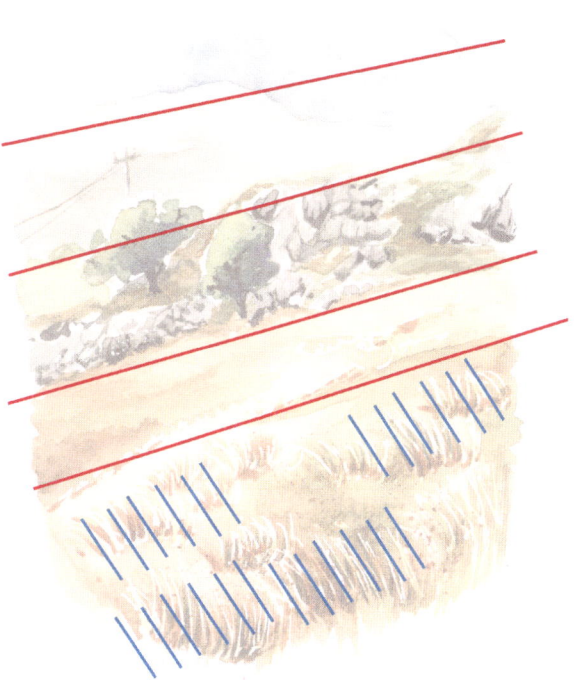

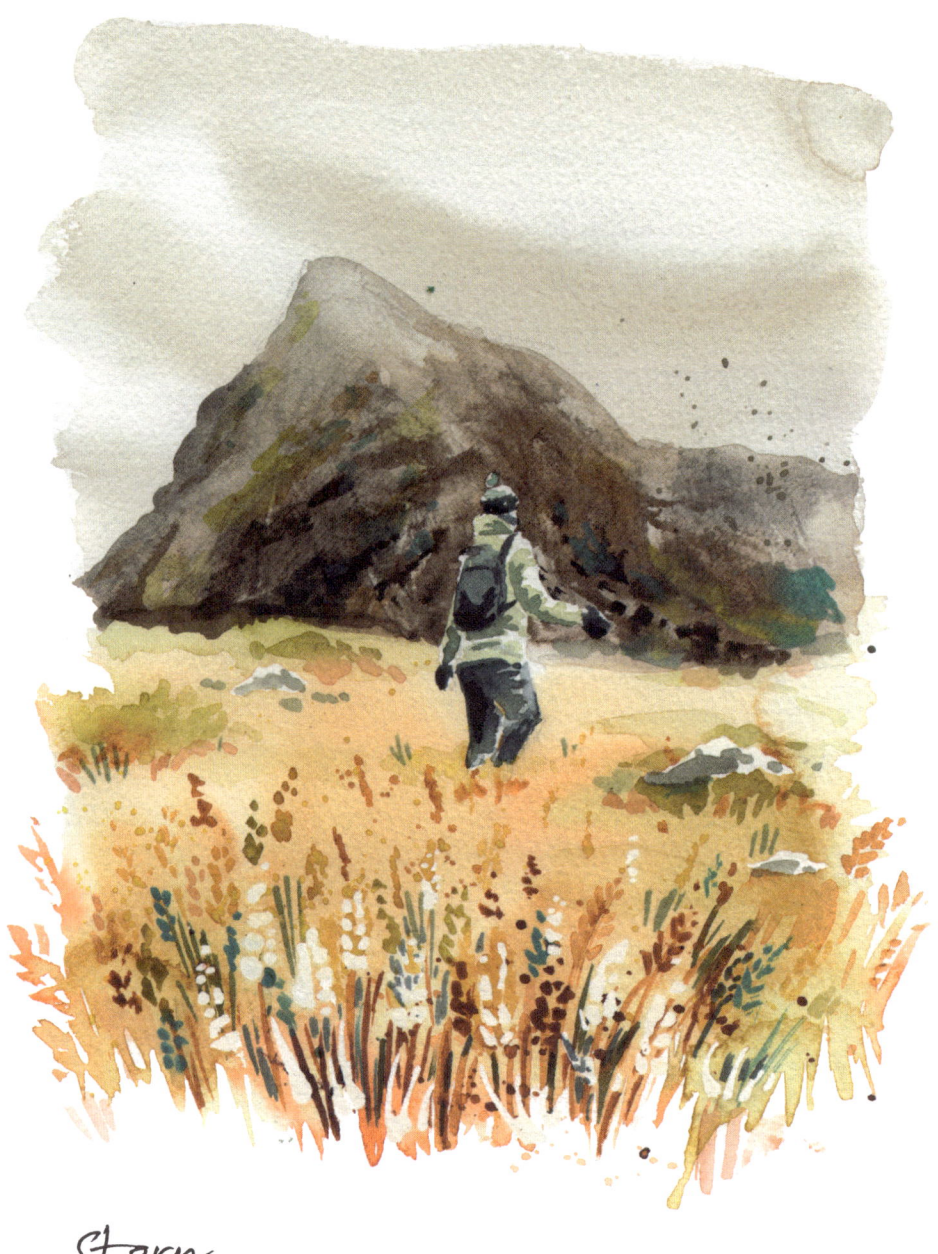

Story

Just like the previous example with the car, I like to add something human-made to my paintings. It can be as small as a fence or a pole, or something more obvious like a building or a person. It makes the painting more interesting, and you can read the story that is happening, as well as show the relationship between human and nature, and how we live side by side.

Framing

Framing makes a painting more intriguing, as if you are looking at it from a different perspective. Use contrasting dark elements around the main scenery, such as rocks, trees and shadows to create a natural frame that invites viewers to peek inside.

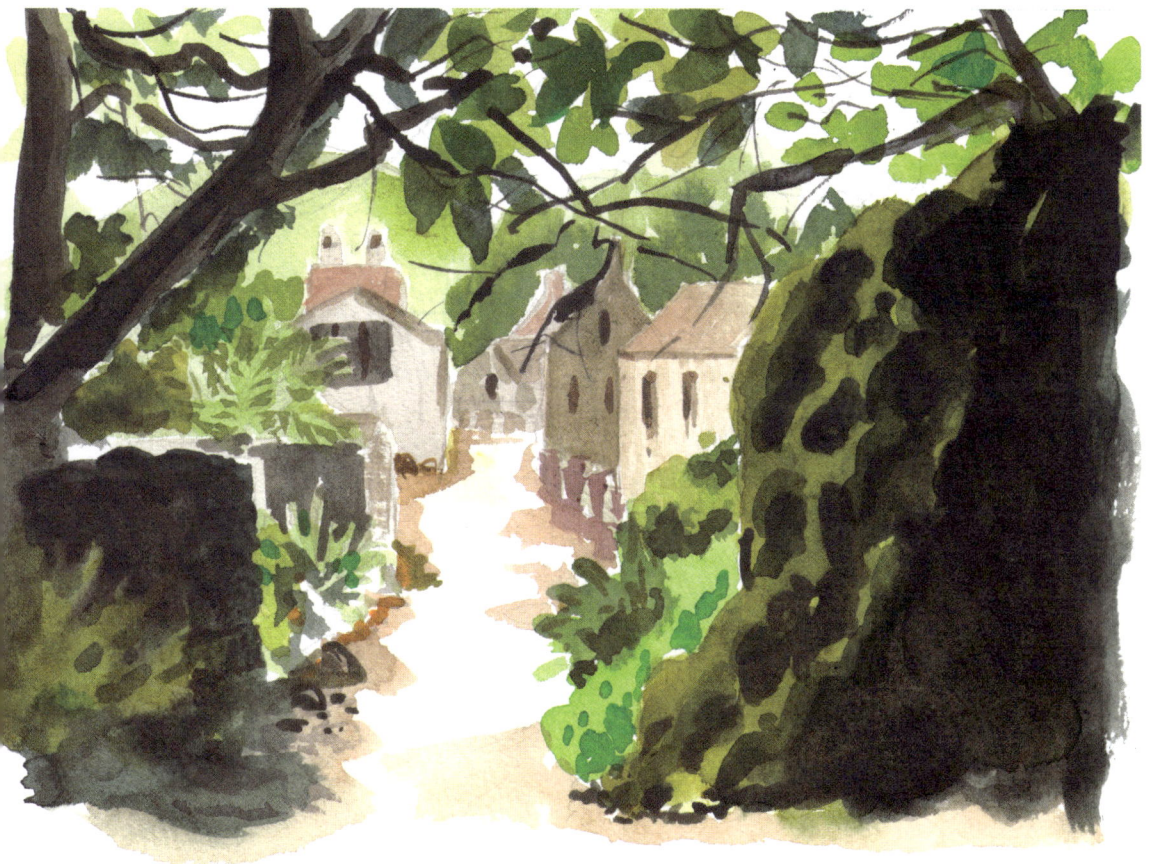

Tonal study

If there was a single exercise that could improve your compositional skills, this would be the one.

Use one colour hue and create a very simple, small thumbnail painting focusing on the contrast of value masses. Consider tone, scale and texture, and add a focal point. Use the compositional guides detailed earlier to help you craft a strong composition.

Use this method to train your compositional skills whenever you can. Start every painting by creating a small thumbnail sketch, and you will see how much your work improves as you learn to think in terms of value masses rather than objects.

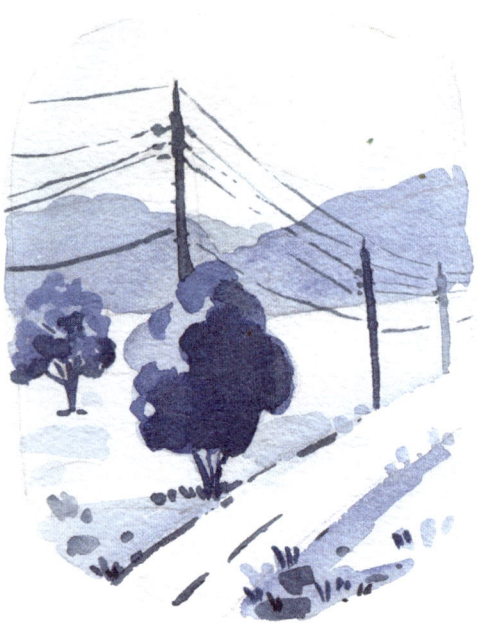
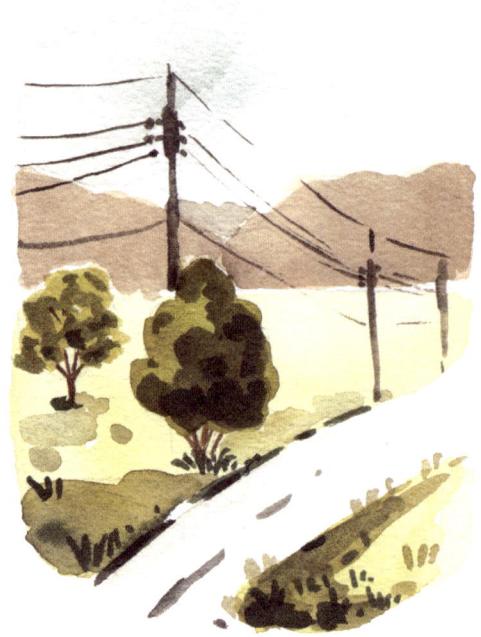

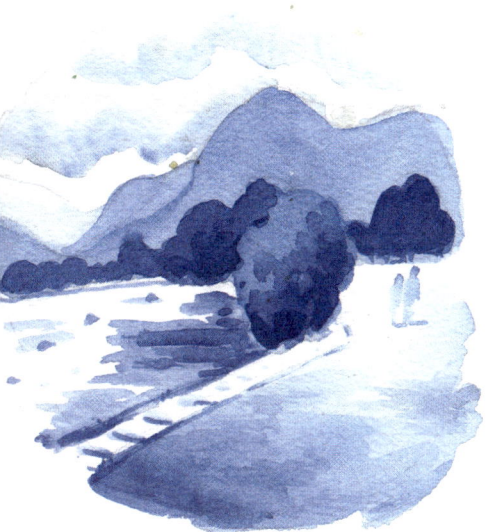

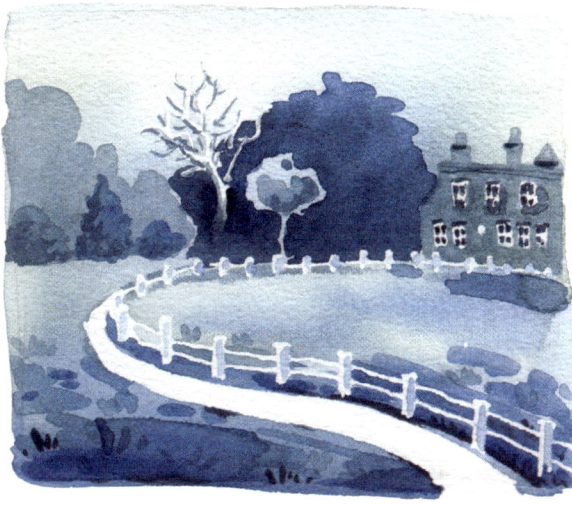

Improving composition

Another way to improve your composition skills is to look at other art mediums. I find movies very helpful, as camerawork relies heavily on good composition. Notice how the film director chooses to arrange the objects in the frame. Look at the scale, shadows and colours. Animated films work very well too.

When visiting museums and galleries, pay attention to the works of the old masters. Don't look at the subject or brushwork, but view the painting in terms of abstract shapes, planes and directional lines.

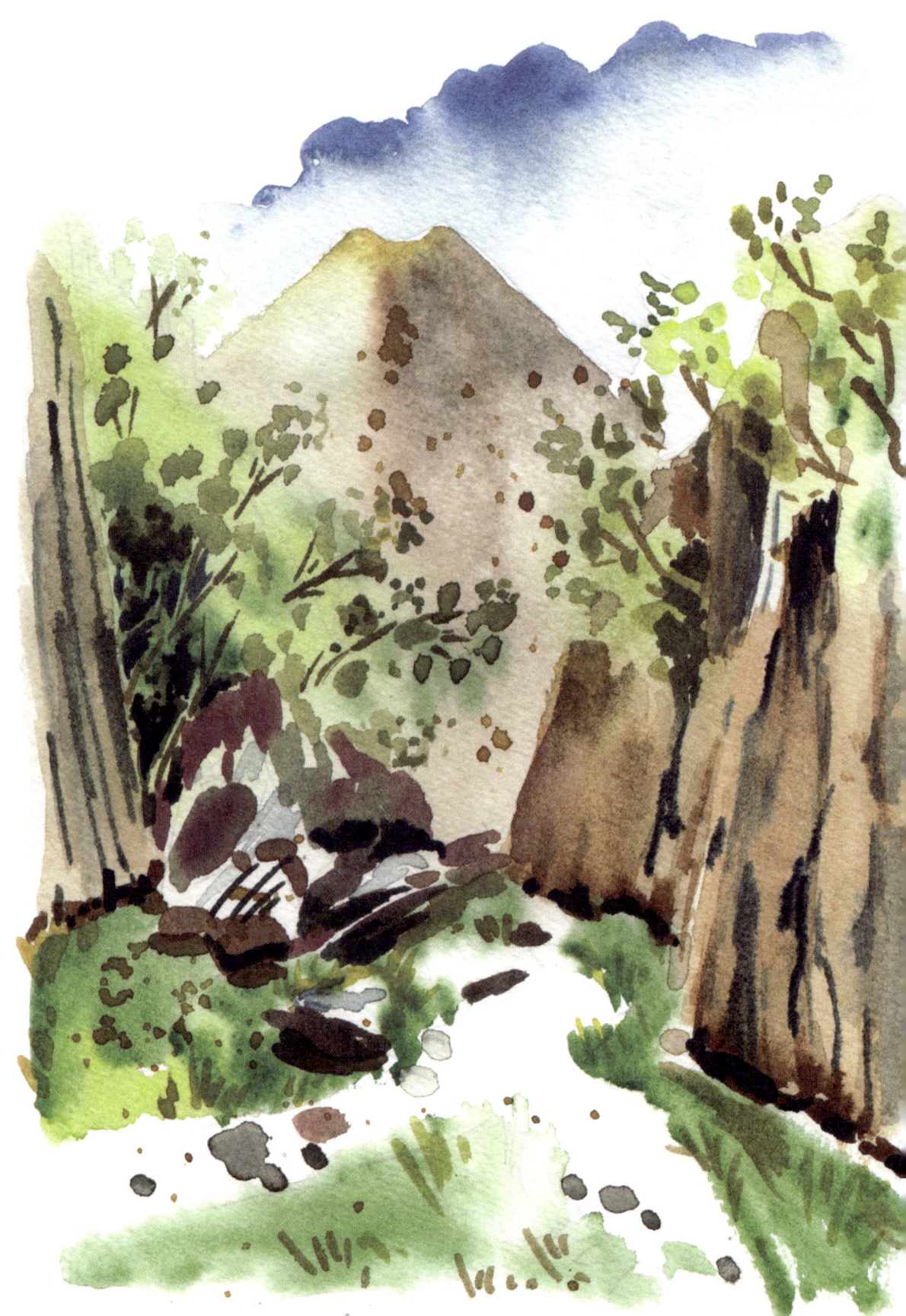

PROJECTS

In this section you will learn the thought processes and techniques behind watercolour painting. I have used a step-by-step approach, which will help you to understand patterns and ideas that are easy to adopt when creating your own landscape paintings. Some of the projects are interpretations of images from my own travels, whilst others are products of my imagination. We will look at various landscape themes – water, mountains, trees, meadows and seasons – and will explore how light, shadows and reflections are applied.

For each exercise I use a size 8 Fuumuui round travel brush with lid, or a size 2 Fuumuui mop brush (these are both the same size and generally very similar). If a brush is not specified in a particular step, it will be one of these. Some exercises may specify extra brushes, including a size 8 Panart flat brush; a size 3 Princeton Heritage round brush; and a size 4 Da Vinci liner brush. You don't have to use the exact same brands as I do, as this is a highly personal choice, so go for anything similar that you like to work with.

The paper I use for the projects is Canson: Moulin du Roy, but you can find other paper suggestions in the resources section on page 156.

To follow along with the projects you will need the recommended tubes swatched at the top of each exercise.

Water

Water has been a popular subject in art over the centuries, and some artists have specialized in this theme alone. What makes water so attractive in paintings is its tranquillity and reflective properties. As the name suggests, watercolour is the perfect medium for painting water, mainly because of its transparency and ability to create soft colour transitions.

I love painting water because there are so many ways in which different effects, brushstrokes and colours can be used to depict it, and there are always new techniques to be discovered. It can be as simple as painting the reflection of an object on or next to the water, or as complex as capturing waves and ripples.

It's always worth having a few tricks up your sleeve when painting water, to make it less intimidating. We will explore some of them in the following exercises.

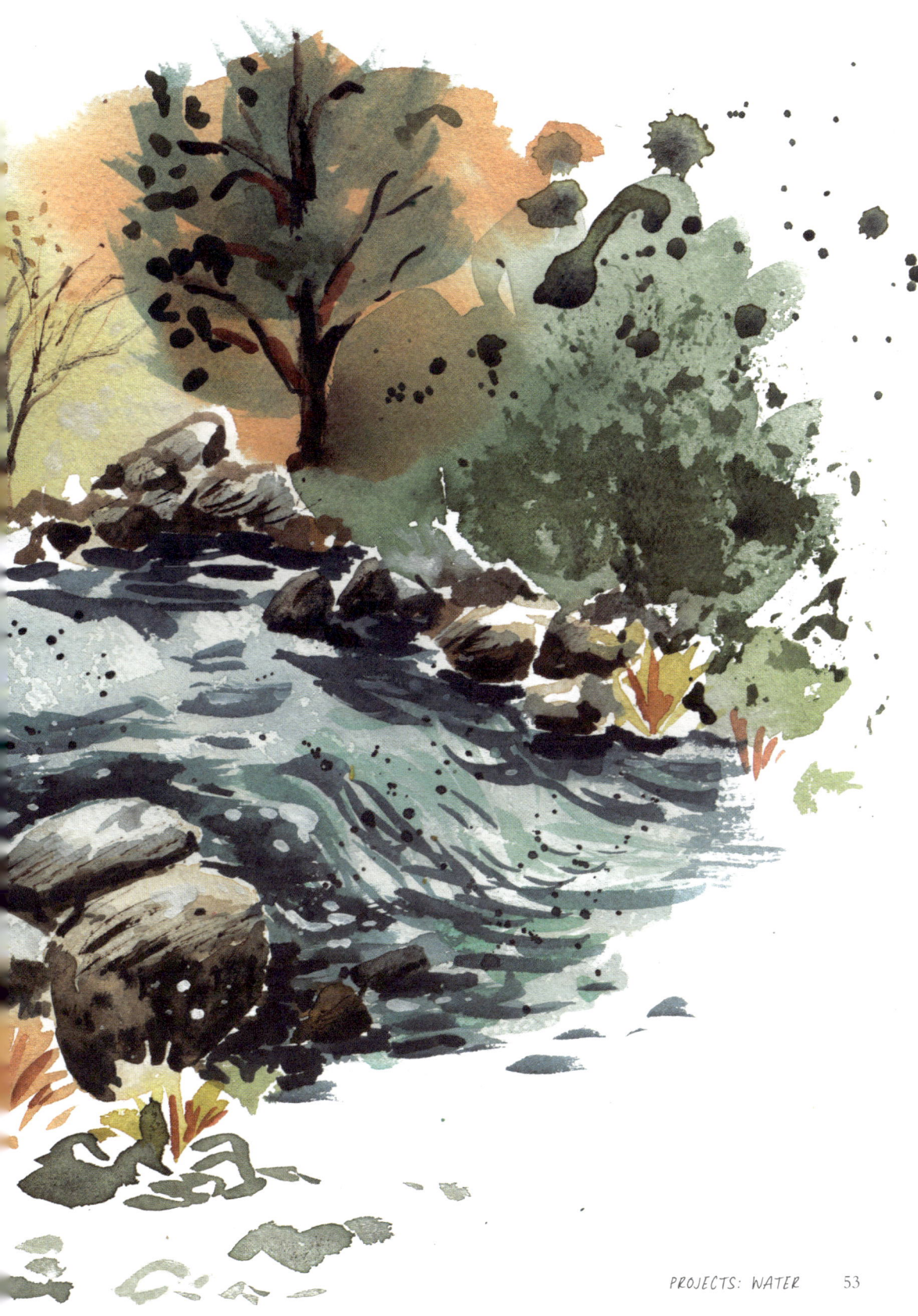

Reflections

As mentioned, water can be depicted showing reflections of surrounding objects. When water is very still, the reflections will be as precise as they would be in a mirror. However, if there are waves or ripples in the water, reflections can range from slightly distorted to almost abstract shapes.

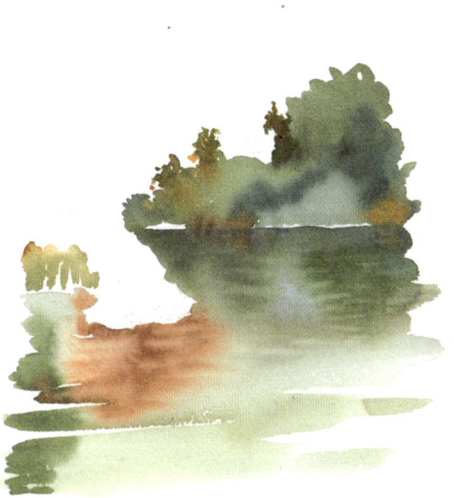

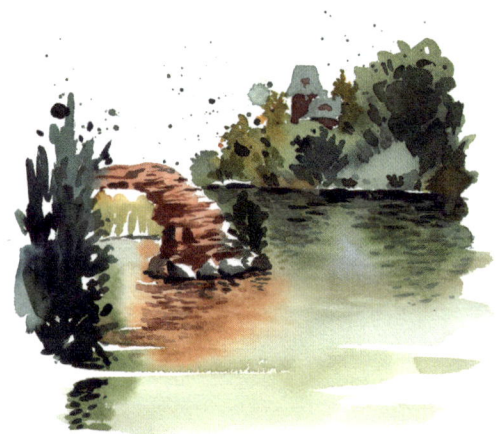

In this example I have painted greenery in the background and in the wetted area of the lake for the reflection. I roughly tried to mimic the same shapes and colours as my subjects. Whilst the paint was drying, I used a flat brush and scrubbed it across the paper to create short highlighted strokes, to represent small ripples.

In the second layer, I added details to the greenery and painted the arch of stones. To define the reflection, I used colours from my subjects and painted short strokes on the water. This way, you combine soft edges of the reflection with more defined ripples of water.

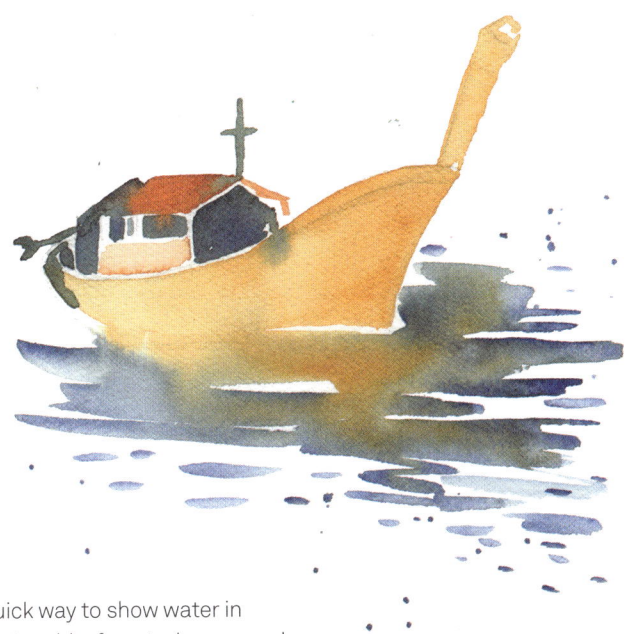

Another quick way to show water in sketches is to add a few strokes around an object. Here I have painted a boat and, whilst it was still wet, made a few larger strokes around it as well as a few smaller ones further from the boat. I used a watered down blue colour for the sea and allowed the colours from the boat to bleed into the water.

On the second layer I painted a few smaller zigzag brushstrokes using more saturated versions of the same colours. A few strokes of white gouache add a shine to the sea.

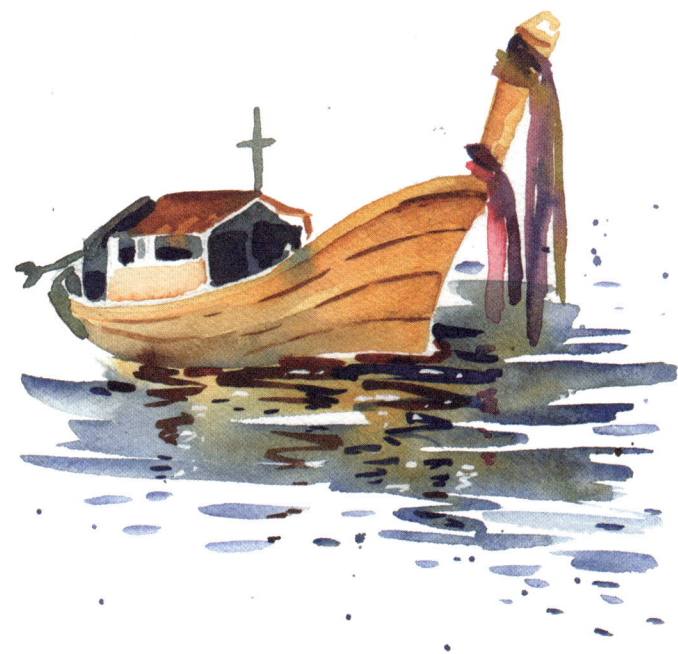

small waves

To paint small waves in the ocean, you can use very short, curved strokes.

In this example, I painted a large area using a very watery mix of turquoise and grey colours.

I then painted a couple of rocks and let the colours from the rocks and ocean mix on the paper.

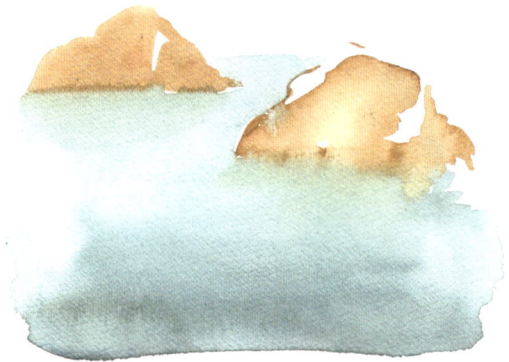

Once this layer was completely dry, I painted overlapping curved strokes using medium-wet ultramarine blue, concentrating darker colours in the foreground and around the rocks. A few drops of burnt umber around the rocks served as their reflection.

Once everything was completely dry, I added a few dots of white gouache to depict the shine from the sun on the ocean.

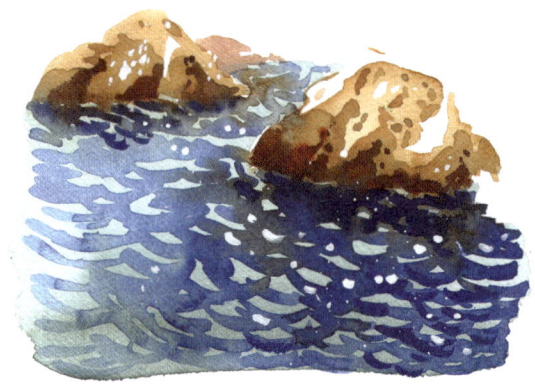

Dry brush

We often think of water as fluid and soft, but a textured dry-brush effect can also be used to depict water.

I used a flat brush to create a dry brushstroke effect (see page 22) and layered strokes of different colours on top of each other, starting with a light blue and gradually building up to deeper, darker blue tones.

To create highlights in the middle, I scraped the paint with sandpaper. To use this trick, your paper should be at least 300 gsm (140 lb).

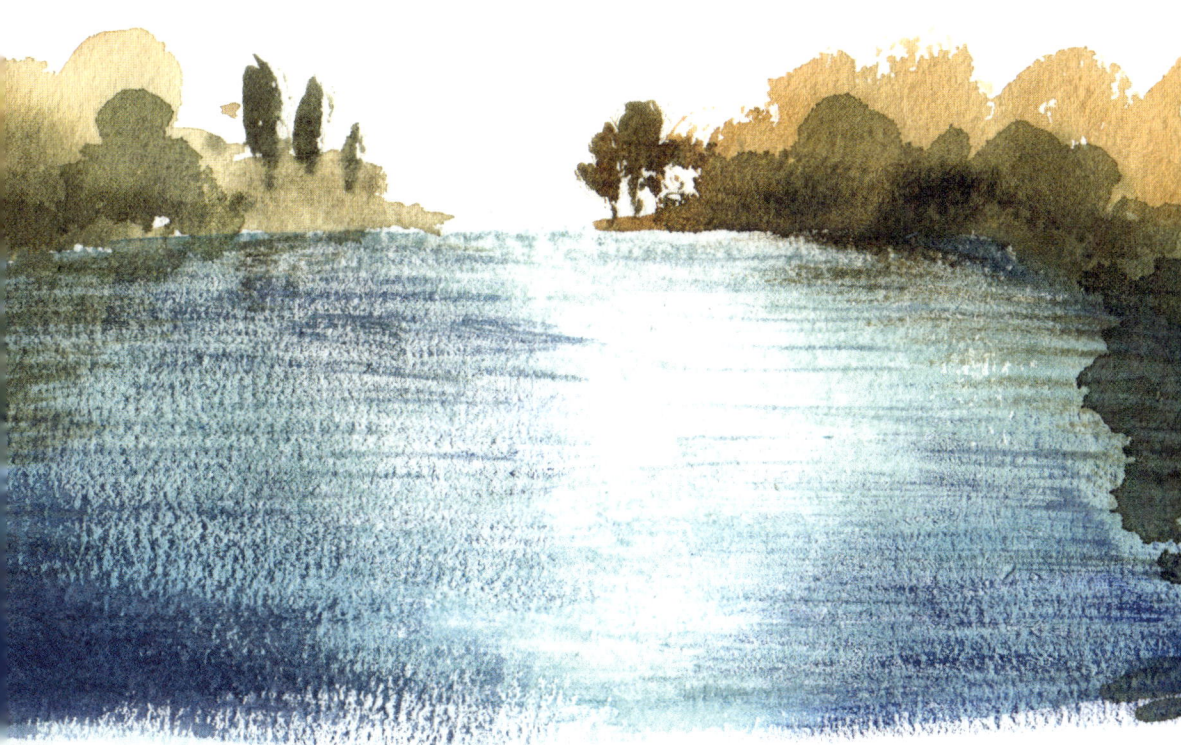

RIPPLES

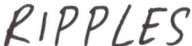

● cobalt teal blue, manganese blue hue, ultramarine blue,
indigo, buff titanium, light red, white gouache

If your painting consists purely of water and there are no shadows or reflections of objects to focus on, you should put effort into defining the shapes of the waves, their shadows and highlights. For this exercise, I suggest finding a good reference photo where you can observe how the ripples appear.

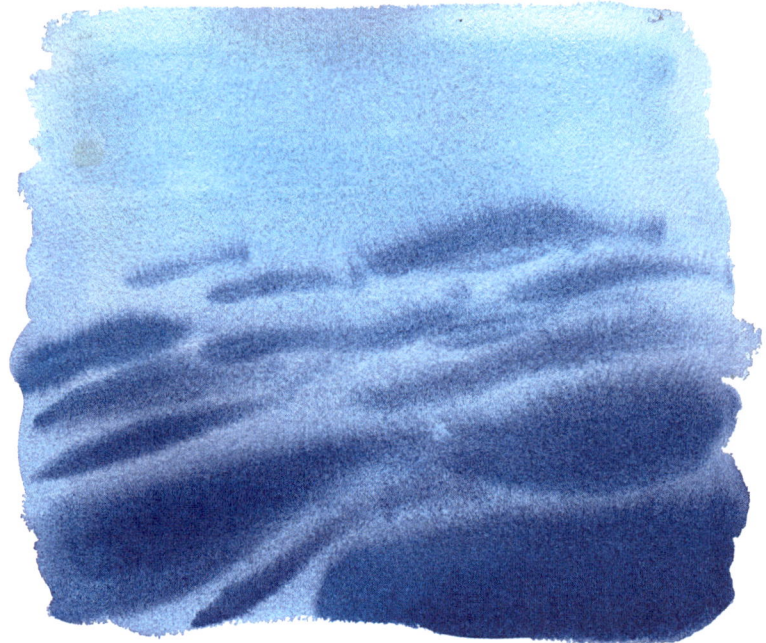

1. Create a very light and watery mixture of cobalt teal blue and manganese blue hue and apply a large wash to the paper (see page 18). Allow it to sit for a little bit, and when you notice the paint starts to lose its shine, use a mop brush to apply large brushstrokes with a thick ultramarine blue. The paint will spread and create a ripple effect with soft edges. There are a couple of things to keep in mind: create larger and more dense brushstrokes in the foreground, and smaller as you move into the background.

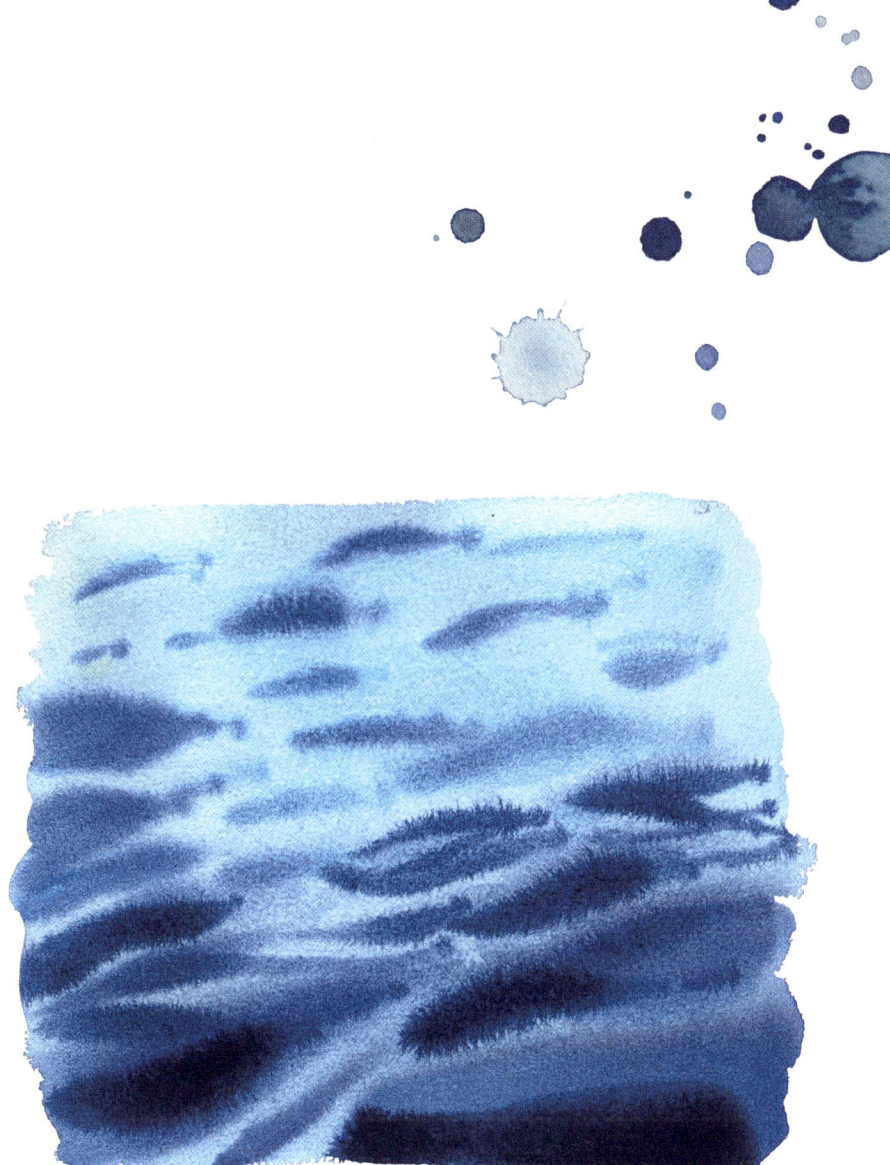

2. In the foreground, add a few very dark indigo strokes using a thick paint straight from the box. Take your time whilst adding darker brushstrokes: let the paint spread, adding more as needed.

If you notice that the paint spreads too much, take a clean wet brush and gently scrub over the wet paint to lift pigments from the area where you want to create highlights.

3. Once you are happy with how the ripples are positioned, it's time to paint the sky. Create a light peach colour by mixing buff titanium with light red and lots of water. Apply this mixture to the bottom of the sky and turn the paper upside down to apply a graded wash (see page 18). Create the wash by adding more water as you work downwards and gradually start introducing a very diluted ultramarine colour. Let everything dry before moving onto the next step.

4. On the dry layer, use the tip of a fine brush with a medium-thick indigo mixture to draw reflections on the water: larger, more detailed and darker in the foreground, and lighter as you move away to the background. Notice how the reflections sit on the highlighted part of the waves.

Allow this layer to dry before adding final touches.

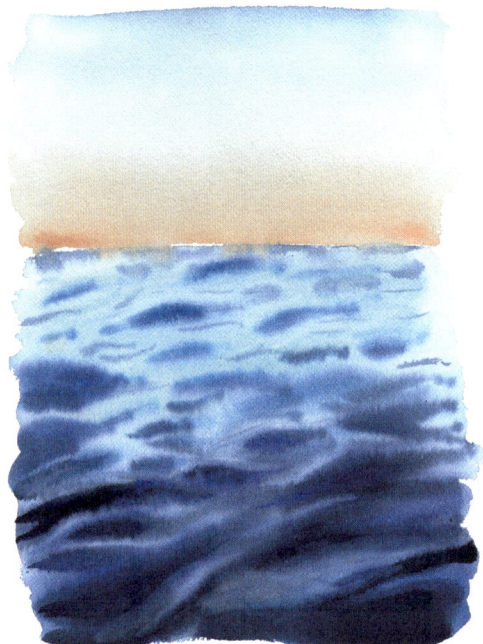
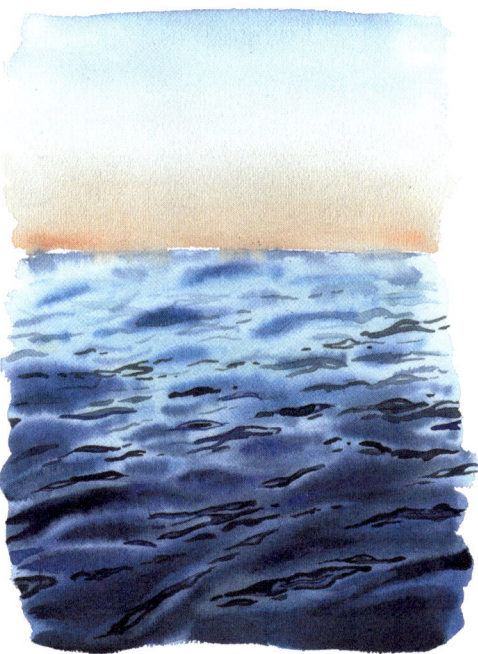

5. Using a small brush and thick white gouache, place shiny highlights on the reflections.

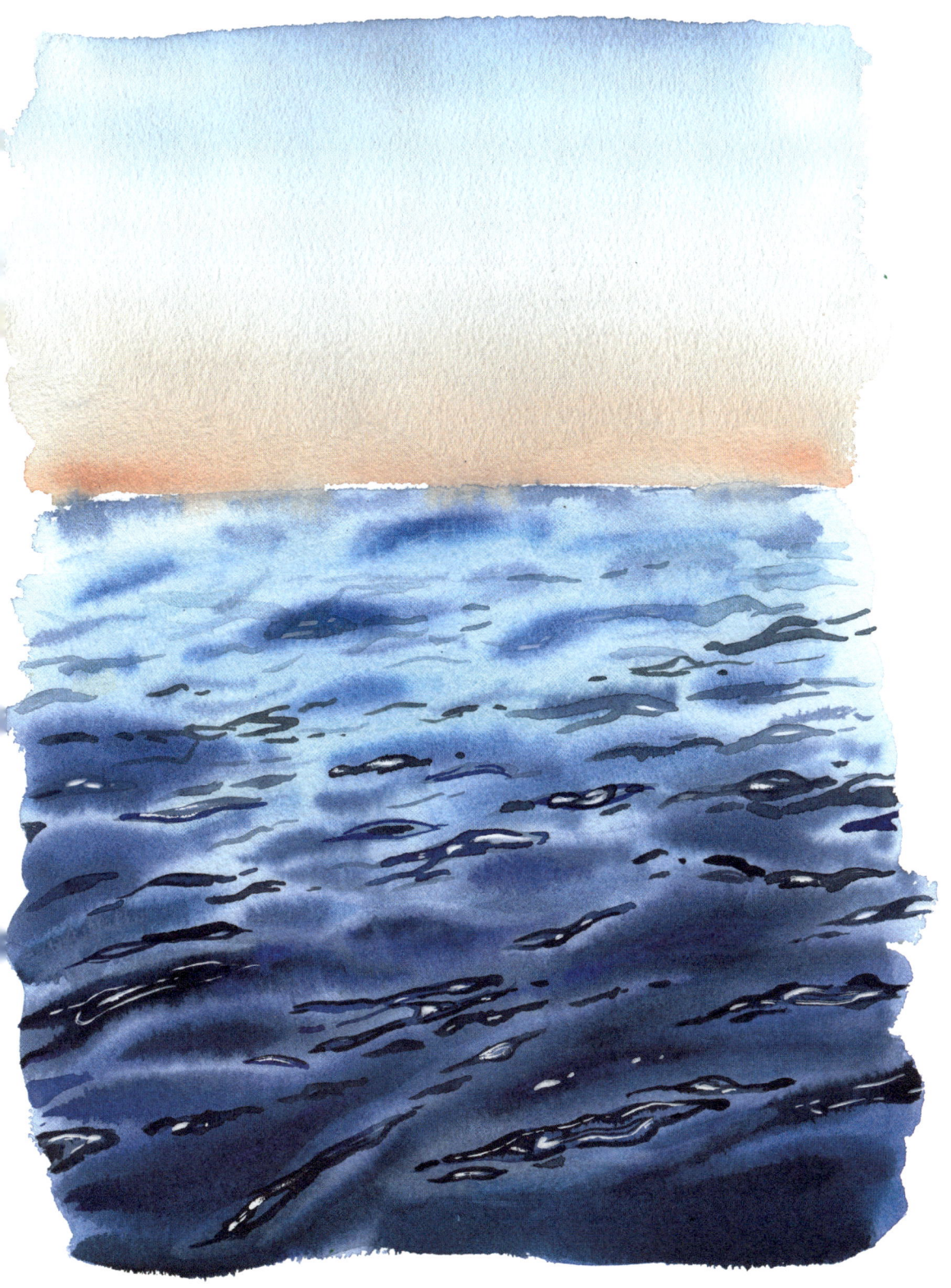

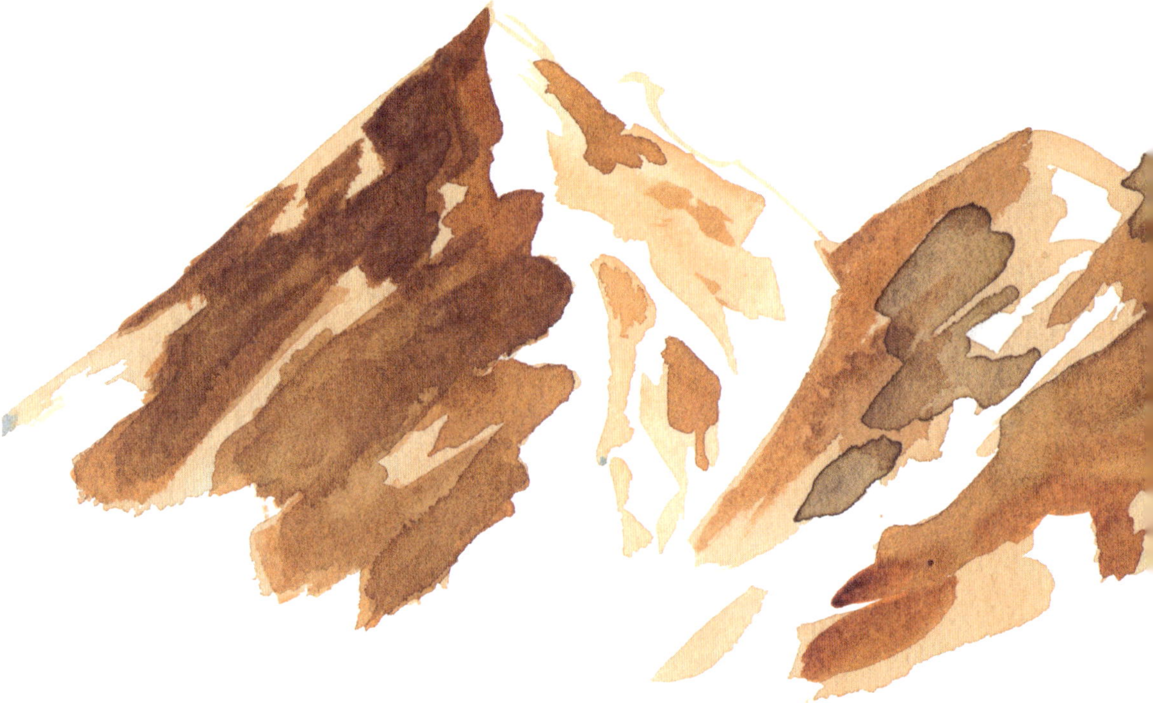

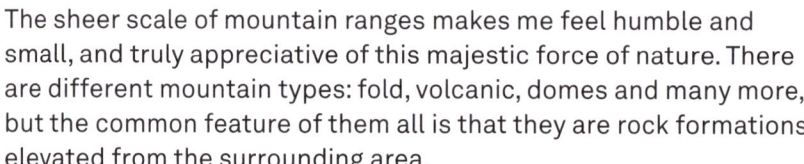

Mountains

The sheer scale of mountain ranges makes me feel humble and small, and truly appreciative of this majestic force of nature. There are different mountain types: fold, volcanic, domes and many more, but the common feature of them all is that they are rock formations elevated from the surrounding area.

In painting, mountains always add depth and volume, emphasizing the scale and spatial relationship with surrounding objects. The contrast between the size of the mountains and everything else makes them perfect to include in the background of a landscape.

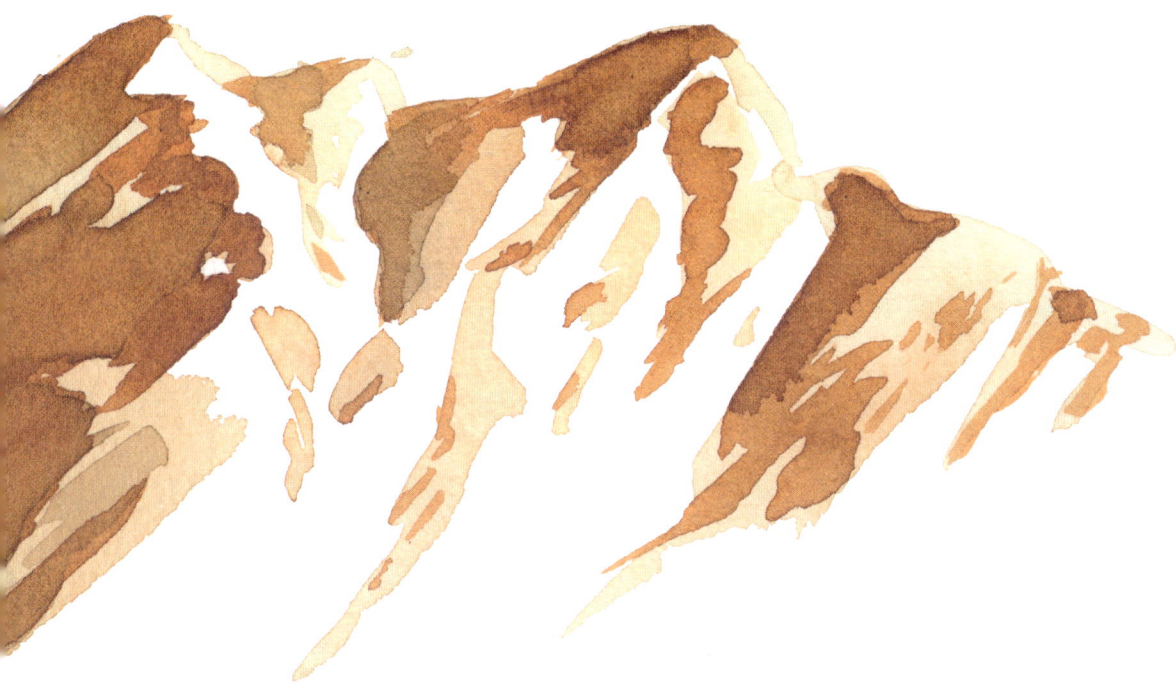

Light and shadow

To paint mountains, it's important to show their rocky texture. The edges should be sharp and clearly defined. This is where your brushstrokes come into play. When you look at mountains in soft light, shadows appear and you can see the shape and texture of the rock.

However, if you try to paint evenly lit rock on paper, it will most likely appear flat and fail to convey its shape. Though our eyes don't have trouble making out three-dimensional shapes, transferring the same image to two dimensions can be tricky – even photography doesn't do it justice! To represent something three-dimensional on paper, you need to accentuate its structure, rather than just painting what you see. Correctly placed areas of light and shadow will help a great deal when painting rocky mountains.

To depict rocky mountains, like the ones above, follow these steps. Using just one colour, paint mountain ridges, applying more saturated paint on one side and leaving the other side white.

Add some brushstrokes of diluted colour to the white parts to show the rocky texture, and use even more saturated colour on the shadowy part.

Snowy mountains

Snow-capped mountains will always have patches of rock texture peeking through the snow. To paint them, apply the same light and shadow principles from page 51, and then build on it.

For the first layer, create an outline of the mountain shape and apply an even wash of your lightest colour. I used a very watery Naples yellow. Let it dry.

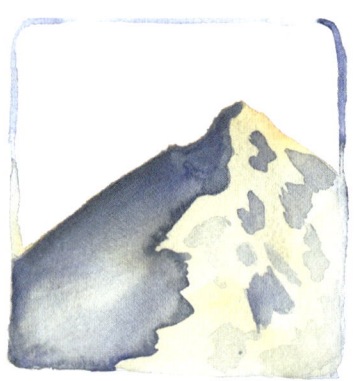

On the dry layer, using medium-wet ultramarine blue, paint a shadowy part of the mountain. The edges should be sharp and defined. Mix the same colour with more water and add darker patches to the lighter part of the mountain using short, scribble-like brushstrokes.

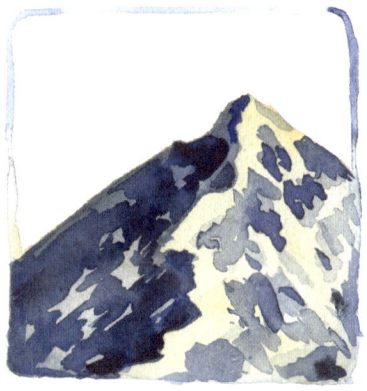

When the second layer is dry, continue applying short brushstrokes to create texture. Add darker patches to the part in shadow, and slightly lighter patches to the lit part of the mountain.

Build a large mountain range by alternating light and shadow on the peaks and slopes.

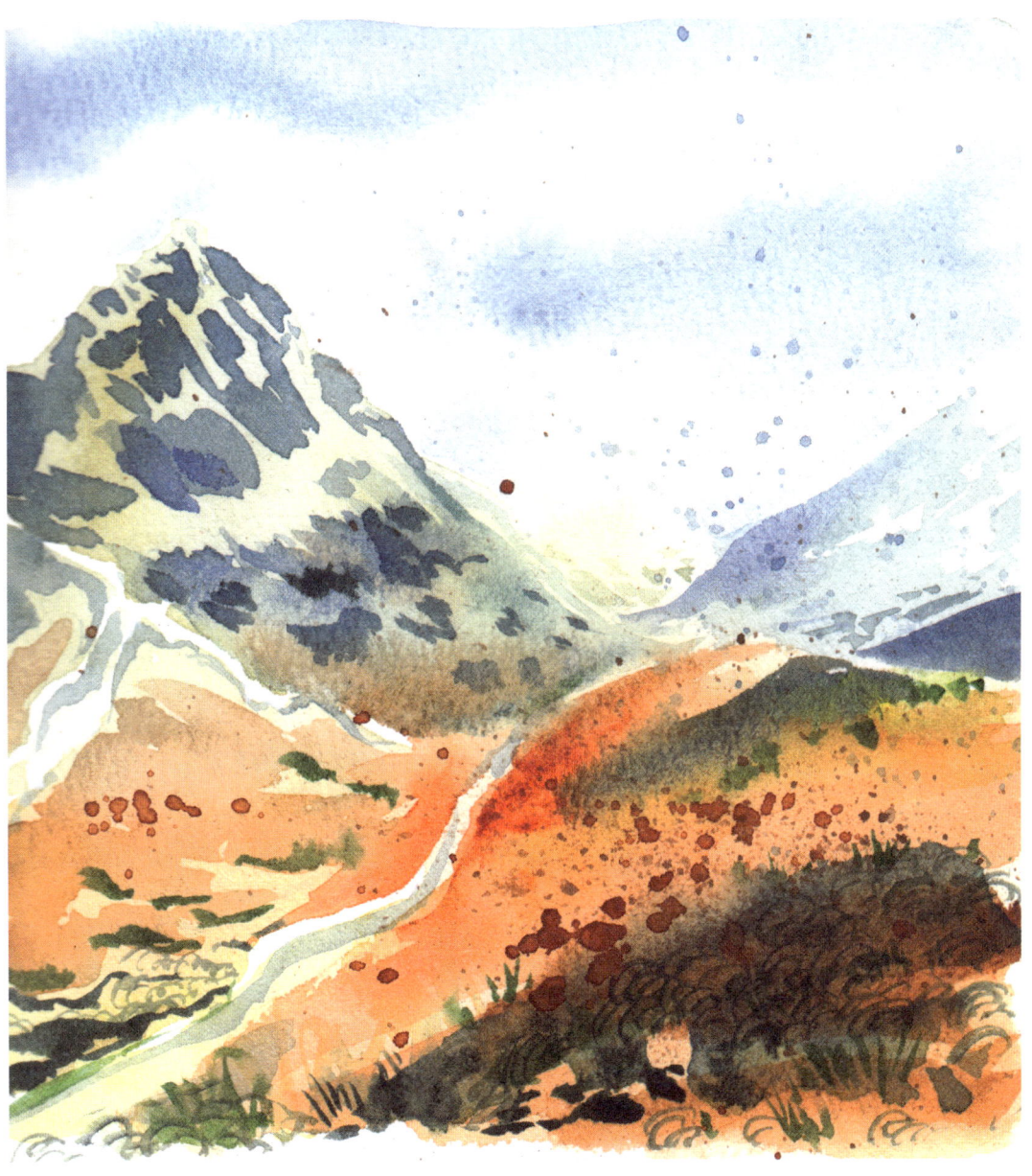

Rocky texture

One of the best features of watercolour is that not everything needs to be 'painted' in order to create cool effects; sometimes just a few simple tricks can be used. A grainy rock texture can be achieved by scraping and moving pigments around with the sharp edge of an old credit card, palette knife, or anything that has a similar hard edge.

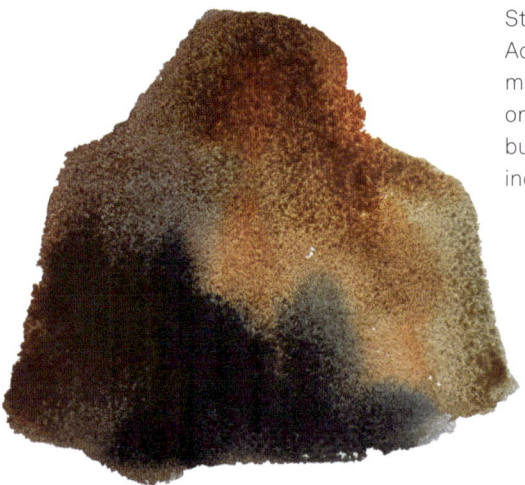

Start by creating a wet wash of the rock. Add different colours and allow them to mix and mingle together using the wet-on-wet technique (see page 19). I used burnt umber, quinacridone orange, and indigo for the shadows.

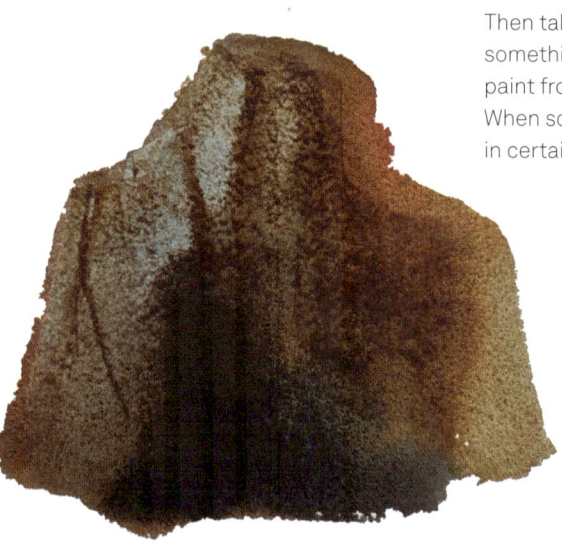

Then take an old credit card (or something similar) and start scraping the paint from the lighter parts of the rock. When scraping, pigment will concentrate in certain areas creating dark lines.

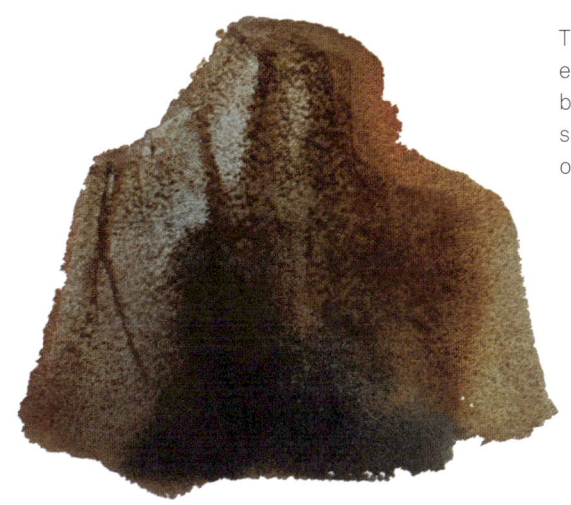

This technique might require some experimentation to find a sweet spot between light and shadow; as you do so, dab more paint on the darker parts of the rock.

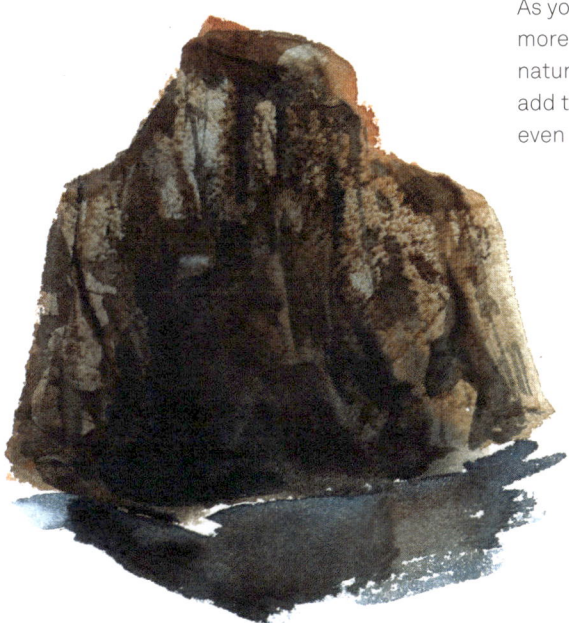

As your rock starts to dry out, adding more defined brushstrokes will create a natural look. Take a small line brush and add thin lines to accentuate the texture even more.

WHITE CLIFFS OF DOVER

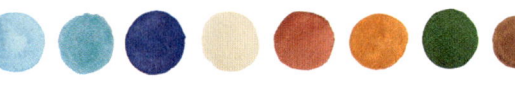

• *manganese blue hue, cobalt teal blue, ultramarine blue, buff titanium, light red, quinacridone deep gold, permanent sap green, burnt umber, indigo*

The famous white cliffs of Dover are situated on the south-east coast of England. Their colour comes from the white chalk and rock, which contrasts sharply with the blue waters below.

1. Mix manganese blue hue with cobalt teal blue and add plenty of water to make a very transparent light colour. Start by painting long, curved brushstrokes to create ocean waves.

Next, add ultramarine blue to the mixture to make it darker and use it to paint waves in the foreground.

2. Rinse your brush lightly, and with a little paint still left on it, draw an outline of the cliff and add a few large brushstrokes around it to define the sky and clouds.

Whilst the paint is still wet, add a few large brushstrokes with a little more blue to create soft clouds.

3. Using a fairly thick consistency of quinacridone deep gold, permanent sap green and burnt umber, paint some greenery on top of the cliff. At the bottom, where you are painting onto dry paper, this will create a hard edge, but the part where the paint bleeds into the wet sky will be satisfyingly unpredictable.

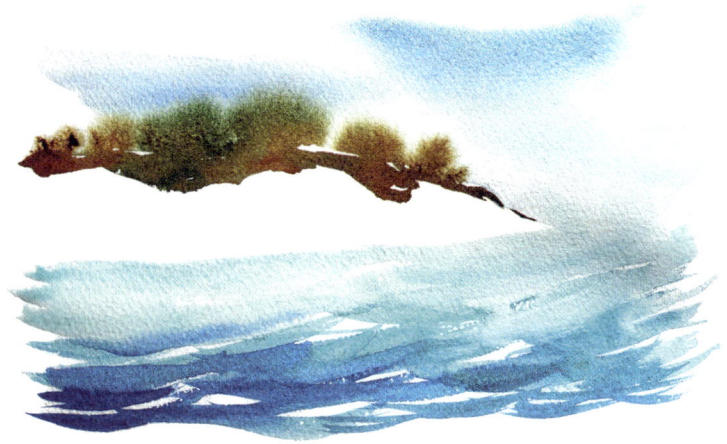

4. Play around, adding more colour to the greenery as the paint dries. Once you are happy with how it looks, leave it to dry completely.

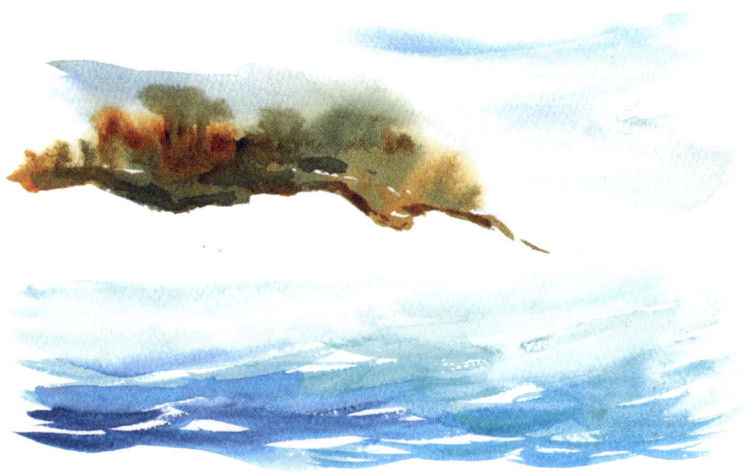

5. Add texture to the cliff using a very light burnt umber. Mix it with lots of water, load your brush, then gently wipe your brush on a paper towel. With the side of the brush, create scribbles using a dry brush effect (see page 22). At the bottom of the cliff, add a darker line to create a shadow; at the top, continue adding darker greenery using thicker paint in permanent sap green.

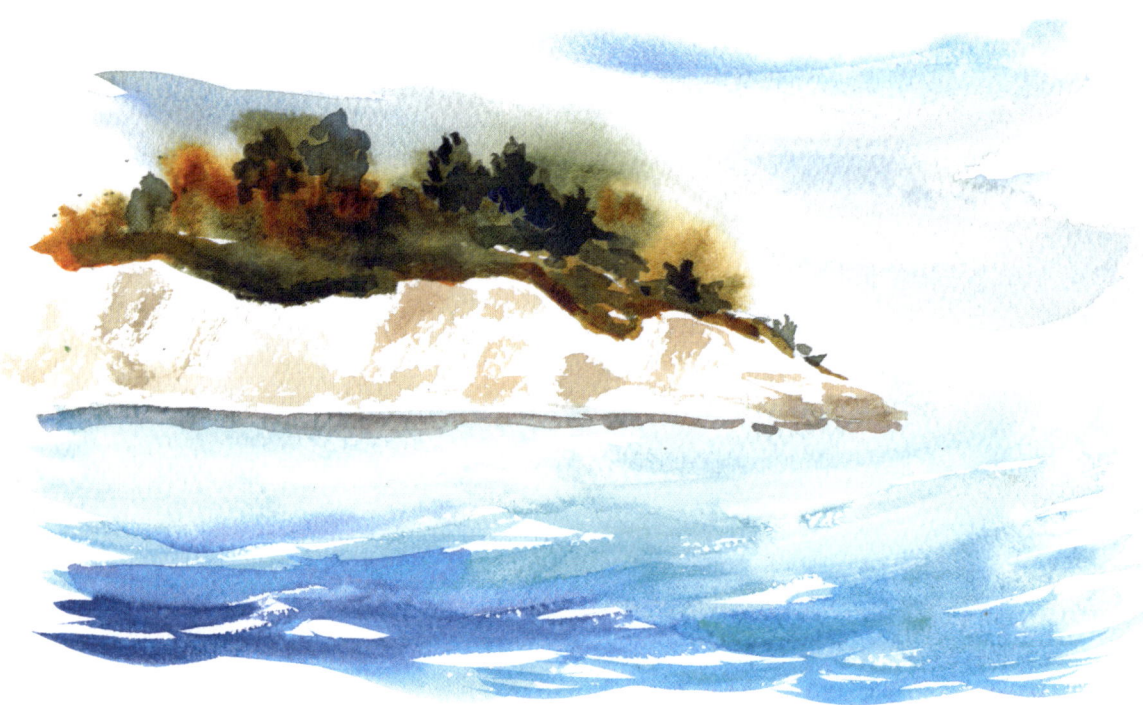

6. For the last step, add more dry brush effect onto the cliffs using darker burnt umber and a dash of indigo. At the top of the greenery add small splashes of cobalt teal blue to create a hazy effect.

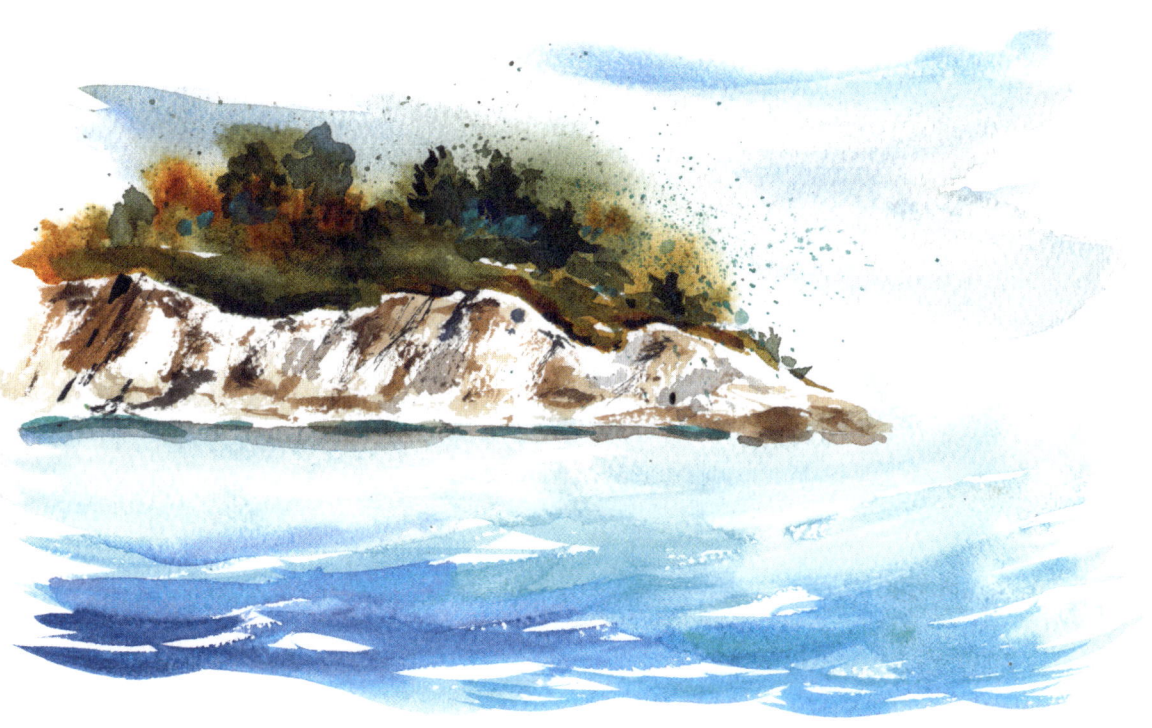

CALM VALLEYS OF SCOTLAND

• neutral tint, burnt umber, cobalt teal blue, manganese blue, rich green gold, deep sap green, mayan blue genuine, scarlet lake, white gouache.

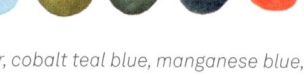

Scotland is a country of striking landscapes, with lochs, rocky mountains and fir trees. The distinguishing colours of the surroundings are a combination of rusty red and moss green.

1. Start by painting shadowy sides of the mountains using a very watery mixture of neutral tint and burnt umber. Make the paint on paper very wet and work through the ridges quickly.

2. Add more water as you go towards the foot of the mountain. Paint the sky using a very light grey wash and adding dashes of neutral tint and cobalt teal blue for clouds. Keep all washes light.

3. At the bottom of the mountain add a thicker but still quite wet wash using burnt umber and rich green gold. At this point, you can also add a few trees in the background. They don't have to be very precise, just enough to be recognizable. Whilst the paint is still wet, sprinkle over some salt, ideally larger crystals such as sea salt (see page 23).

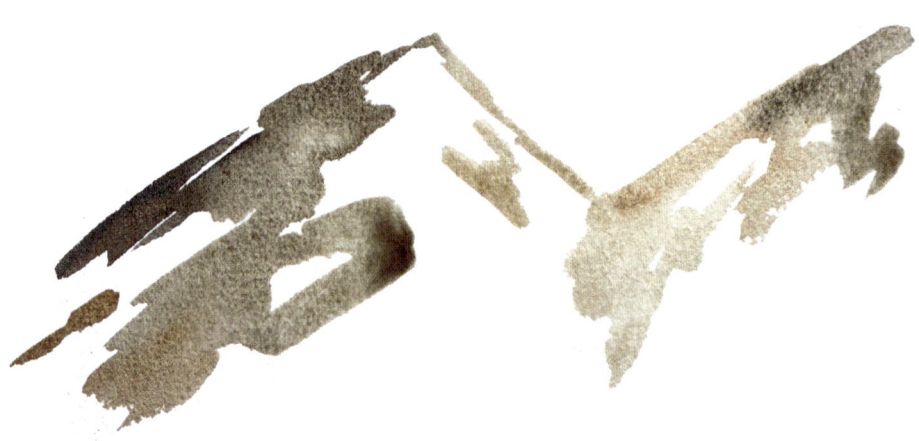

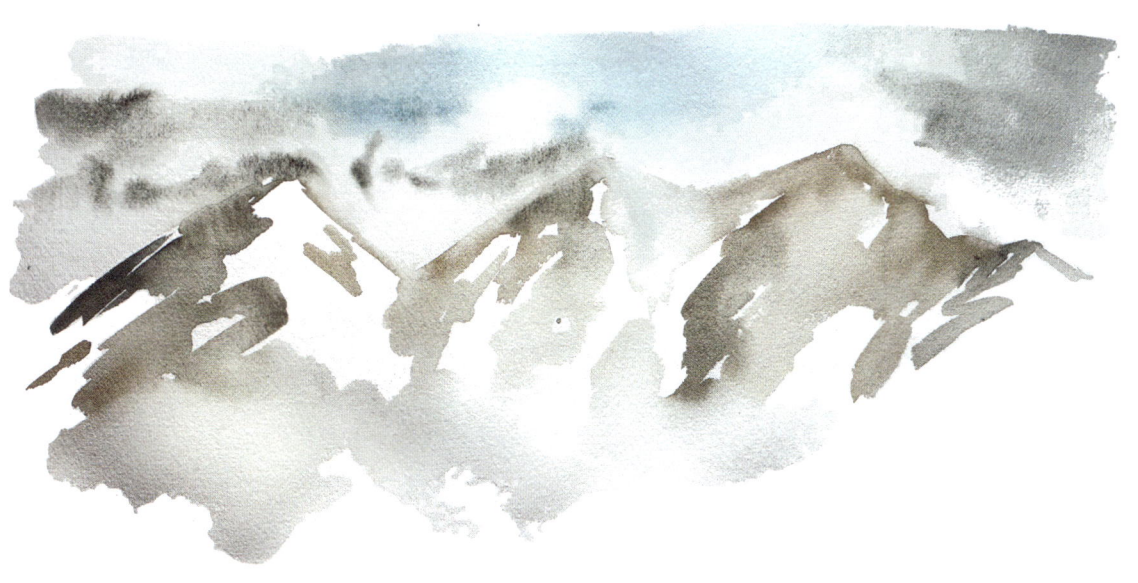

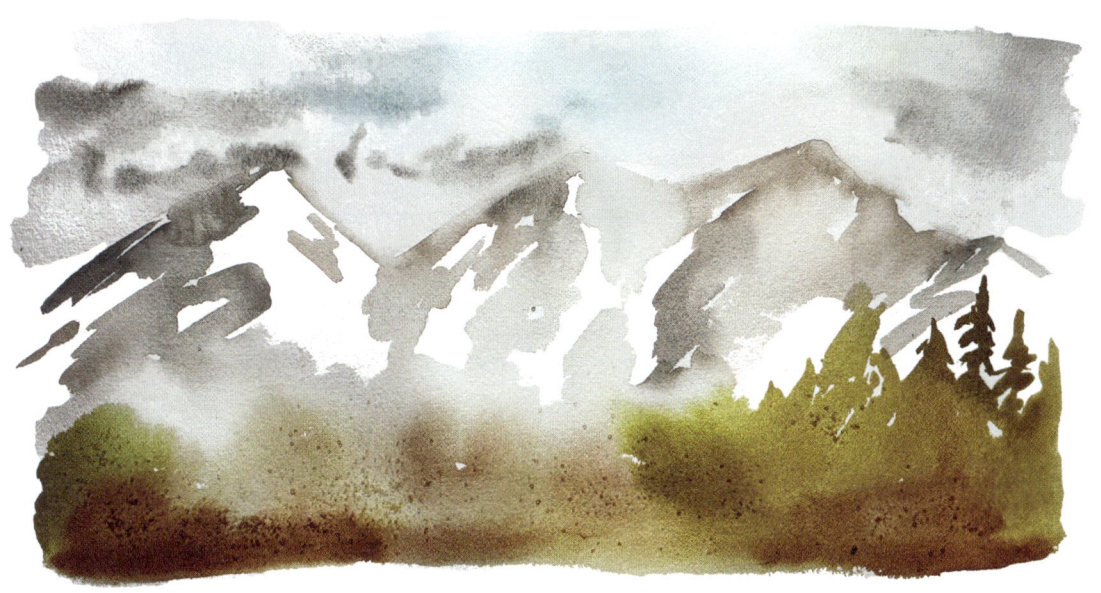

4. Continue working towards the bottom of the page, painting long horizontal lines with a mixture of cobalt teal blue and manganese blue hue, and also allowing paint from the shore to bleed into the water. Add a few drops of your greenery colours to the water to show their reflection. Let this layer dry completely before moving onto the next step.

When painting fir trees, start from the top and use short, scribbly brushstrokes.

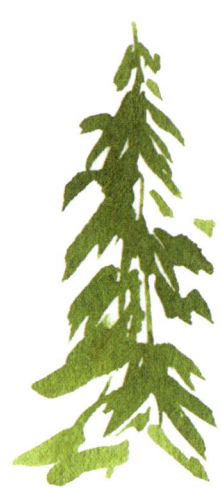

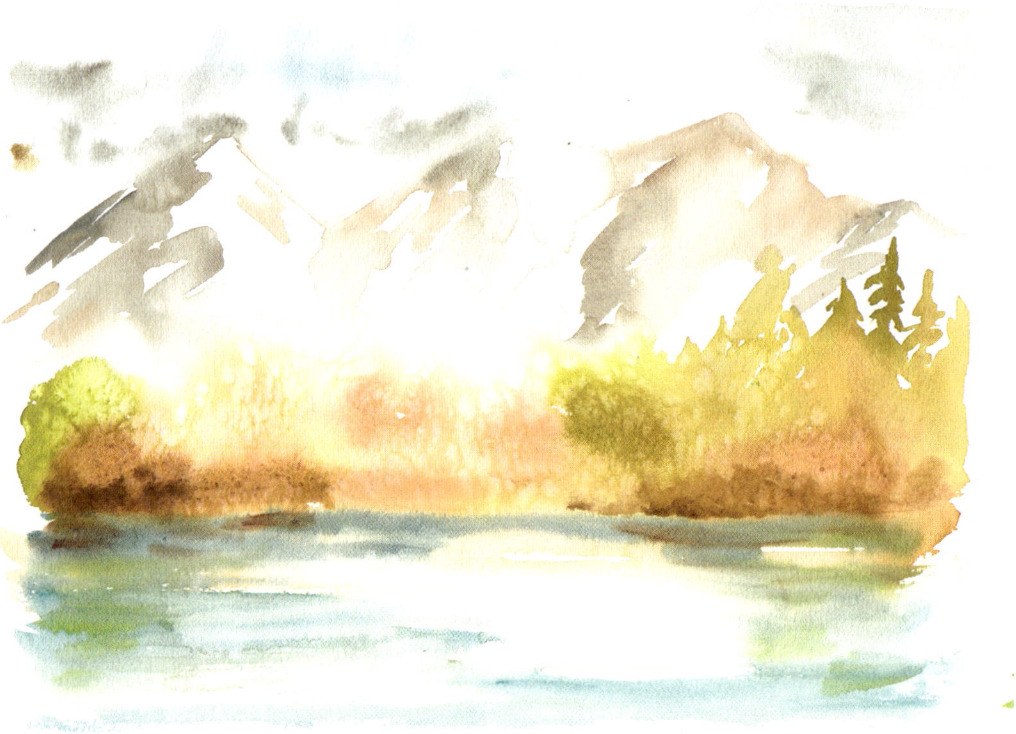

5. Load your brush with medium-wet deep sap green mixed with rich green gold and use this mixture to paint trees, alternate this colour with mayan blue genuine for some trees. When the trees are painted, load your brush with lots of water and pull the paint down from the bottom of the trees to the coastline, creating a very soft transition of colour (see page 22).

6. For the mountains, add more shadows using the same colours as before but with a slightly thicker consistency. For the foreground, use a very thick mayan blue and deep sap green to create a dry brush effect (see page 22), layering it with burnt umber. Take a small liner brush and load it with water, then pull the colour from the ground to create long blades of grass.

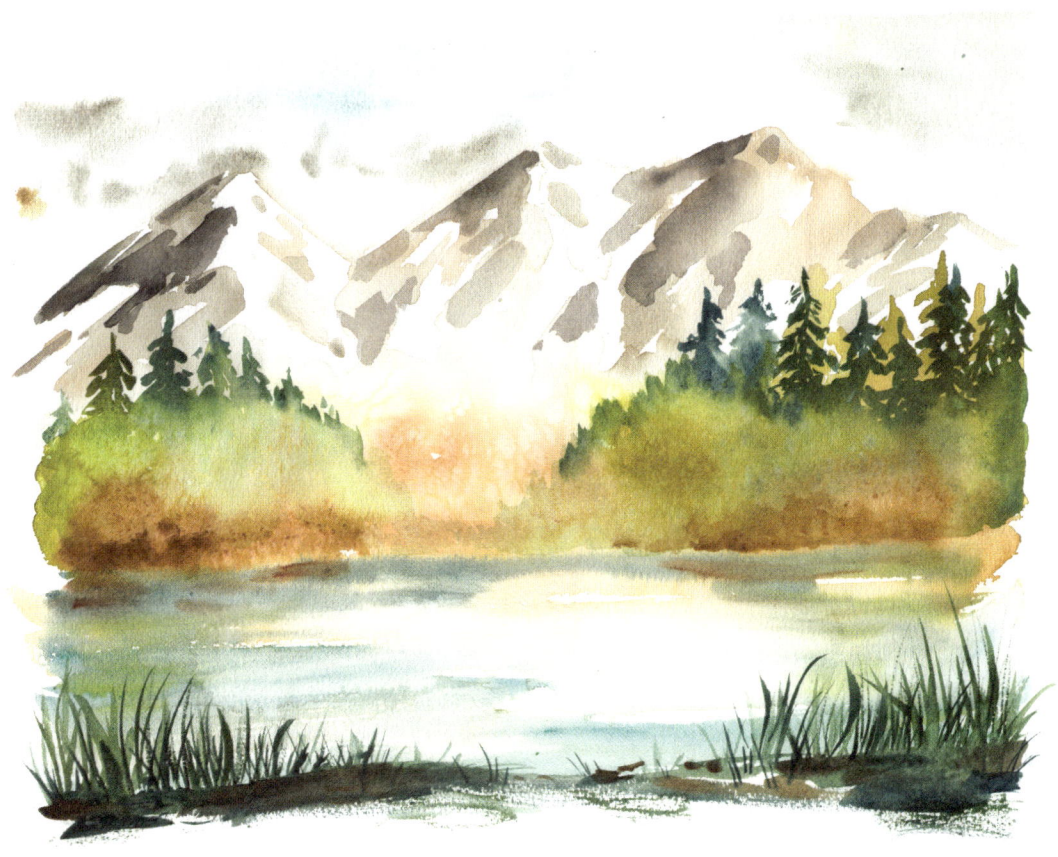

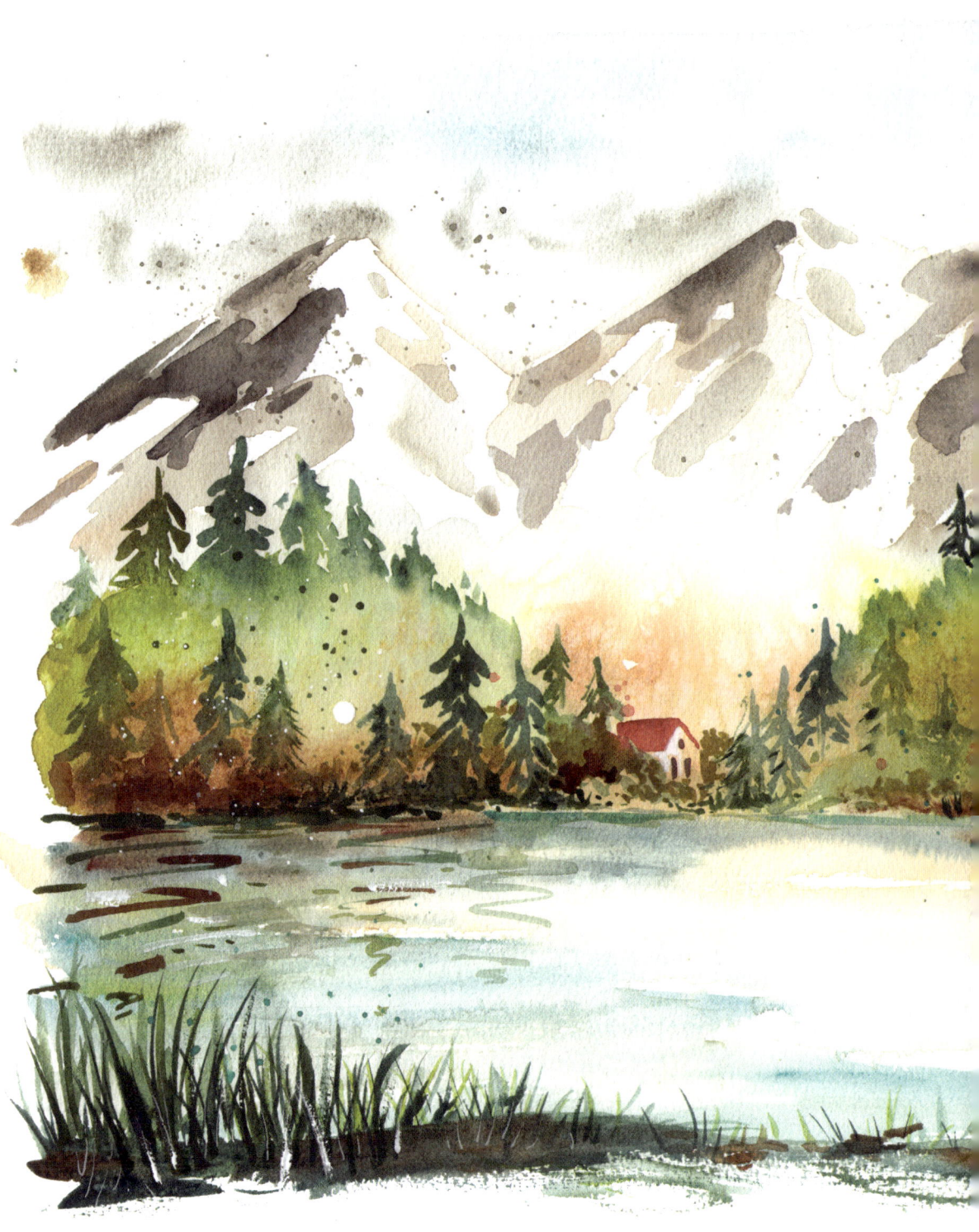

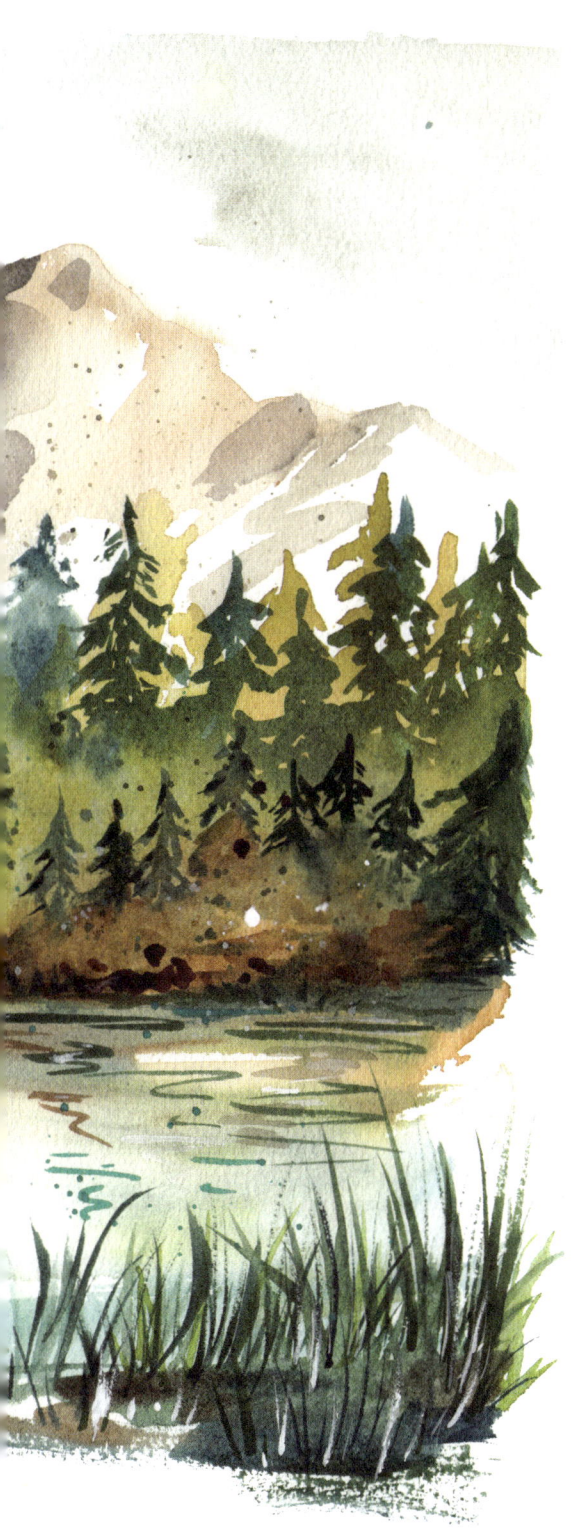

7. For the final step, paint a very simplistic house using scarlet lake for the roof and burnt umber for windows. Add a few more fir trees around it. Add darker blades of the grass in the foreground and a few white ones using white gouache.

To add more defined reflections to the water use a small brush loaded with thick colour and create zigzag lines. After adding a few splashes your painting is finished.

WINDY MOORS OF YORKSHIRE

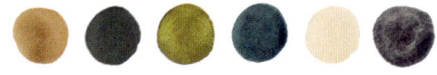

• raw umber, perylene green, rich green gold,
mayan blue genuine, buff titanium, lunar black, white gouache

The Yorkshire moors consist of many beautiful, undulating hills. They look different to the rockier mountains we've been painting so far, and we will use much softer edges and brushstrokes to depict them.

1. Start by creating a very wet wash using raw umber, perylene green and rich green gold, allowing the colours to mix directly on the paper. Concentrate darker colours in the foreground. Paint around a path, rocks and grass in the foreground and leave them white (see page 21). Allow this layer to dry completely.

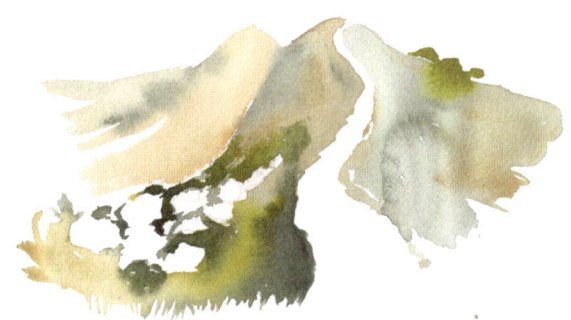

2. To paint the sky use a very wet mayan blue genuine, and paint large, curved strokes to depict clouds in the wind. Add some buff titanium to the wet sky and allow the paint to create soft edges.

Start adding more depth to the now dry hills, using the same colours as previously. Remember that objects closer to you will appear darker and more defined. Leave the hills further away untouched.

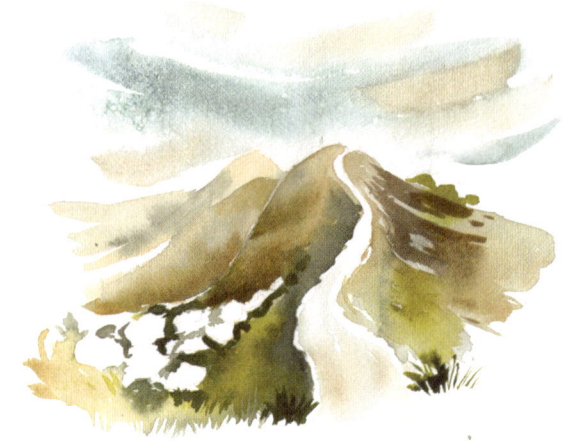

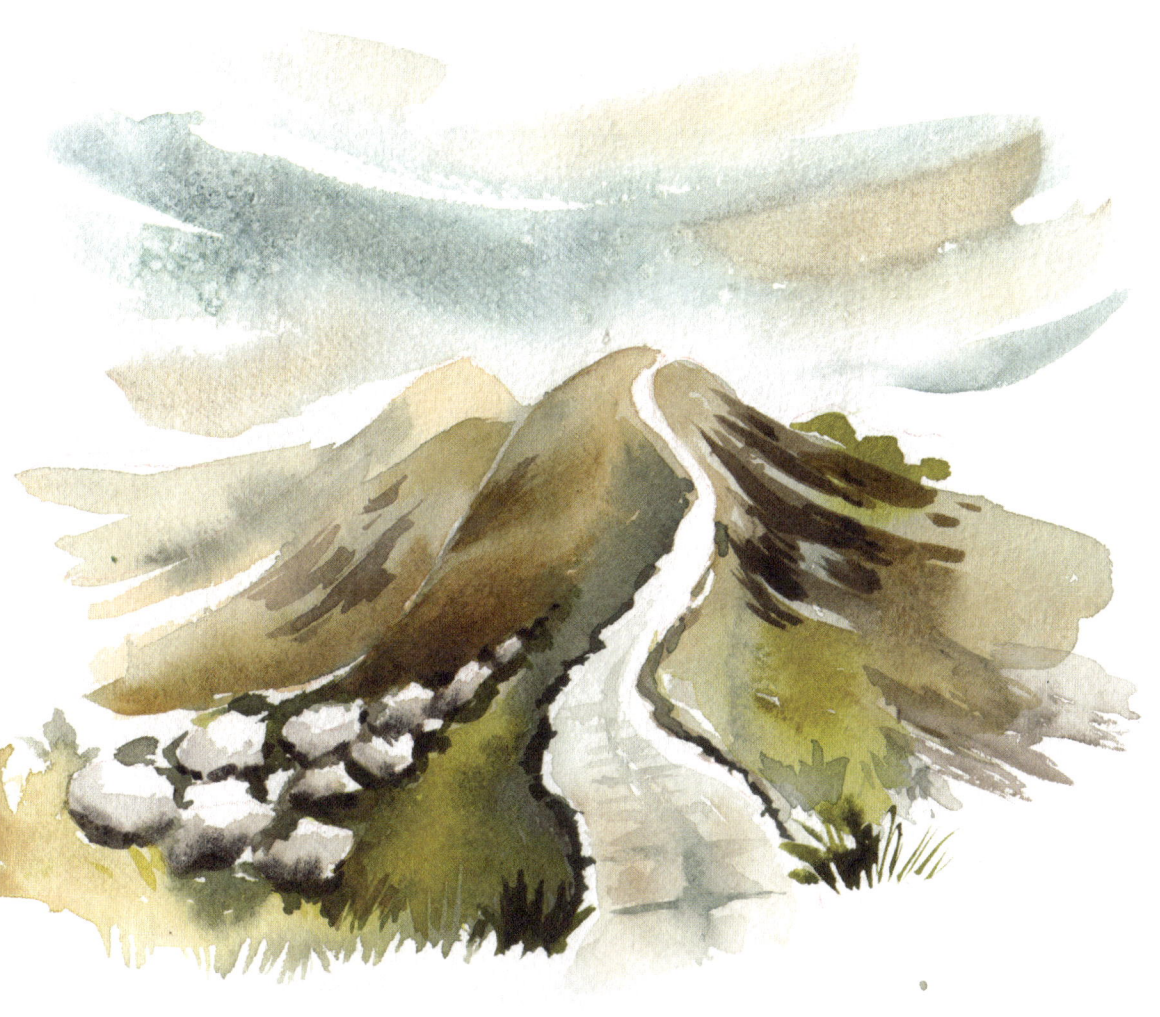

3. Using the same colours from the sky in a very light wash, define a few stones on the pathway in the foreground, which disappear as they move towards the peak.

Keep adding washes to the hills to sculpt their rounded shapes. Using lunar black, paint shadows on the rocks, but leave the top parts untouched.

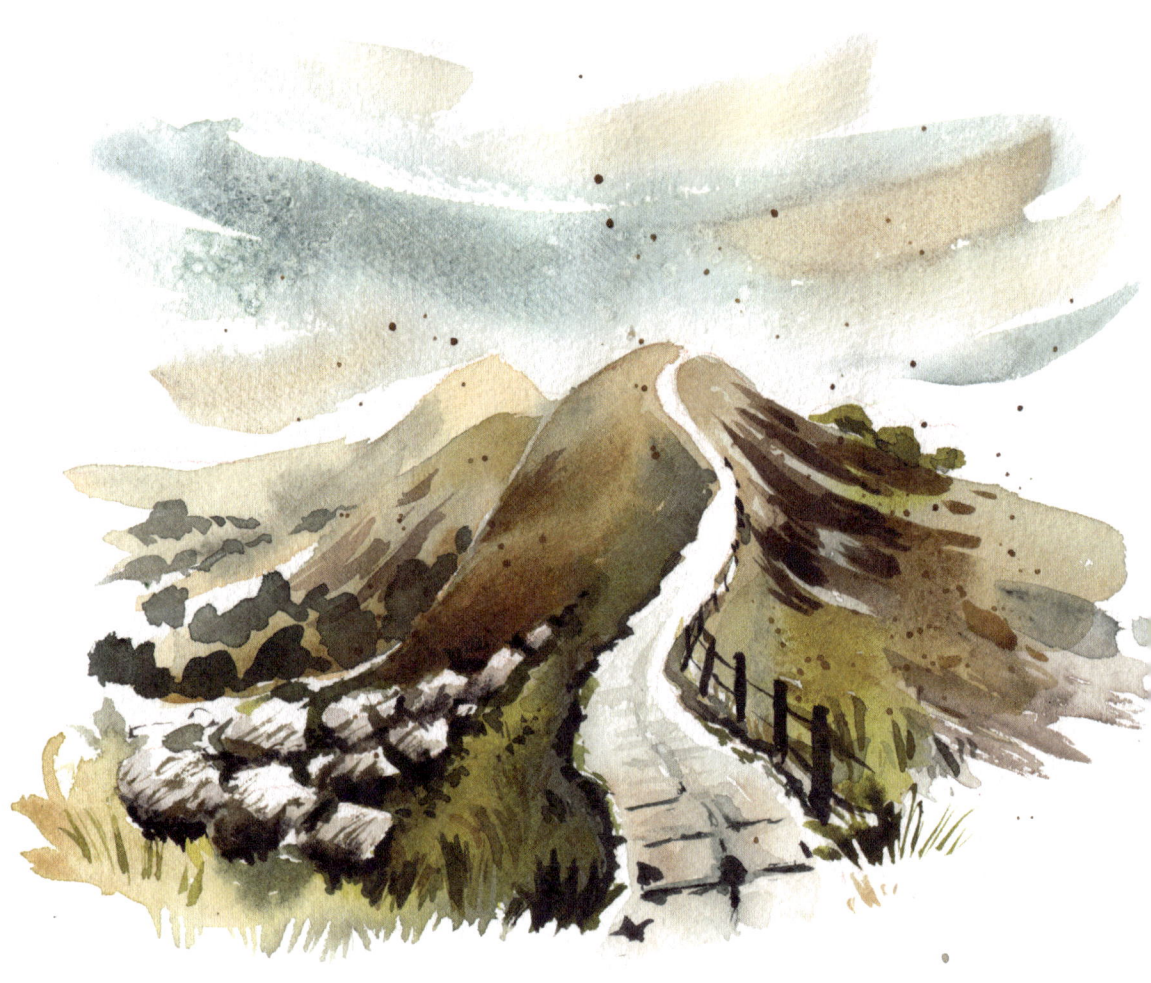

4. Now that the larger shapes are in place it's time to add smaller brushstrokes to create texture. For the grass in the foreground use short, swift strokes with a fine brush or the tip of a mop brush. Concentrate details in the foreground and let them disappear into the background.

For example, paint large poles for the fence at the beginning of the path and just a few dots towards the end. Using a small brush add a few textured strokes to the tops of the rocks. For the trees in the background use light perylene green and circular brush scribbles.

5. Lastly, add shadows to the faraway trees using thicker perylene green, and use white gouache to paint another side of the poles. To make the painting more interesting, you can add the silhouettes of two people in the distance.

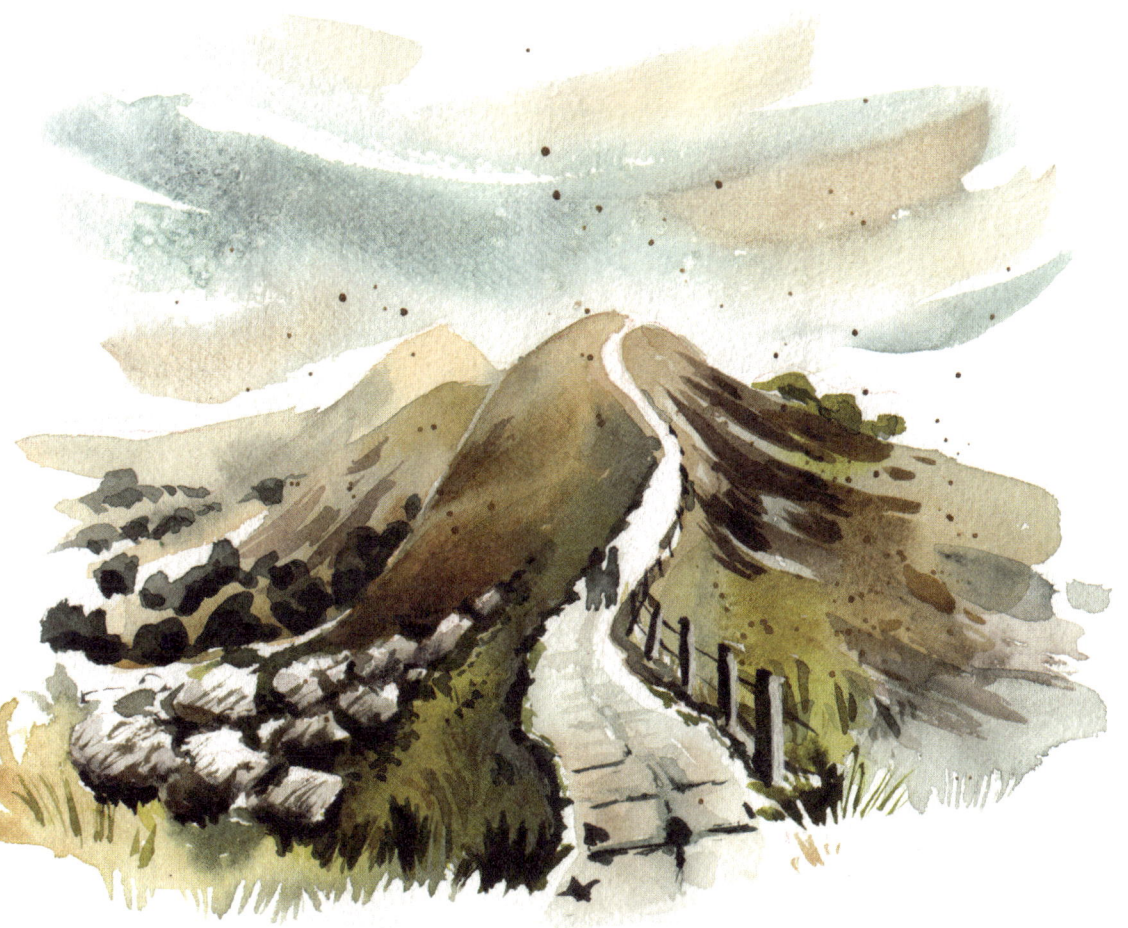

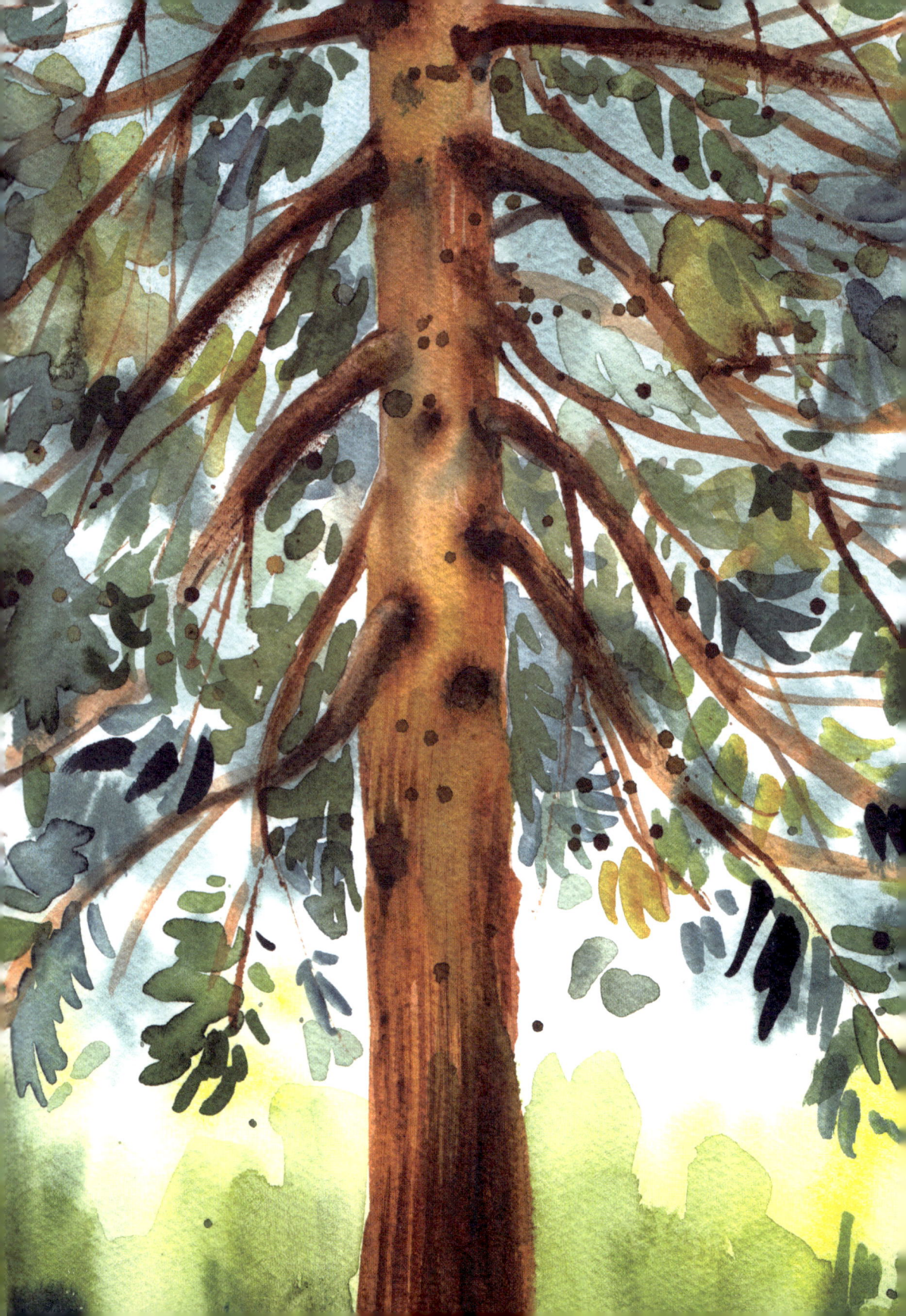

Trees

It's hard to imagine a landscape without trees or any sort of greenery. When painting trees in a landscape, I usually approach it in two ways: using simple blobs of paint to represent clusters of trees in the distance, and more detailed trees in the foreground, showing the texture of leaves and trunks. But first, let's cover the basics.

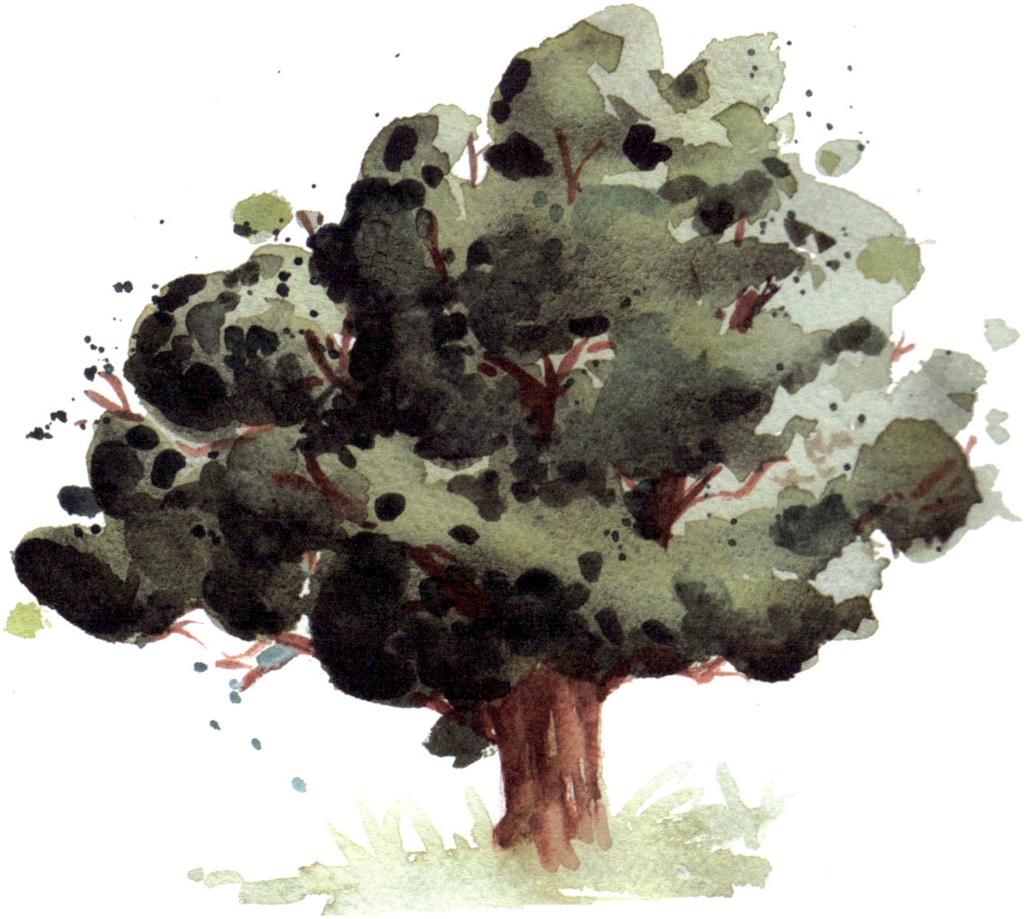

Basic shape

If you can paint a sphere, you are already halfway to painting a tree. Look at this example: when the light source is coming from the top right side, the sphere will also have a lighter part on the top right. The shadow will form in the opposite direction to the light source. In this example, it forms into the shape of a crescent on the bottom left side.

If you elongate the sphere into something like a rounded cone, the same rule still applies, but the shadow will follow the new shape.

If you add an uneven edge to this shape, along with a trunk, you have created a basic tree. Remember that the cast shadow (the shadow on the ground) will always be on the opposite side to the light source.

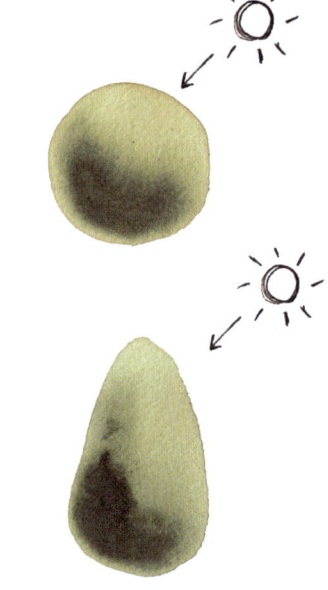

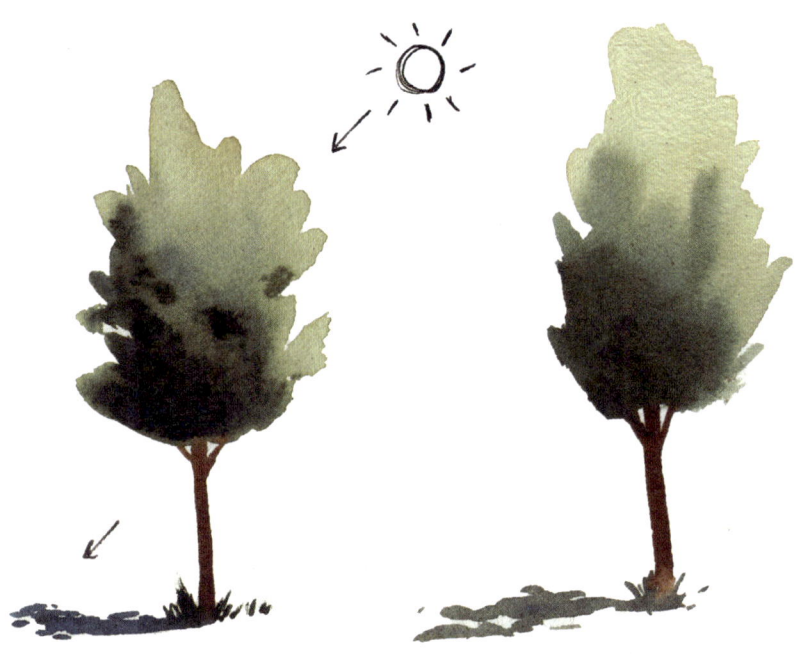

Complex shape

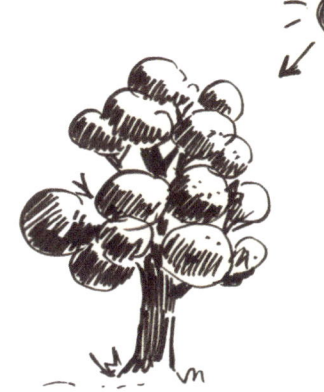

Let's break down the structure of a more complex tree. Think of a tree as one large sphere made up of many smaller ones. By visualizing clusters of leaves as individual spheres grouped together, it becomes easier to understand where light and shadow should fall. The lower clusters of a tree will have more shadow and the top leaves more light.

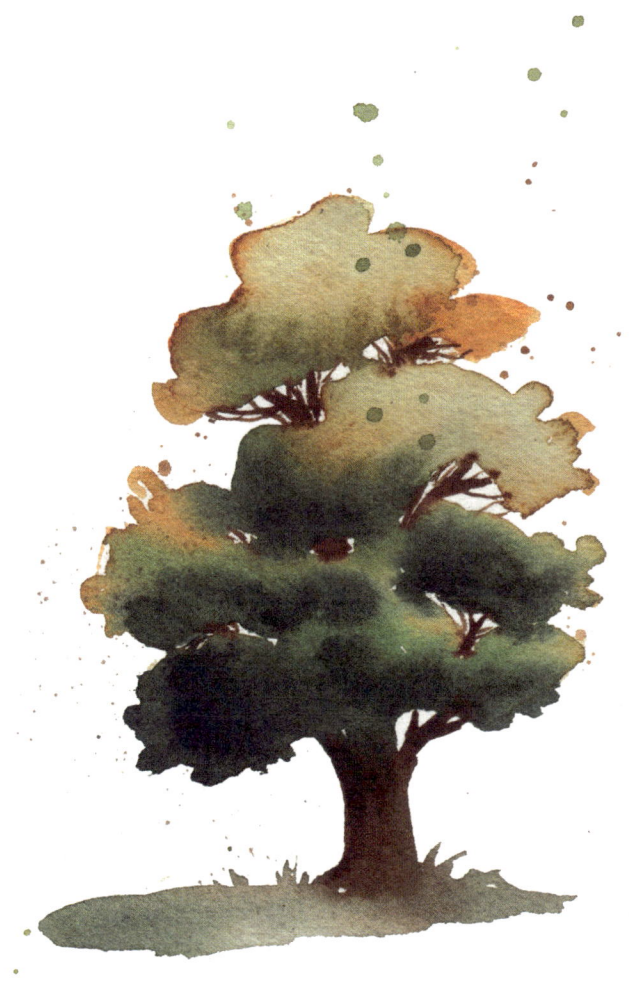

Different types of tree

JAPANESE MAPLE TREE

Japanese maple can be depicted using small brushstrokes of a round brush placed close to each other to create clusters of leaves.

When the tree is young it will have a more uneven shape and you will see more of its branches.

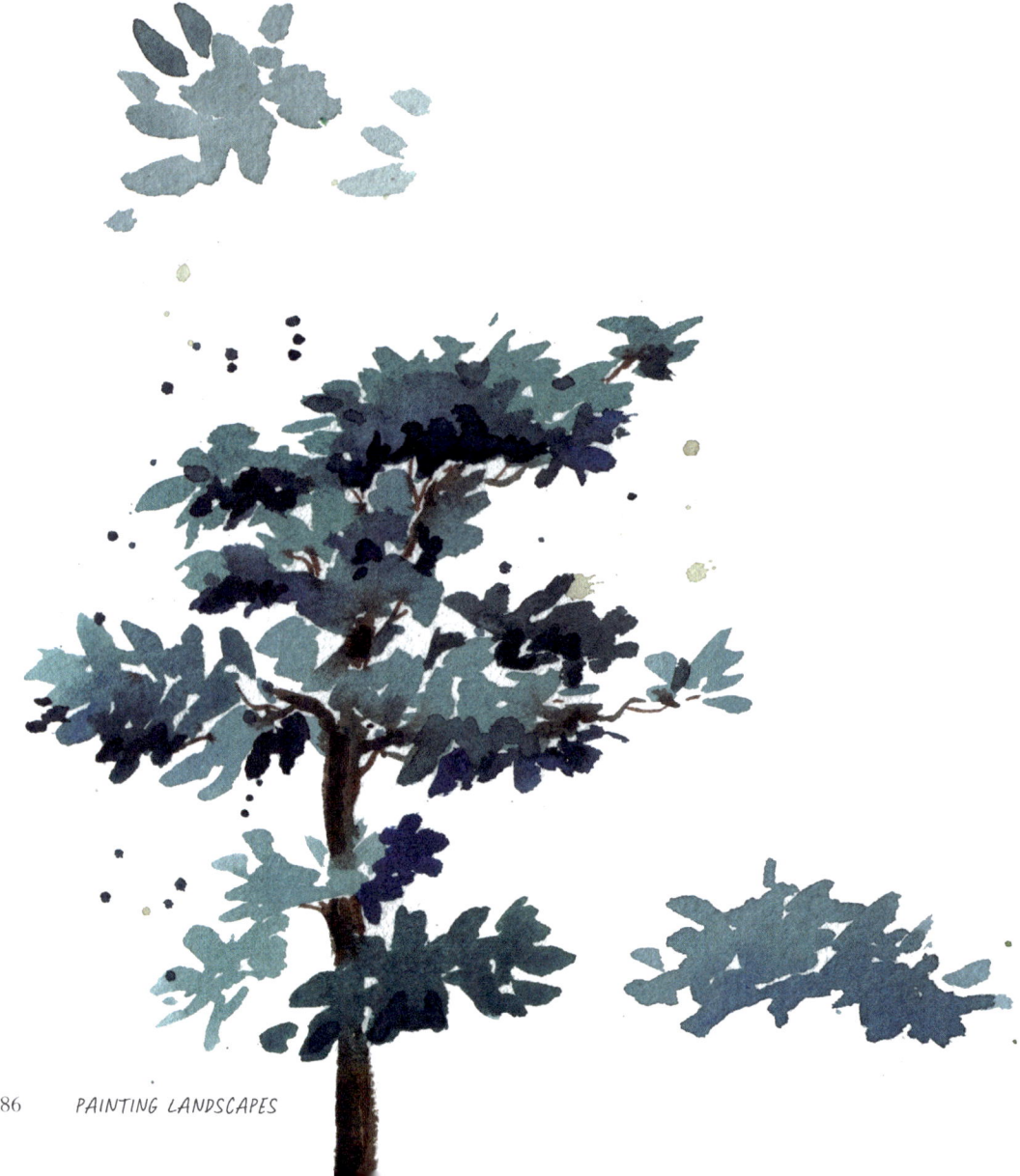

PINE TREE

Pine trees are usually very tall, with curvy branches extending outwards. Unlike a 'typical' tree, it will have a more elongated shape rather than a spherical shape. To paint clusters of leaves use circular scribbles with shadows added at the bottom.

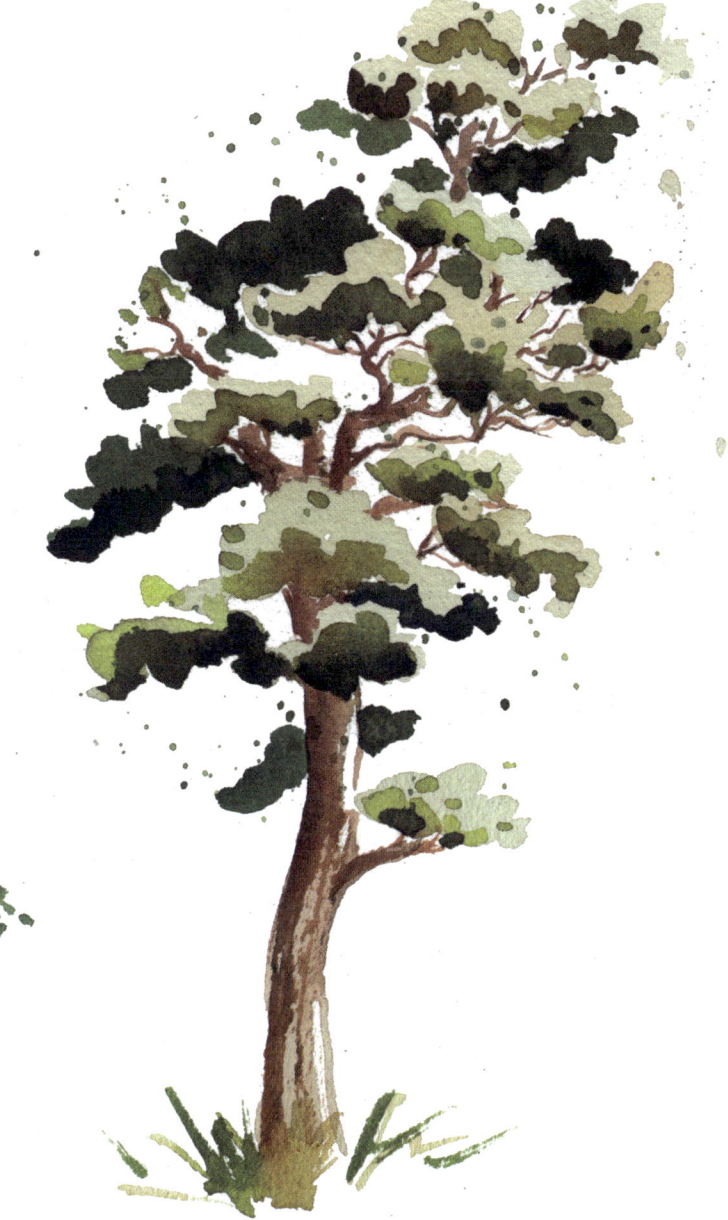

WINTER TREE

A winter tree may seem like an overwhelming subject when you see all the overlapping branches. But to paint it you don't need to be very precise; it's enough to convey the overall impression.

Use a very swift motion of the hand to draw branches in all directions, remembering that branches are always thicker nearer the trunk of the tree. Using a dry brush effect is also ideal to create the impression of lots of branches.

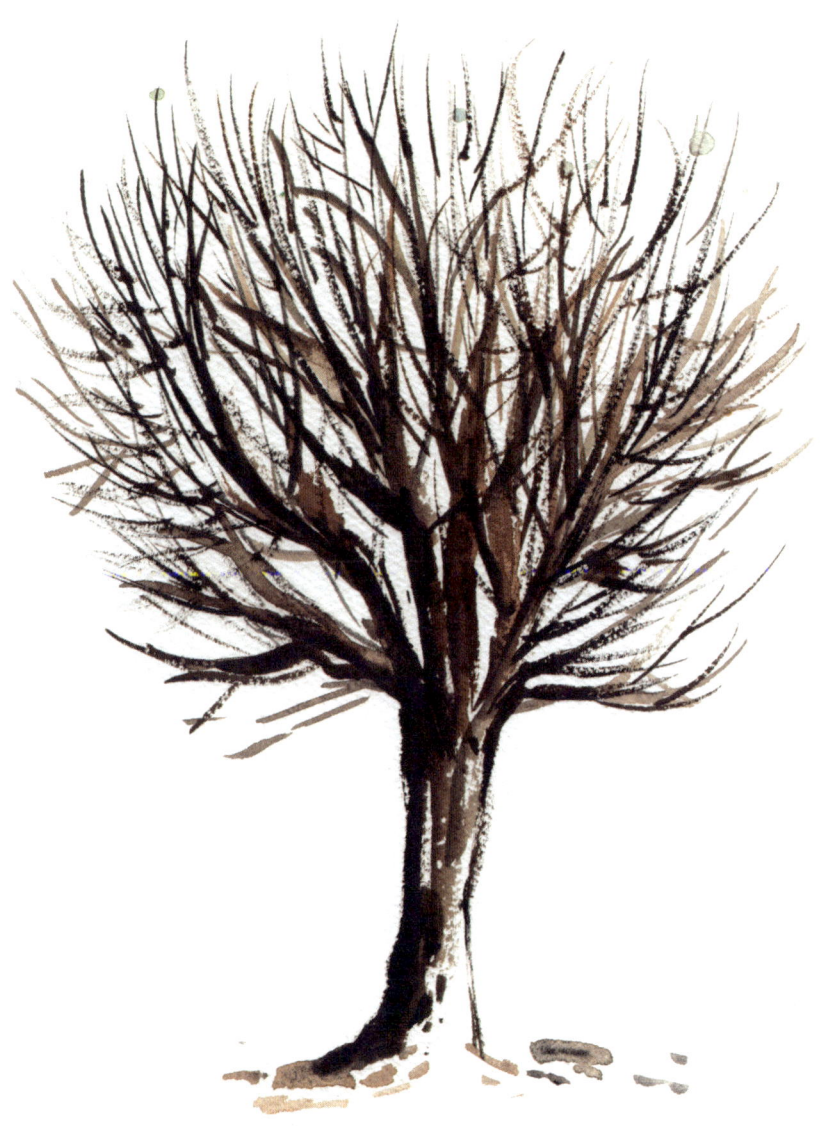

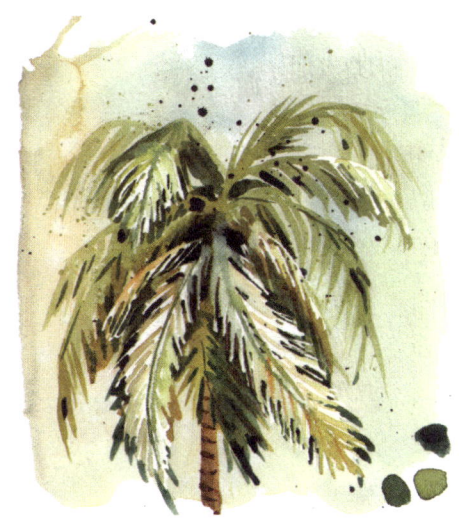

PALM TREE

A flat brush is ideal for painting a simplistic palm tree. Use the side of the brush to pull out fan-shaped leaves. Typically, palm trees have some yellow leaves situated at the bottom of the canopy.

To create a more detailed palm tree, use masking fluid to protect the front leaves from the paint (see page 24). Once you are finished painting the leaves at the back, peel the mask off and add a very light colour to the front white leaves.

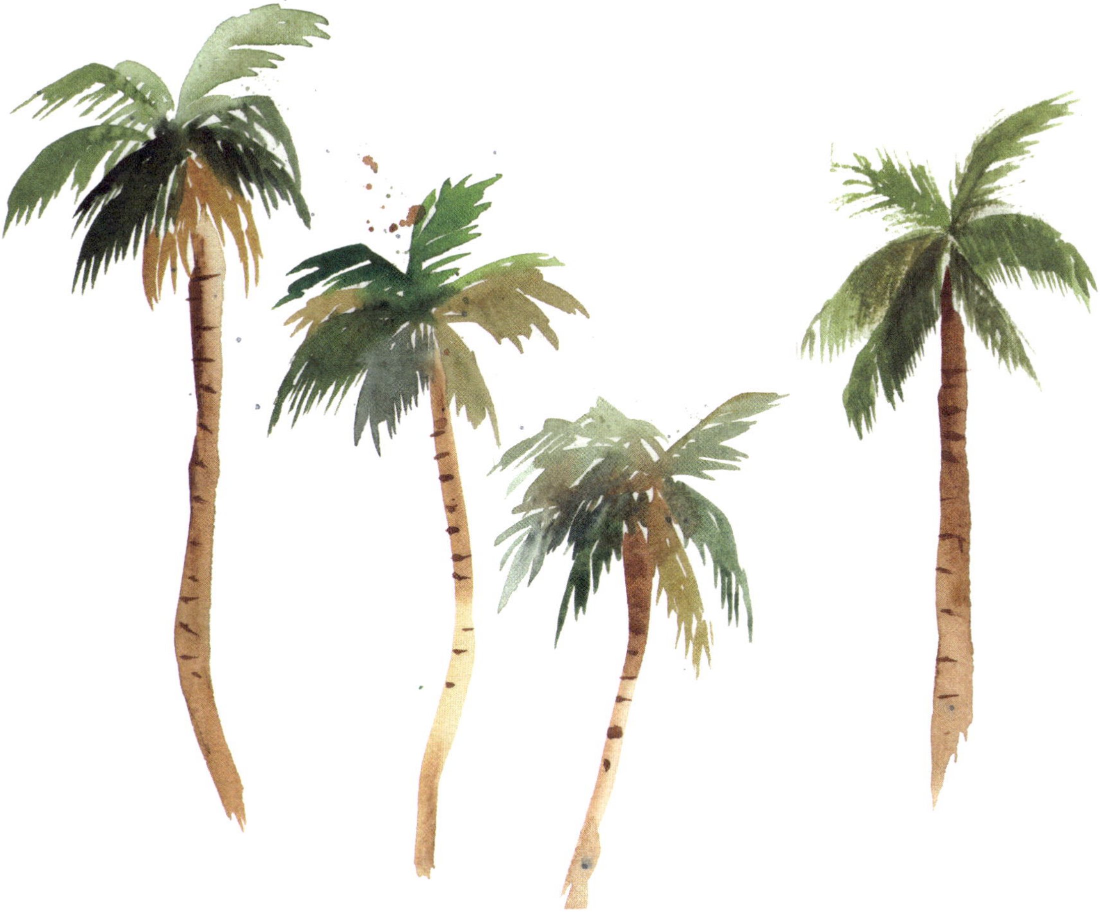

Creative tips

Layering expressive brushstrokes alone can be a perfect way of depicting leaves. In this example, I used the side of a filbert brush to create a curved teardrop shape. The tree looks very lively and vibrant.

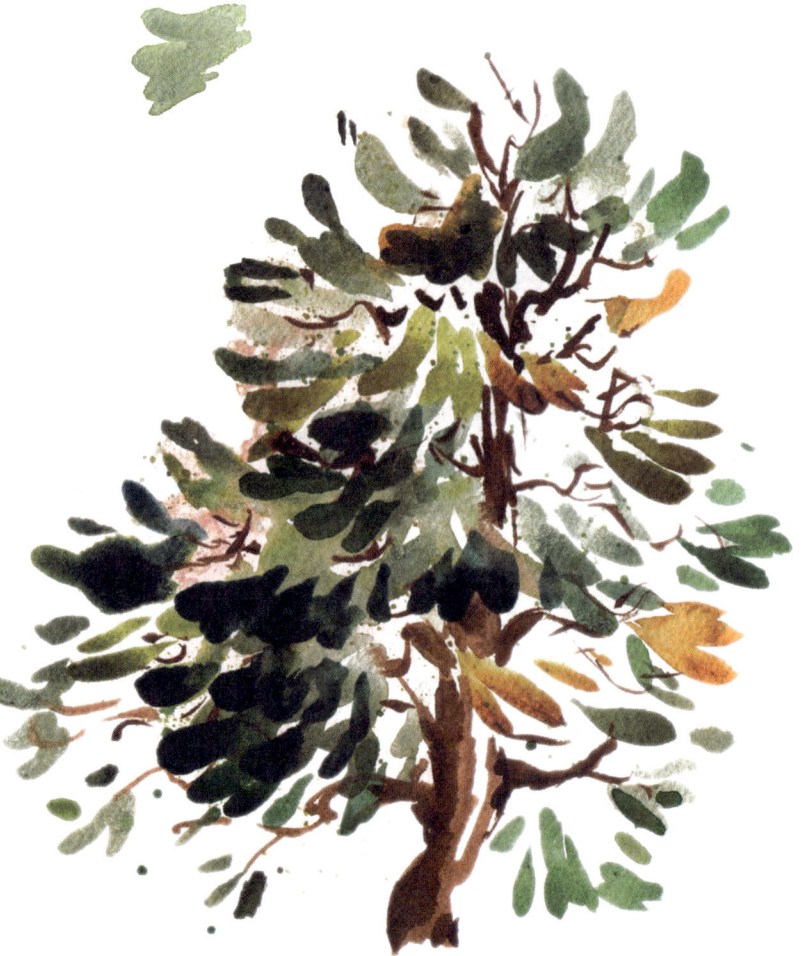

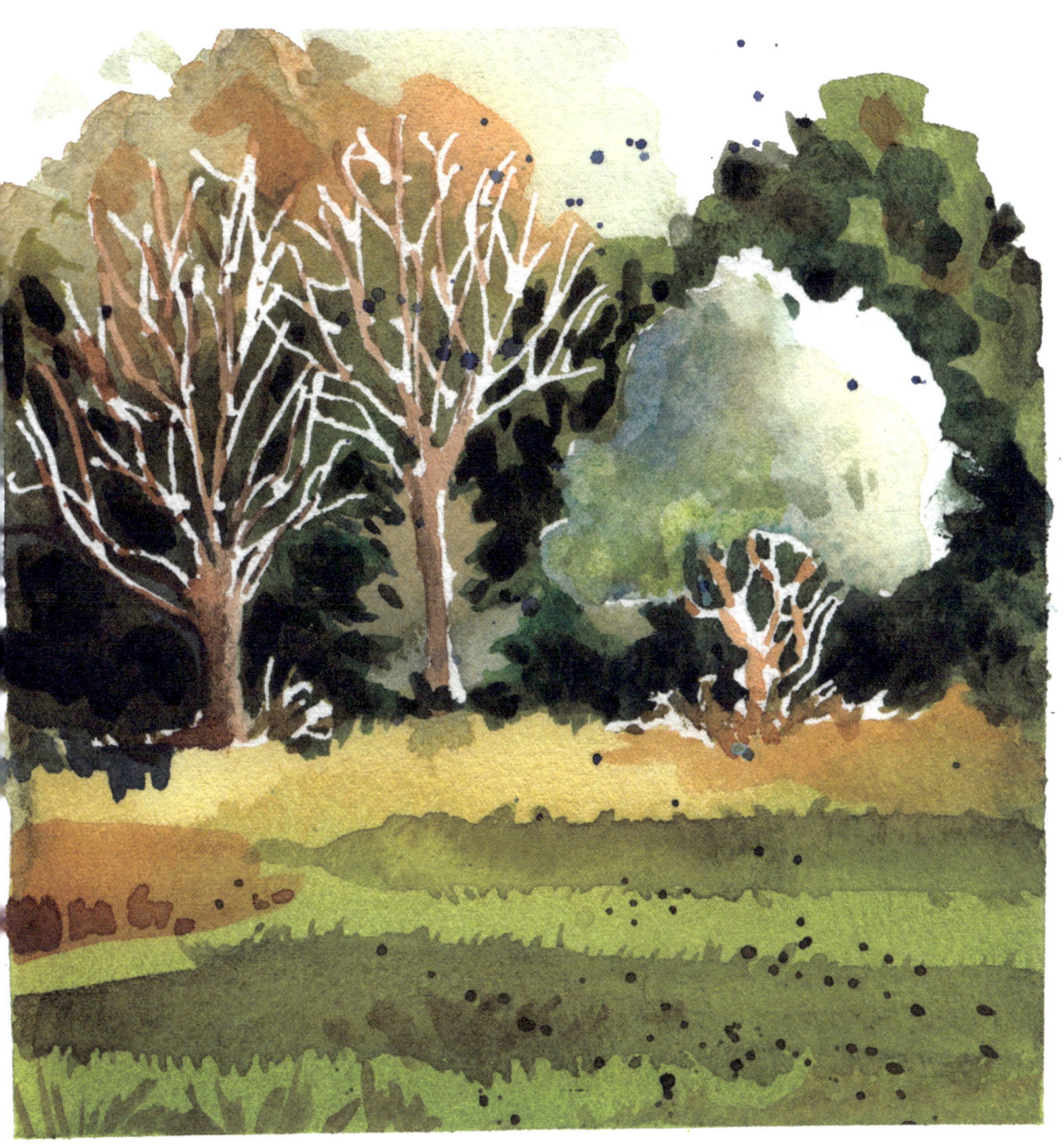

Use masking fluid to protect the trunk and branches whilst creating highlights on the branches.

When the mask is peeled off, add colour to the trunk and branches, leaving one side white to create highlights.

BIRCH GROVE

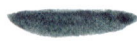

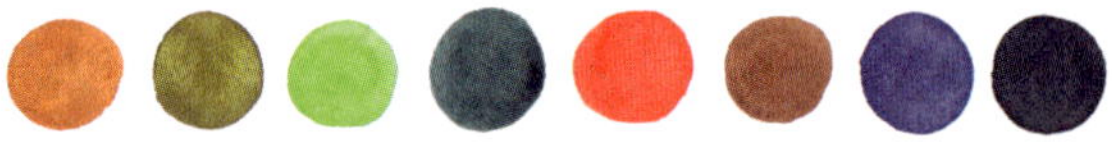

• *quinacridone deep gold, rich green gold, sap green light, mayan blue genuine, scarlet lake, burnt umber, ultramarine blue, indigo*

With this exercise it's important to practise painting birch trunks a few times before moving onto a larger piece. It might take some experimentation to find the best way to make marks. Take an old credit card, or something with a similar sharp edge, then dip its shorter edge into a very wet paint and drag it across dry paper. You will get an uneven striped mark that resembles the pattern of the birch trunk. Try dipping different card edges into various colours and see the effects you create.

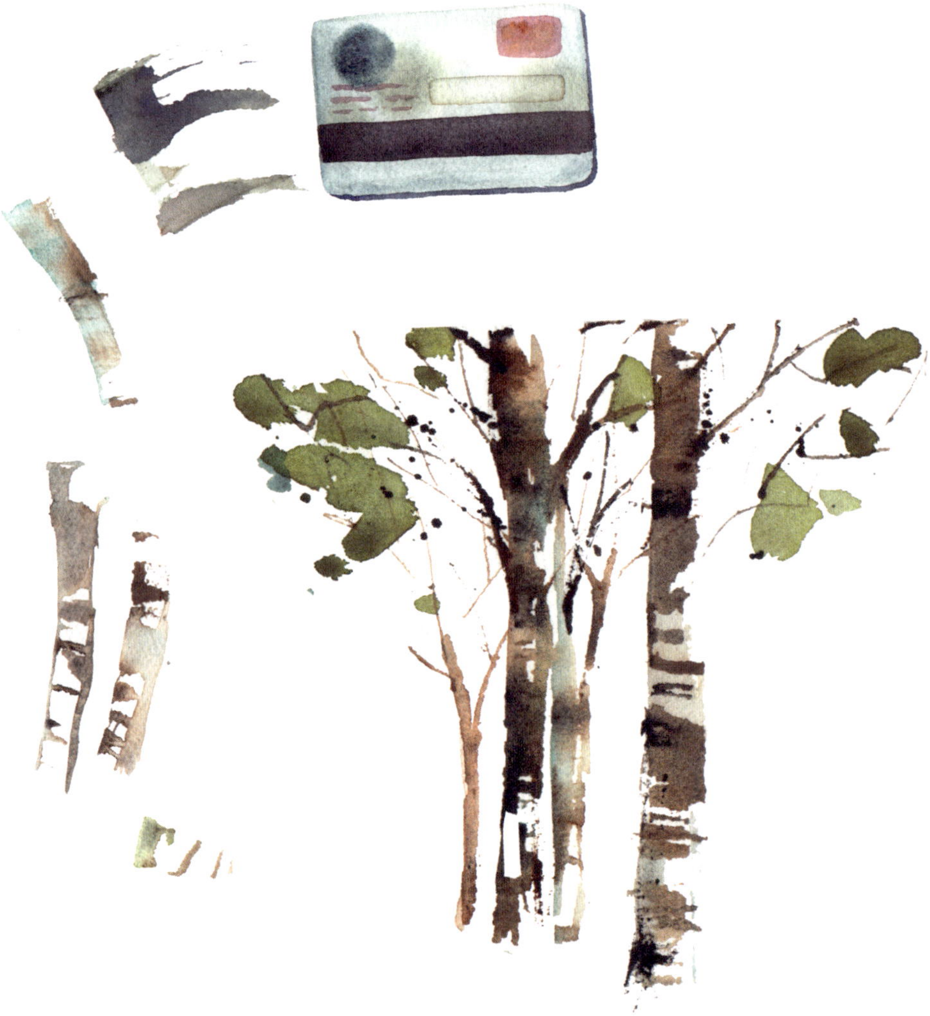

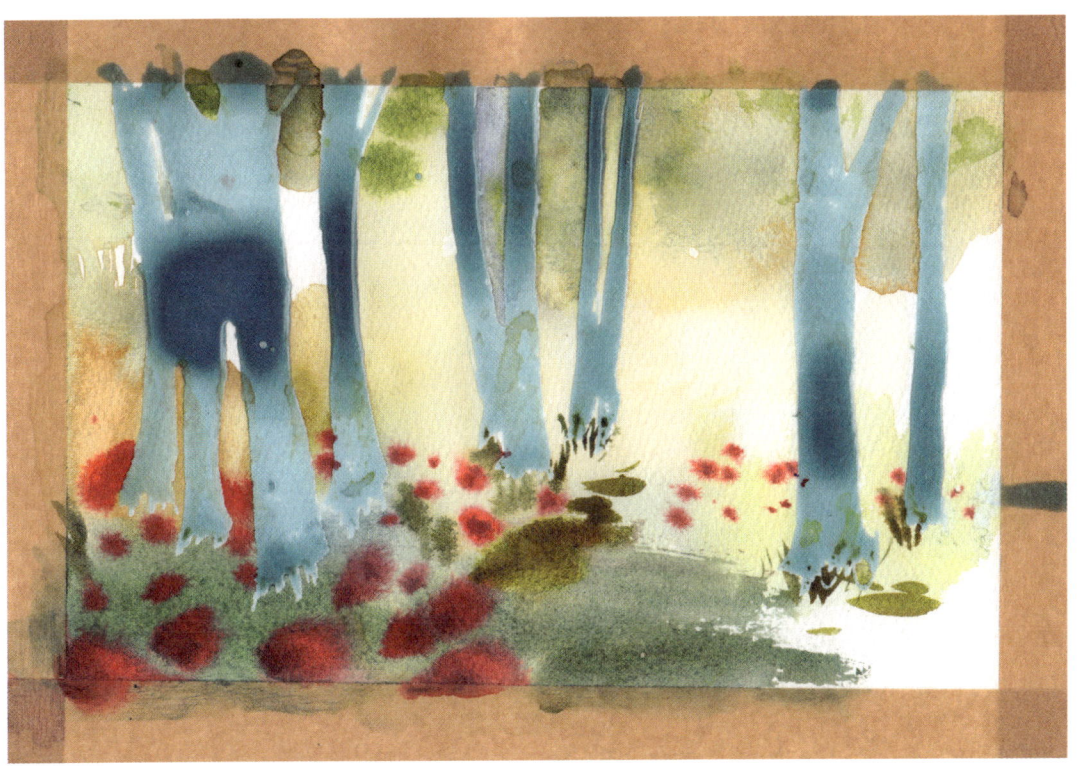

1. Use masking tape to secure your paper to your work surface. Draw simple tree trunks with a pencil, then protect them with masking fluid (see page 24).

2. When the masking fluid is completely dry, take a very wet paint and create large washes around the tree trunks. Use quinacridone deep gold, rich green gold and sap green light at the top, letting the paints mix on paper, and introduce mayan blue genuine towards the bottom of the painting. This step can be very intuitive and bring quite unexpected results.

3. For the flowers, use scarlet lake. It is important to not add the red paint too early. When the previous layer starts to lose its shine, but is still wet, then add a few drops of thick paint. The red paint will spread, creating soft edges.

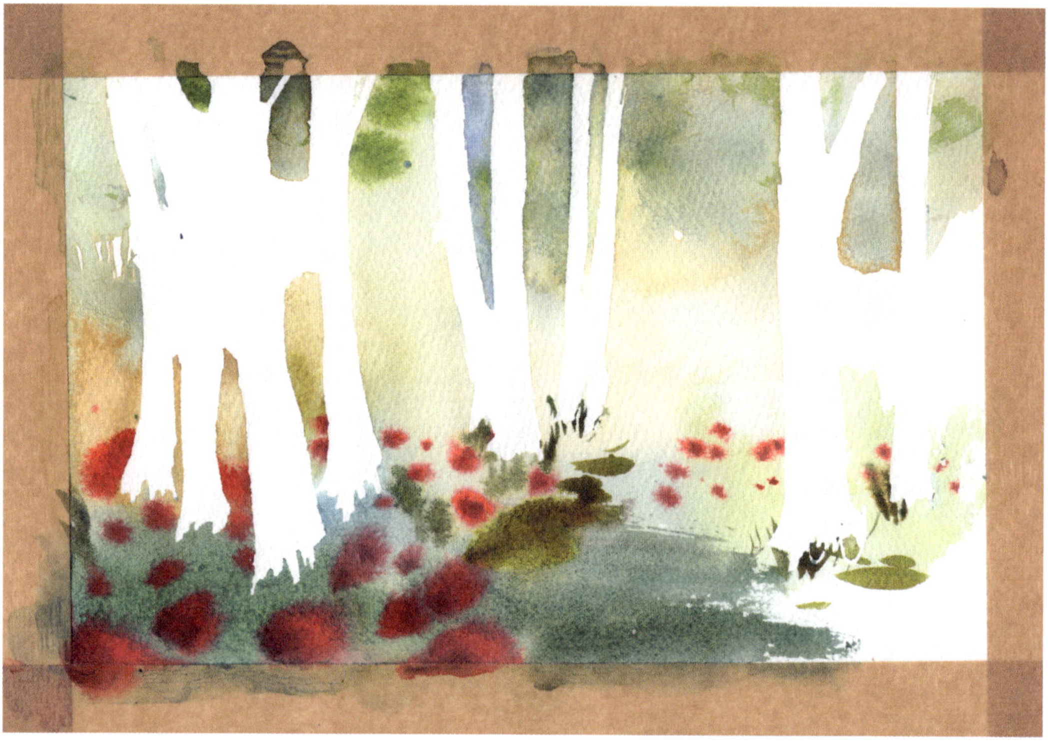

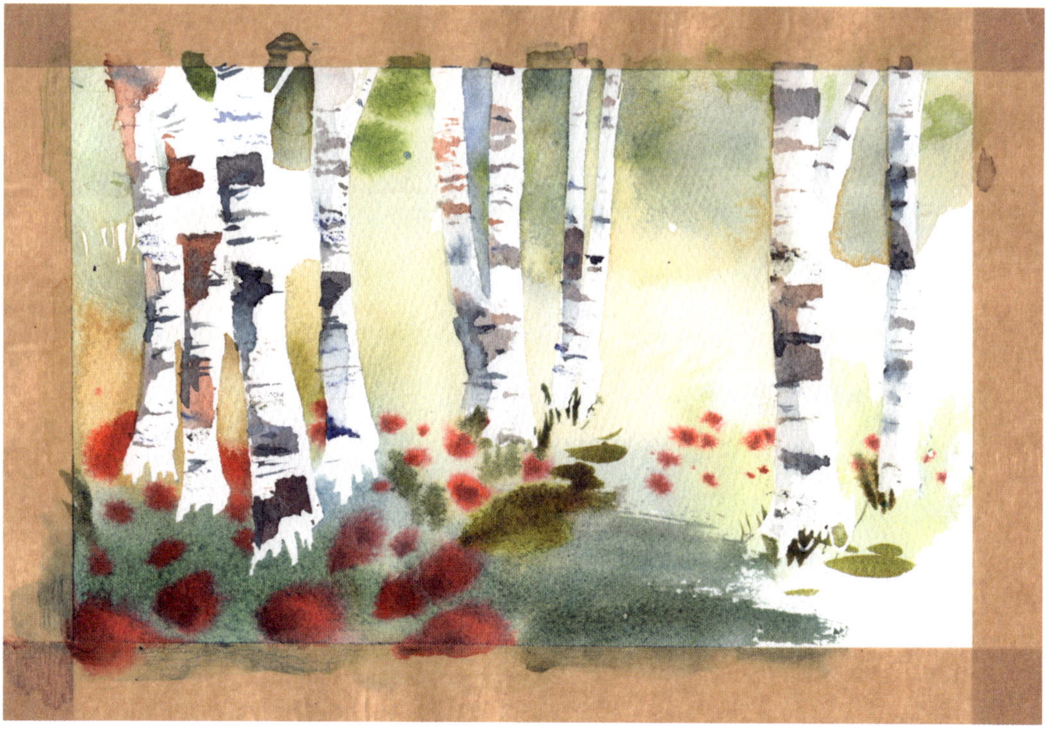

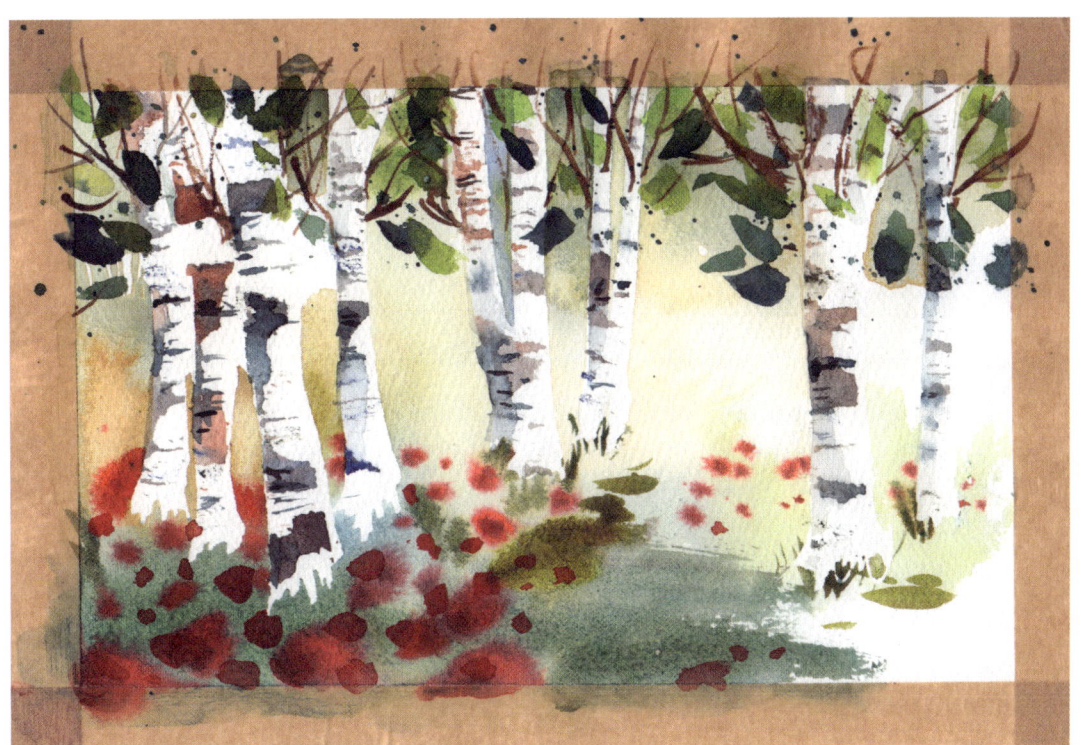

4. When the painting is completely dry, peel off the masking fluid.

5. Use credit card marks to create the texture of the birch trunk in burnt umber and ultramarine blue. Occasionally 'help' the colours to mix together by adding some darker lines to the wet paint.

6. Take a thin liner brush and load it with burnt umber straight from the box. With a swift motion, paint long branches coming from the trunk. For the leaves, alternate rich green gold, sap green light and a mixture of sap green light and indigo for darker leaves. Create short brushstrokes, almost like a stamp. Add a few more red flowers on the ground.

7. Mix a very dark colour using sap green light and lots of indigo. Paint a few blades of grass between the flowers and a few behind the trunks to make them stand out. Once the paint is dry, remove the masking tape.

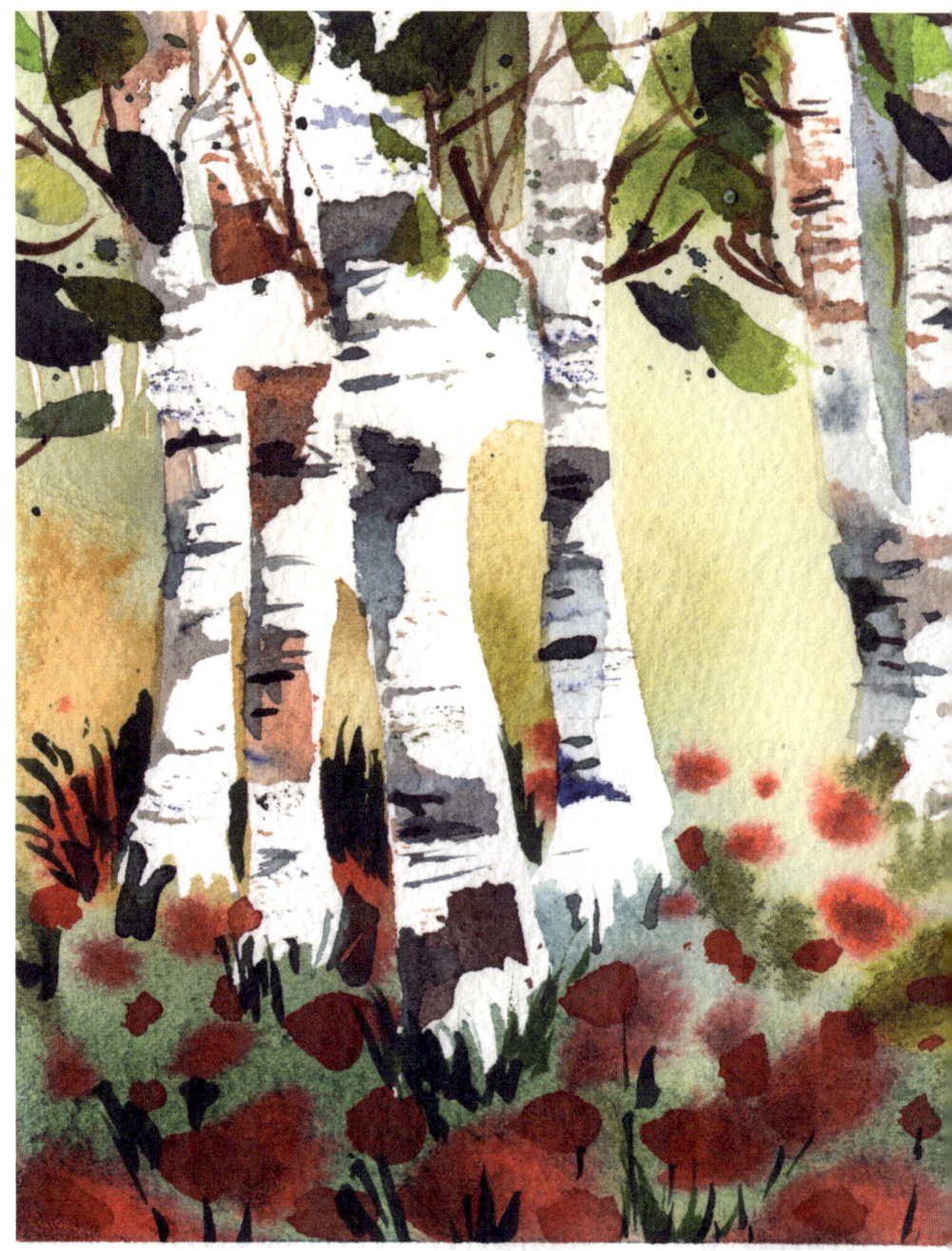

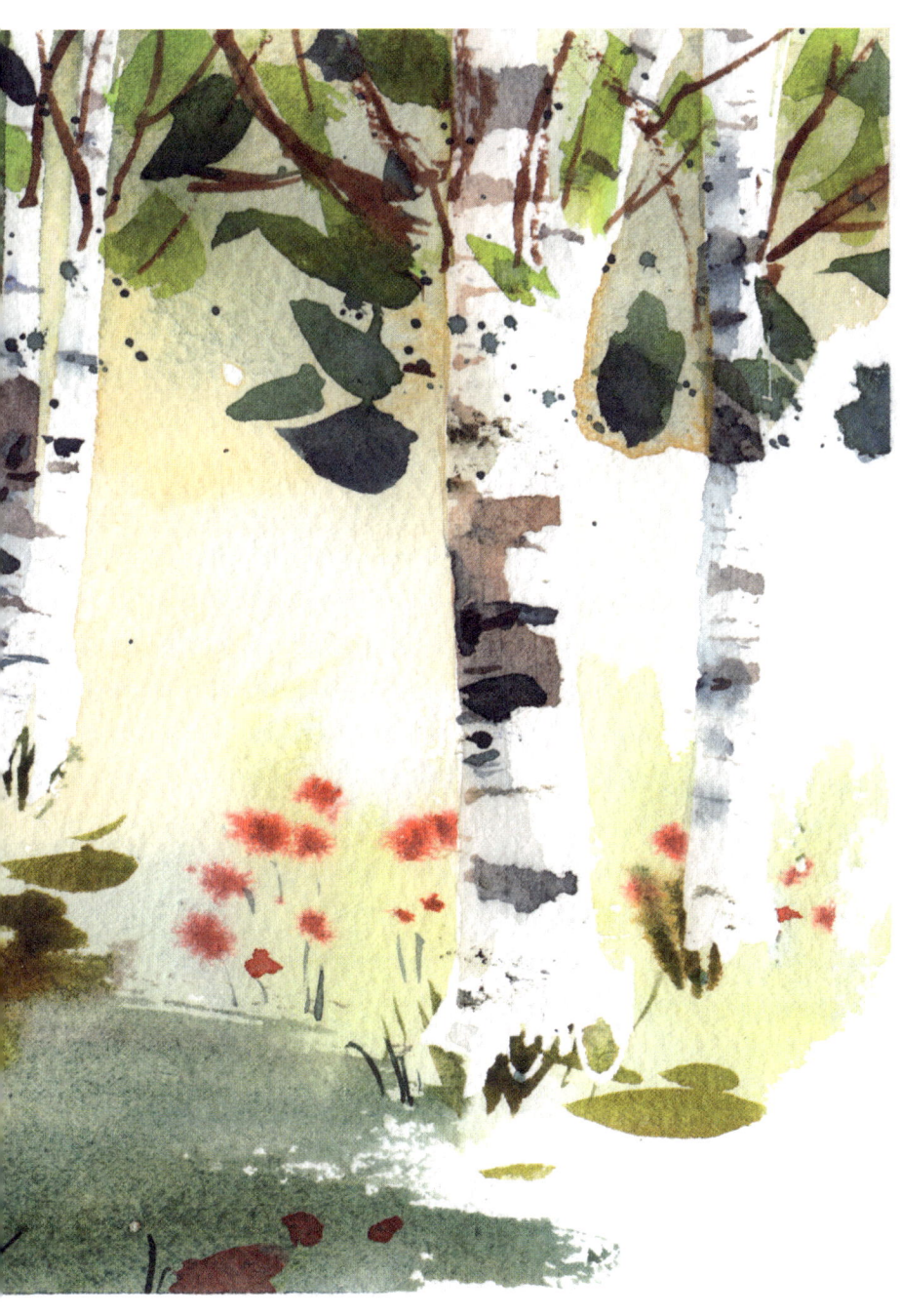

LUSH GREENERY OF THAILAND

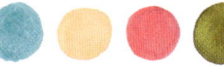 

• cobalt teal blue, Naples yellow, permanent rose, rich green gold, deep sap green, ultramarine blue, quinacridone orange, burnt umber

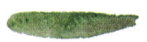

Thailand is a country of rich tropical forests with thick vegetation. It might seem like an artist's dream to transfer those vibrant landscapes onto paper, but at the same time, it can be overwhelming to see so much green foliage, that you can get lost in it. It is important to remember that, as the creator of your painting, only you choose what to put onto the paper.

1. Use masking tape to secure your paper to your work surface. Start with a very light drawing that indicates a few main objects: the ocean line, an island in the background, a few trees and buildings. Then wet the paper almost completely, avoiding only a few buildings. Using the wet-on-wet technique (see page 19), add paint to the wet paper. Start with the less defined parts, such as the ocean and the sky. Use cobalt teal blue for the ocean and a very light mixture of Naples yellow and permanent rose for the sky.

2. To achieve a very soft colour transition effect, as if the colour almost disappears, hold your paper upright so the paint start flowing down creating a soft graded wash effect. Keep the paper tilted until it dries.

Once this paint dries, paint greenery using rich green gold for the lightest parts, deep sap green for medium areas, and a mixture of deep sap green and ultramarine blue for the darkest elements. Add a few flowers using drops of quinacridone orange.

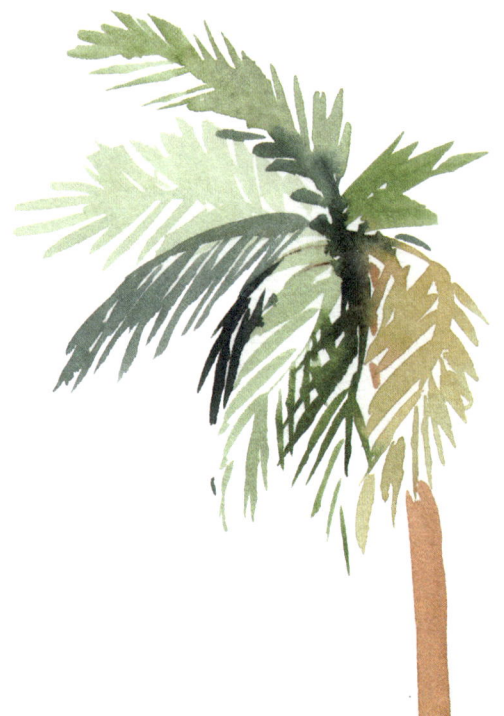

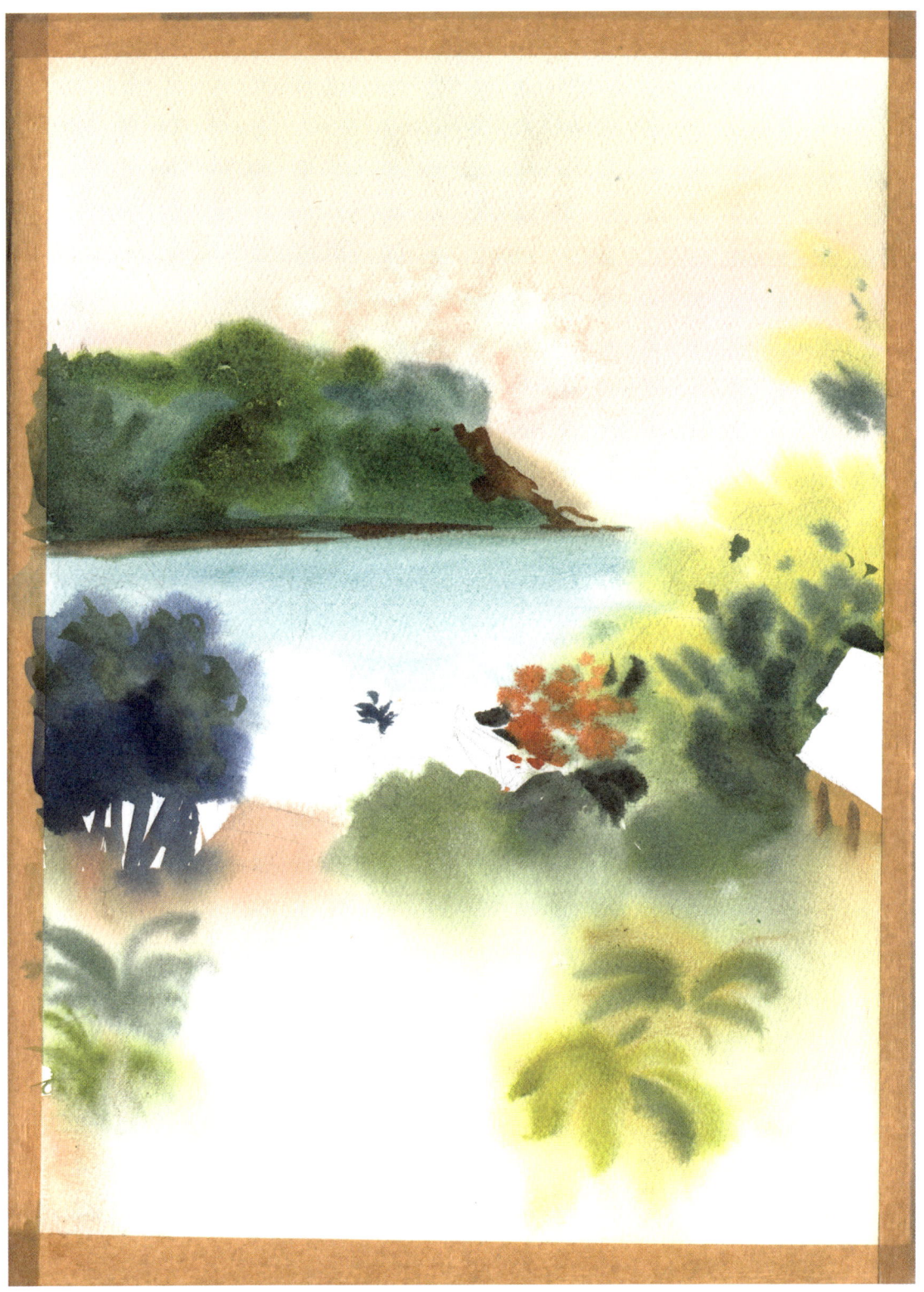

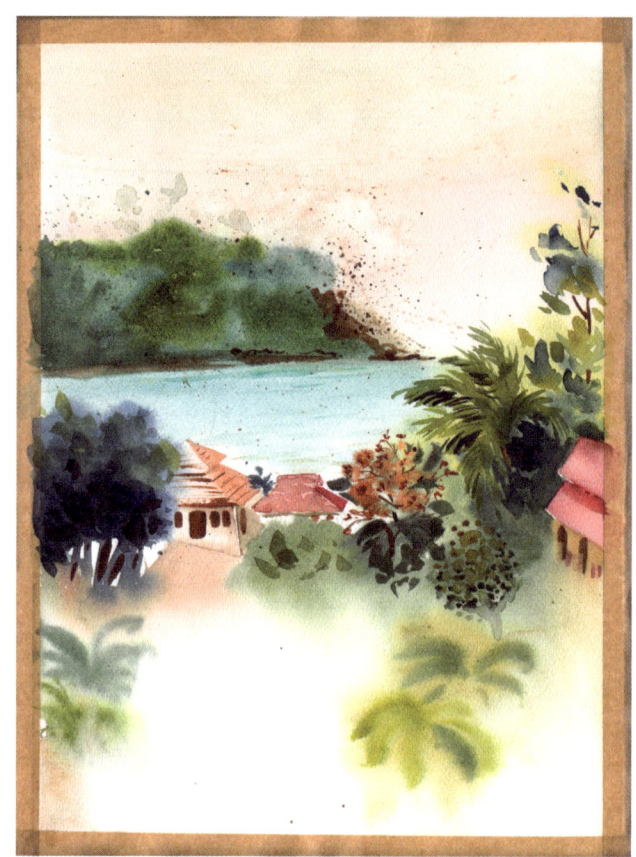

3. Once the layer is completely dry, start adding some details to the greenery. Be careful not to cover over all of the greenery from the first layer. Use different types of brushstrokes to show a variety of foliage and flowers. Palm trees will have fanning leaves (see page 89) and a blooming bush will have small flowers created with the tip of a mop brush.

For the buildings, use rich permanent rose and burnt umber.

4. Now it's time to add the finishing touches. Define the leaves of the palm trees that overlap the island using thick ultramarine blue and deep sap green. Use deep sap green to add some banana leaves in the foreground. With the very tip of a mop brush, use a thick mixture of burnt umber and ultramarine blue to paint silhouettes of boats parked next to the shore. Add the shadows cast onto the water from the boats and a few lines to show waves using a very light cobalt teal blue. Remove the masking tape.

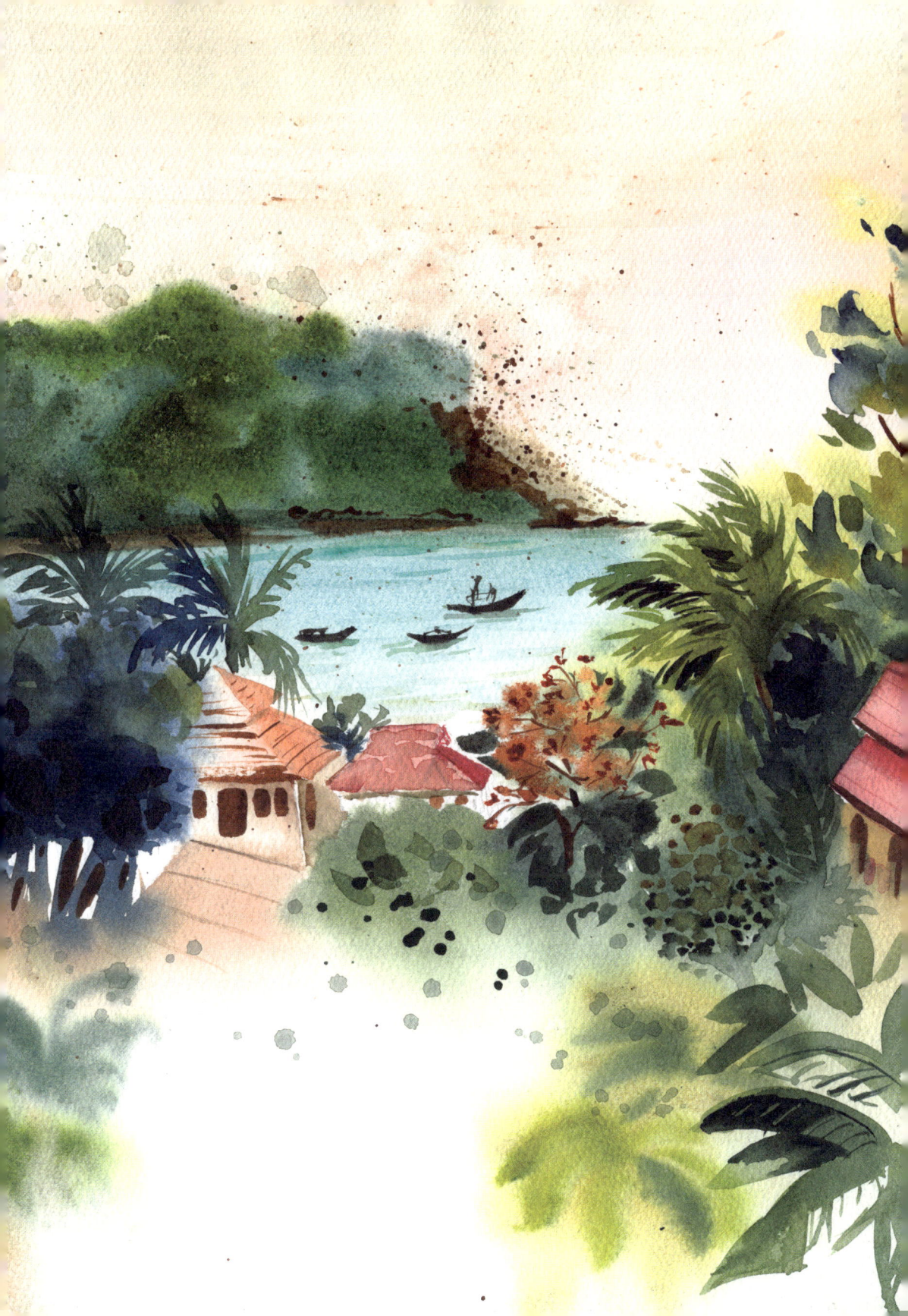

VINEYARD IN BURGUNDY

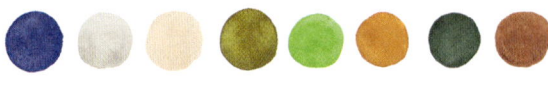

● ultramarine blue, Davy's gray, buff titanium, rich green gold, sap green light, quinacridone gold, deep sap green, burnt umber

The French region of Burgundy is not only famous for some of the world's finest wines; it is also characterized by rolling hills and picturesque landscapes. In this exercise you will use a combination of wet and dry techniques to create clouds (see page 19).

painting clouds

Practise painting clouds using the wet-on-wet technique. Start by wetting your paper with clean water and allow it to dry a little bit. Whilst still damp, create an outline of the cloud by adding a blue colour into areas surrounding the negative space where the cloud will be (see page 21). As the paint starts spreading, use a clean, damp brush to lift the pigment from the top part of the cloud.

Mix some very light grey and add it to the bottom of the cloud to create shadow.

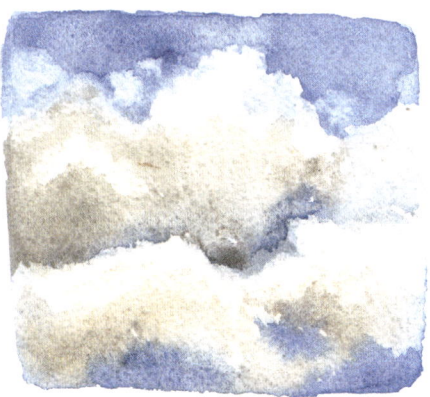

Another way to paint clouds with hard edges is to follow the same steps as above, but while the paint is still wet and spreading, gently dab a paper towel onto the wet surface to lift pigment around the cloud, creating more defined edges.

1. Start your painting with a very light sketch. The final painting will have some buildings in the distance, but for now you can just draw a horizon line of the buildings. Wet the top part of the painting and start adding clouds. Use a light ultramarine blue for the sky and a mixture of Davy's gray and buff titanium to create shadows.

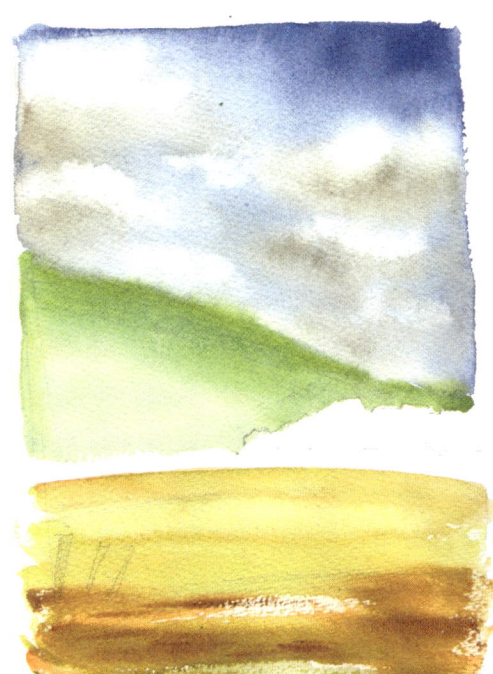

2. Use a mixture of rich green gold and sap green light to paint the top line of the hill, then use a clean brush and water to pull down the paint to create an even gradient from dark to light (see page 22). The grassy area is painted with quinacridone gold, lighter at the back, and a thick layer using the dry brush technique in the foreground. When this layer is dry, move onto painting trees.

3. Using a deep sap green mixed with rich green gold, paint clusters of trees in the background as well as some single trees. Whilst the trees are still wet, use ultramarine blue at the bottom for shadowy areas. To create interest, make some trees more green and others more blue.

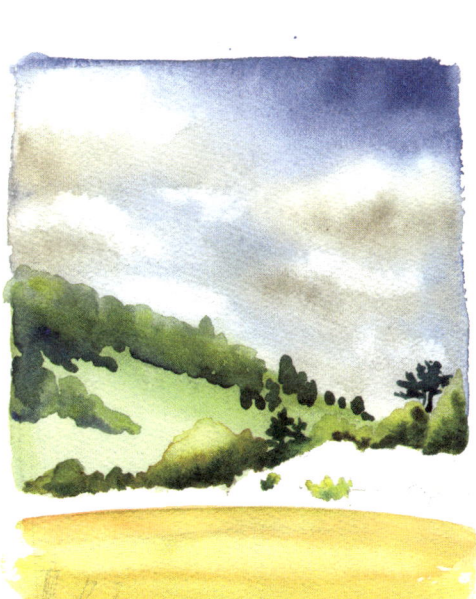

4. Create a medium-wet mix of quinacridone gold with a little bit of deep sap green, and use it to paint rows of grapevines, leaving negative space at the bottom for grass, as well as for fence poles (see page 21). Use more water and lighter colours to paint rows that are further away. Add a mixture of deep sap green and sap green light at the bottom of rows for a shadow.

For the buildings, use burnt umber to paint the roof, windows and the stone wall.

5. Once dry, deepen some of the greenery and grapevine shadows. Using a very thick burnt umber and some ultramarine blue, mix a very dark brown–grey colour and paint vertical lines for fence poles. Add a few blades of grass in the foreground.

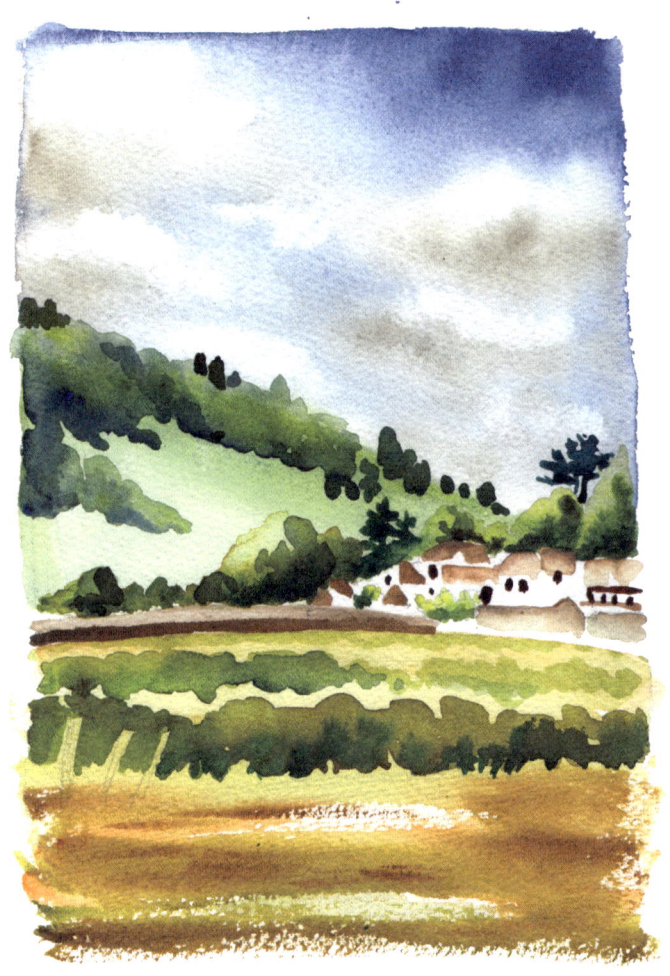

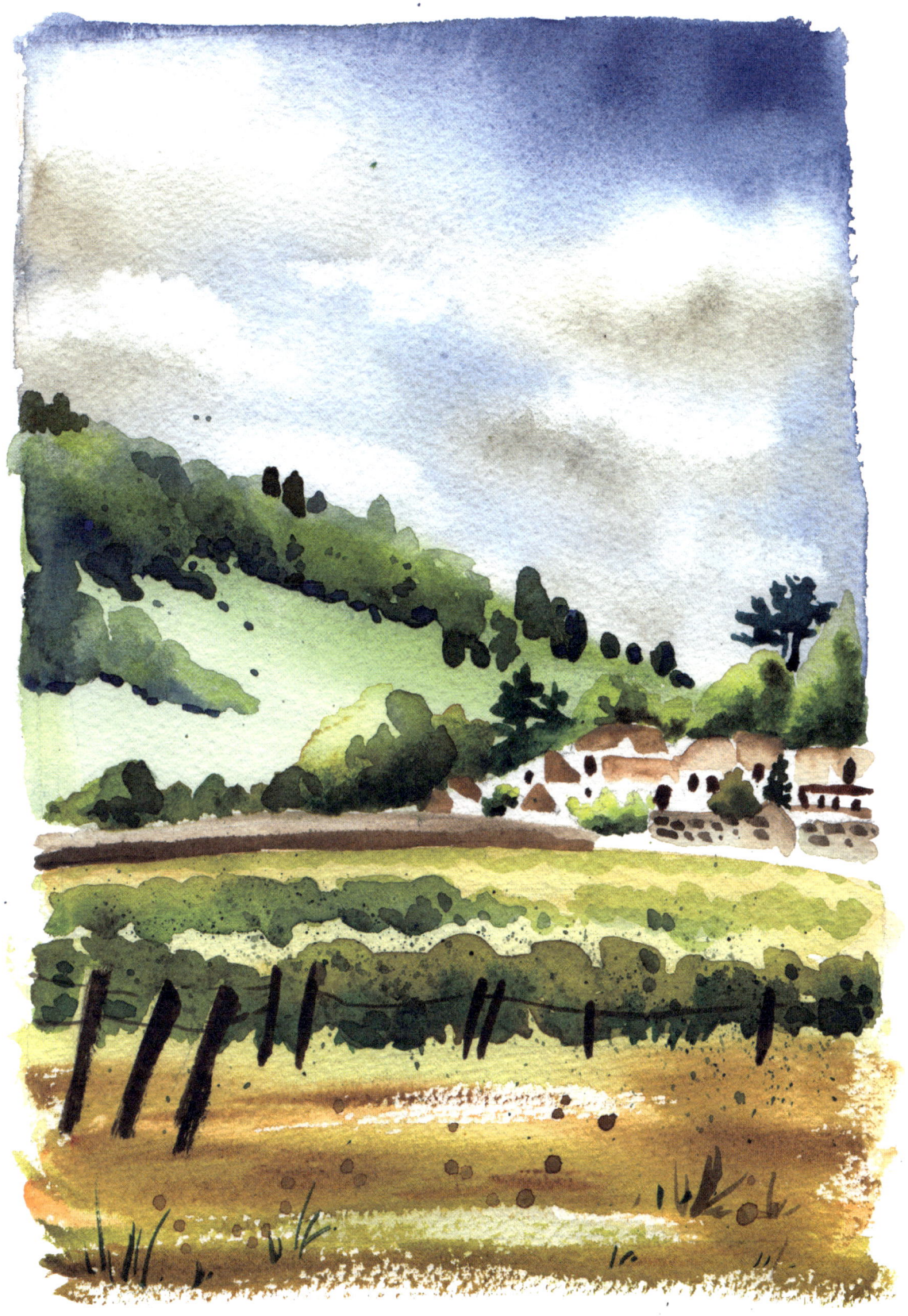

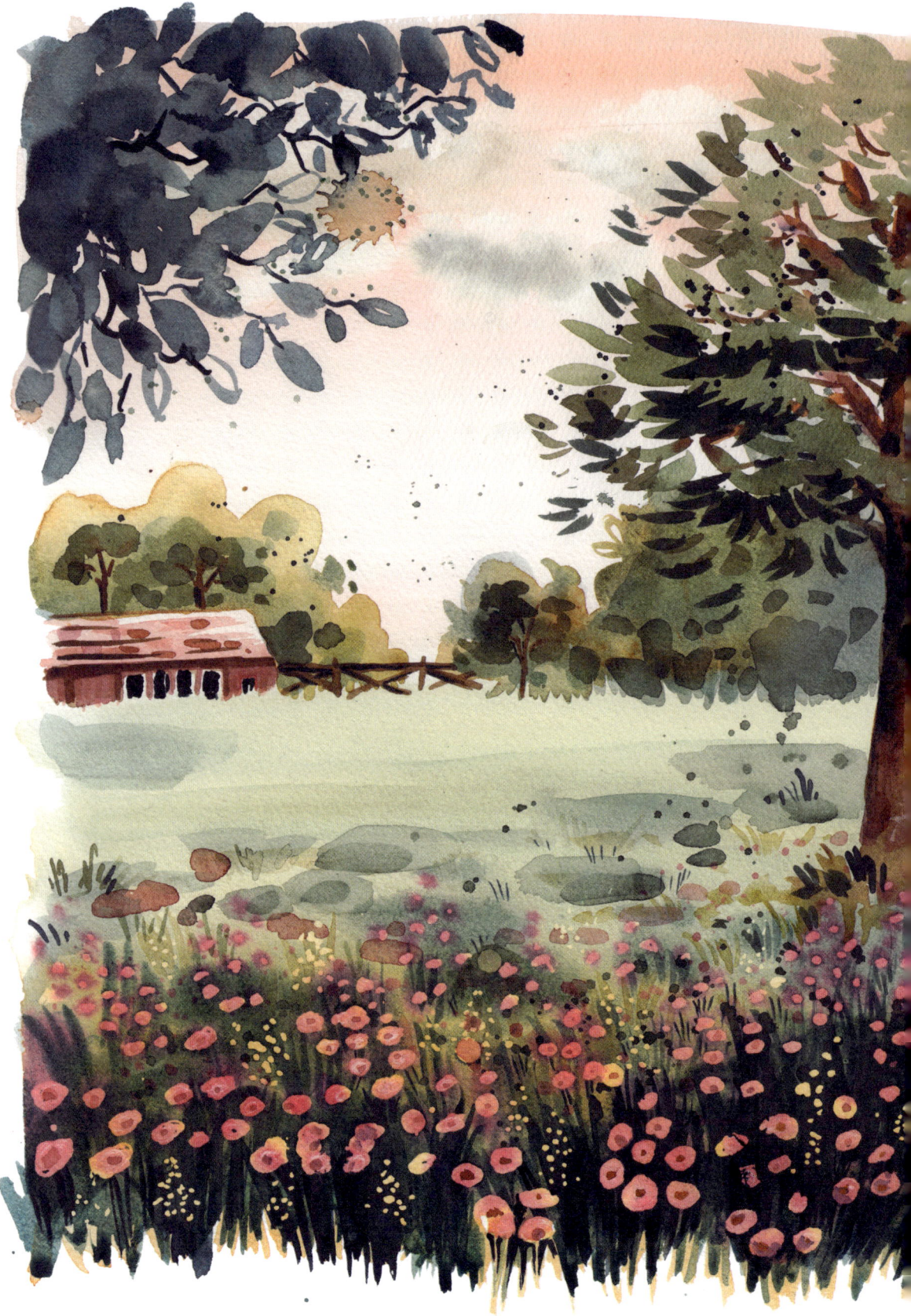

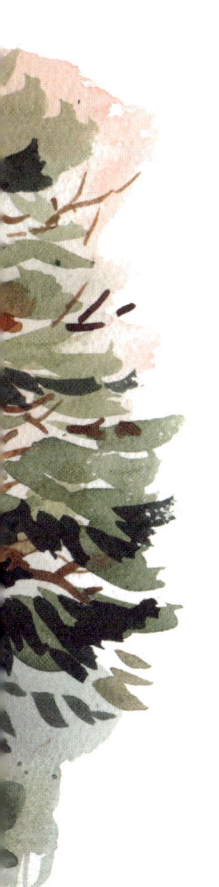

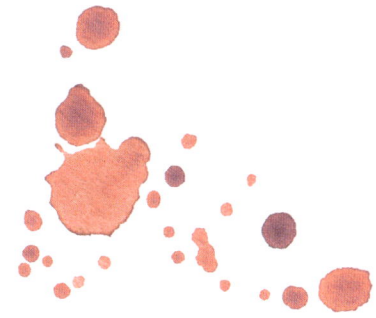

Meadows

I find painting a meadow of flowers delightful. Flowers bring so much colour to an otherwise green landscape. You can't help to be moved by the beauty of flowers – for me, they represent joy and celebration.

As with everything watercolour, there are numerous different ways of painting this subject, and I want to share my favourite, using masking fluid and the layering technique. Before we jump into the projects, I want to touch on perspective, as it's crucial to depicting a realistic meadow.

perspective

The use of perspective creates the illusion of depth in a painting. This is achieved through a variety of optical tricks, using colour tones and object scales. Let's consider the anatomy of a painting of a meadow of flowers.

First, you need to choose the good angle. Imagine you are looking at the meadow not from the top down, but as if you were almost on the same level as the flowers; this angle will enhance the contrast in scale, with blooms in the foreground bigger and brighter than those further away.

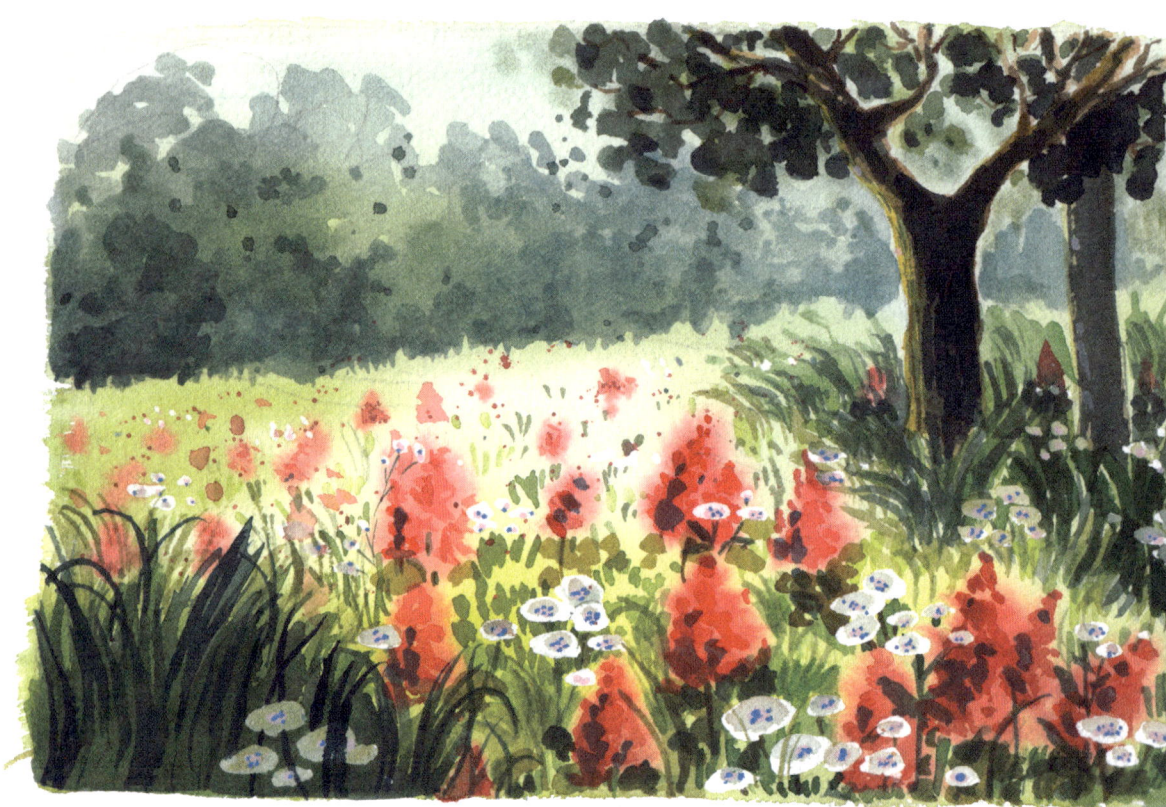

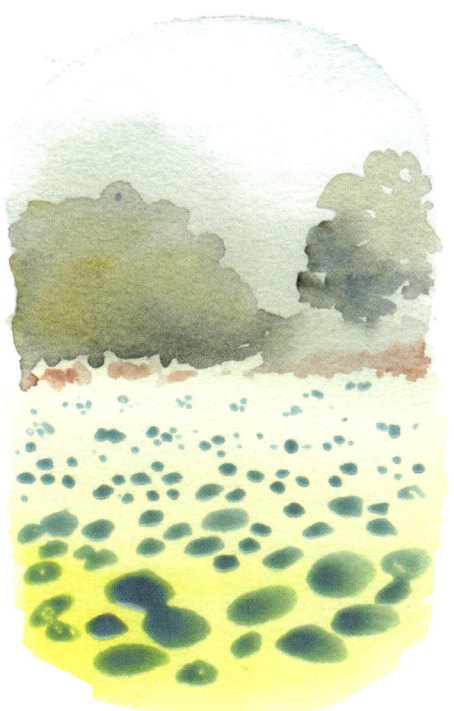

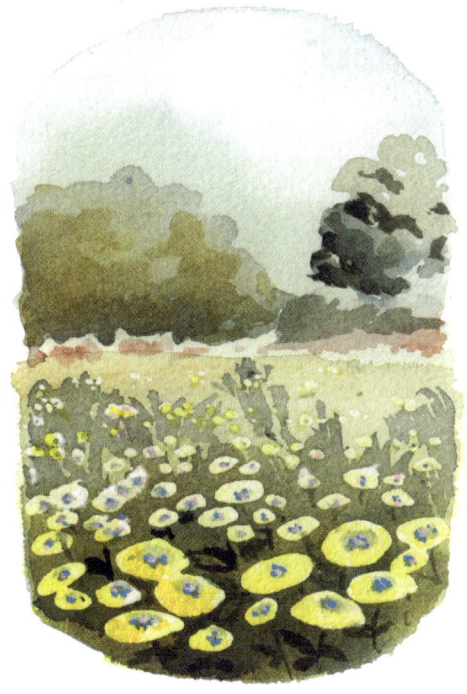

In this example, an easy way to create the illusion of perspective is to apply a wash using your chosen flower colour, which fades into the distance. Once the wash was dry, I applied masking fluid in the shapes of blooms to protect these areas whilst painting further layers. I kept them very simple, just rounded blobs rotated in different directions. Notice how the bloom size recedes into the distance.

Next, I applied a few more washes, concentrating darker shades in the foreground. After peeling off the masking fluid, my flowers began to show. To achieve a sense of depth, I added more details to the foreground flowers, like leaves and pollen, whilst keeping flowers in the distance as abstract dots.

Now let's apply the same principles to a more complex meadow.

MEADOW

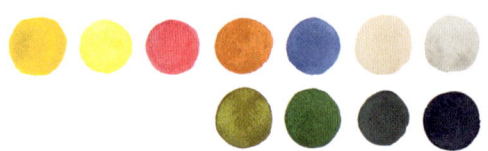

- *winsor yellow, lemon yellow deep, permanent rose, quinacridone deep gold, cobalt blue, buff titanium, Davy's gray, rich green gold, permanent sap green, perylene green, indigo*

1. Apply three large washes. Start with the meadow and use a very wet mixture of winsor yellow and lemon yellow deep. Add a few drops of medium-wet permanent rose and quinacridone deep gold and let them spread unevenly. Don't worry about how the paint spreads, as parts of it will be covered in further layers.

For the sky, use a very wet wash of cobalt blue to create a lighter shade, so it doesn't detract attention from the flowers. I followed the same principle with the path, using a very light mixture of buff titanium and Davy's gray.

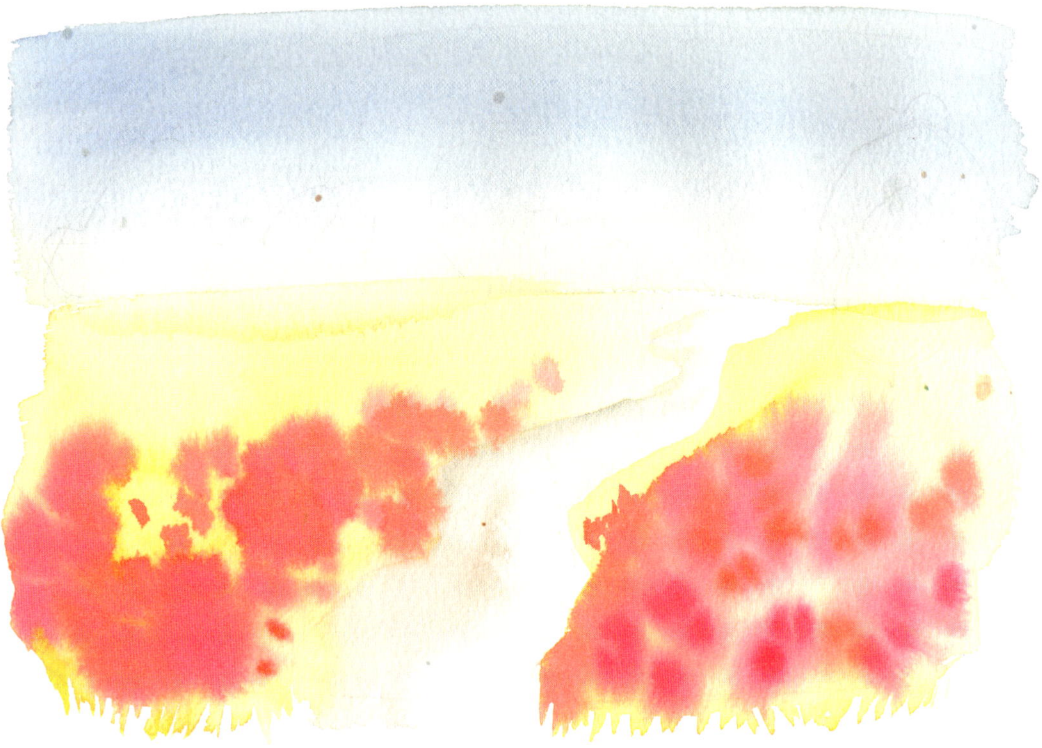

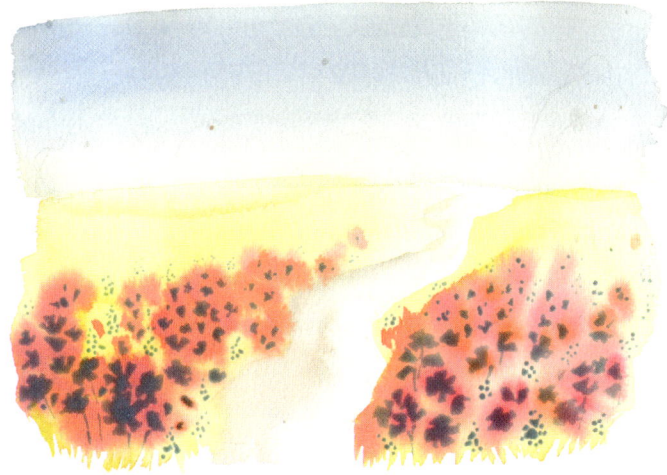

2. Once the first layer is dry, draw the shapes of flowers using masking fluid. Create larger blooms on the pink parts of the wash and clusters of small dots on the yellow parts of the wash. The beauty of this method is that no two paintings will be the same – you will get a different placement of the flowers every time, depending on how the previously painted wash turned out.

3. When the masking fluid is completely dry, apply another wash to the meadow using medium-wet rich green gold and a few drops of sap green. Concentrate darker tones in the foreground. With the tip of a round brush, add a few strokes to create blades of grass on the sides and others slightly covering the path. Then, using a very light and watery mixture of perylene green and rich green gold, paint abstract scribbles in the background to represent greenery in the distance. Allow this layer to dry.

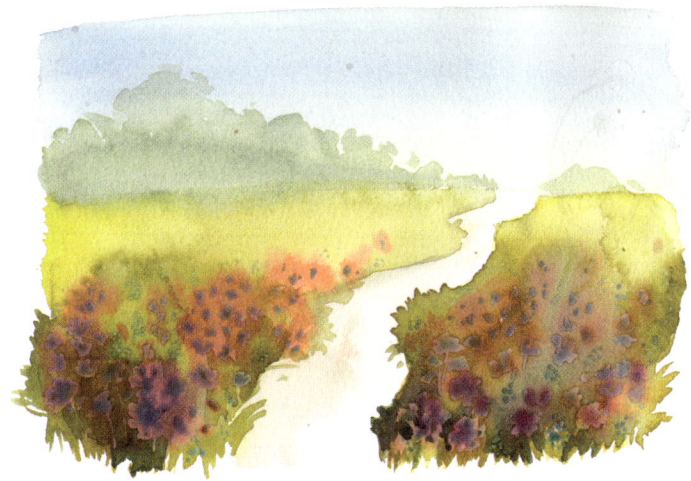

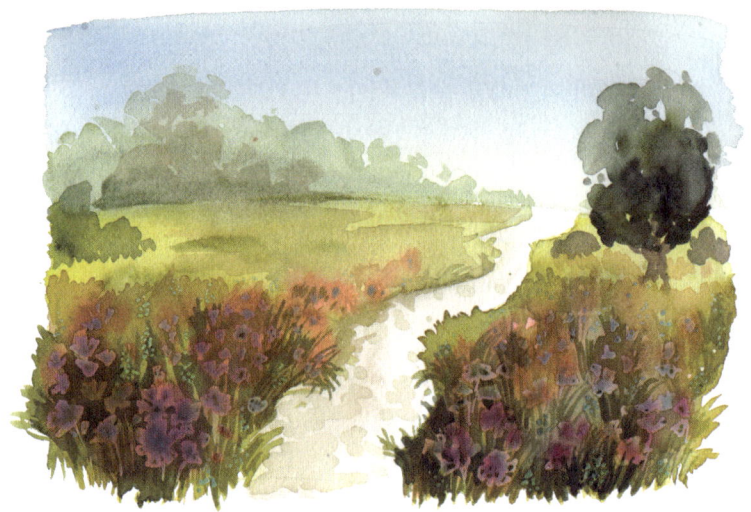

4. Using permanent sap green and perylene green separately, add short strokes to create more grass stems. Again, most prominent and dark brushstrokes should emerge in the foreground. Using the same, but very diluted, greens, add more greenery and a tree in the background, but keep brushstrokes light and abstract. Allow this layer to dry.

5. Darken shadowy parts of the grass using a thick mixture of perylene green and indigo. With a very thick mixture of perylene green and permanent sap green, add shadow to the tree to enhance its three-dimensional shape. When the layer is fully dry, peel off the masking fluid.

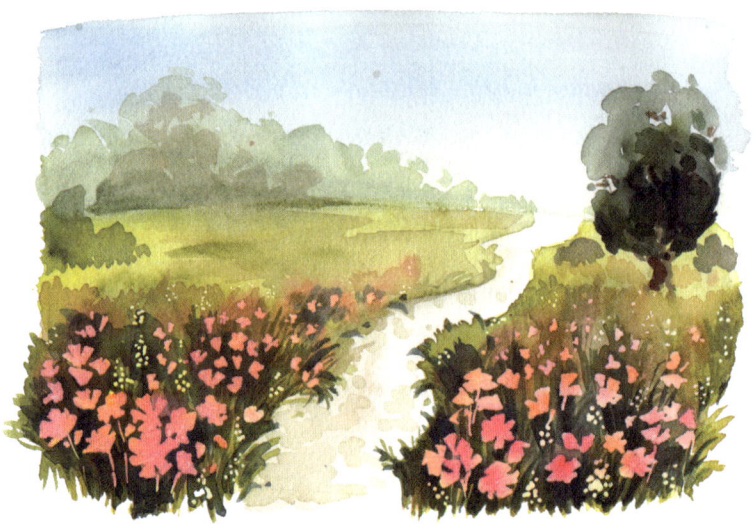

6. Add some details to the flowers, as well as some shadows and splashes. Use permanent rose to add dots to the middle of the flowers and, once dry, add another dot of a very thick winsor yellow. Using the same flower colours as previously in a medium consistency, paint more flowers on top of the grass stems.

7. Paint a few strokes at the back of the field representing different imperfections of the grass, use all the greens from before in a and medium-wet to very wet consistency. Finally, use a medium-wet indigo to cast shadows on the path and under the tree.

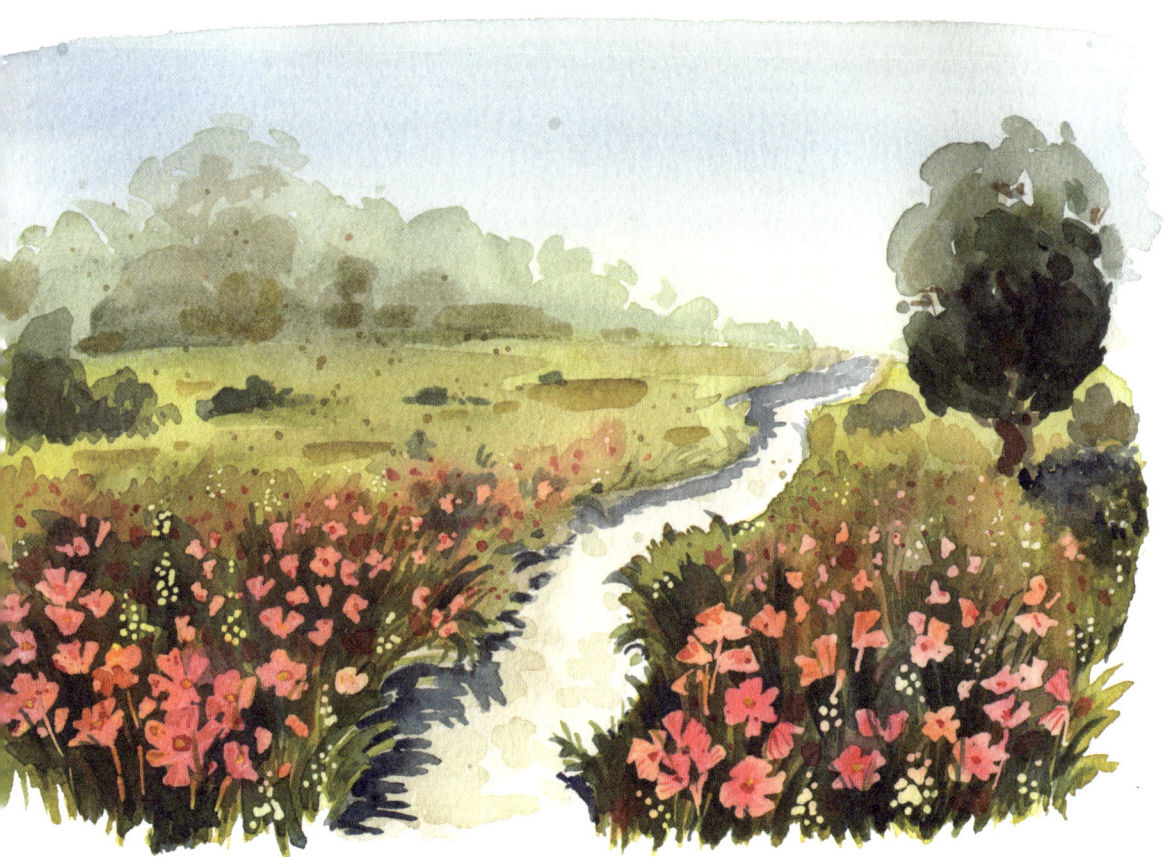

Seasons

Observing the different seasons reminds us of the natural cycles and the changes that happen in nature. The same place can look completely different at various times of the year. In autumn, for example, you might notice a wide range of natural hues from the changing colours of the leaves and the sun sitting lower in the sky, casting a warmer light over the landscape. Seasons provide us with even more of a variety of subjects to paint, often without the need to travel far. In the following exercises, we will explore how to paint landscapes across the seasons, combining techniques we've already learned with the distinct characteristics of each time of year.

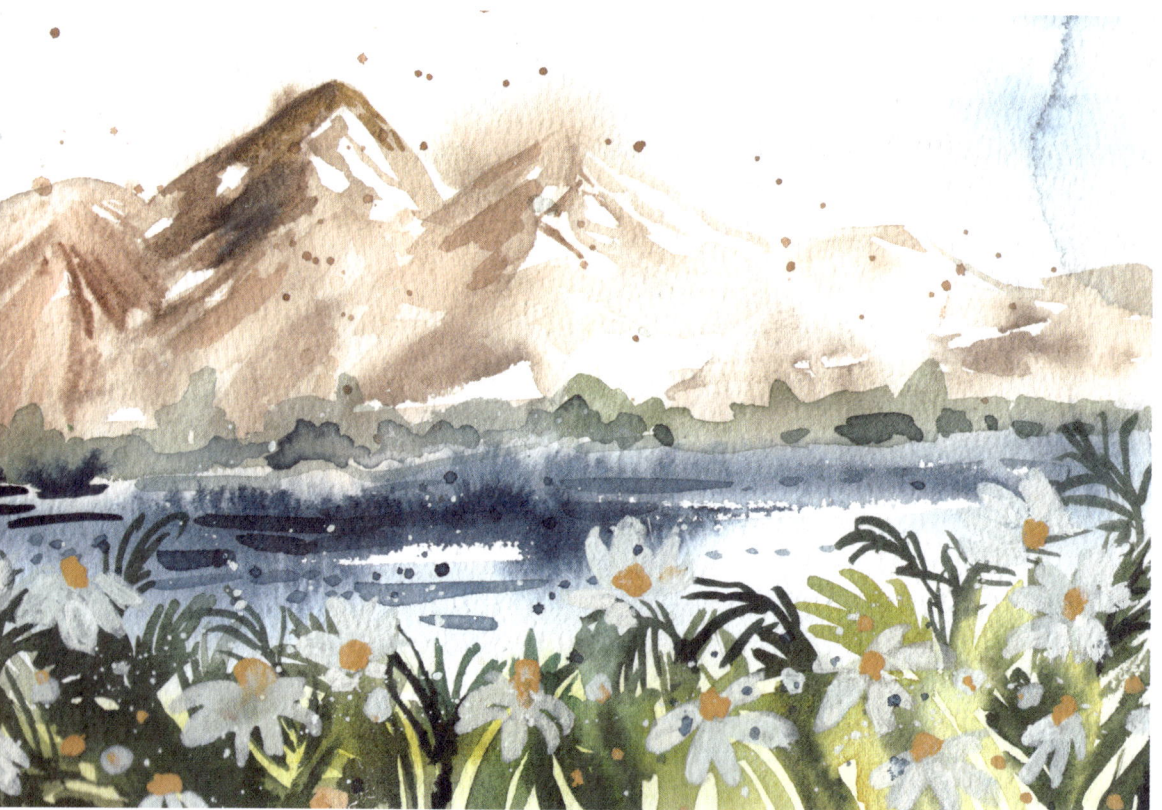

Spring

Spring is the season when nature goes through the cycle of rebirth. It is also when, after the dark winter months, we finally start going outside more often and enjoying the longer days.

Foliage in the spring tends to be very contrasting, varying from the light greens of newly grown leaves to the very dark, almost blueish leaves of evergreens that stopped growing around autumn and darkened over the winter.

The most distinctive feature of this season is the blossom on trees, and nothing blooms more beautifully than cherry trees. People everywhere enjoy taking photos in front of blossoming sakuras, and artists reach for their tools to capture the scene.

I, too, can't resist the opportunity to paint a spring landscape featuring a blooming cherry tree.

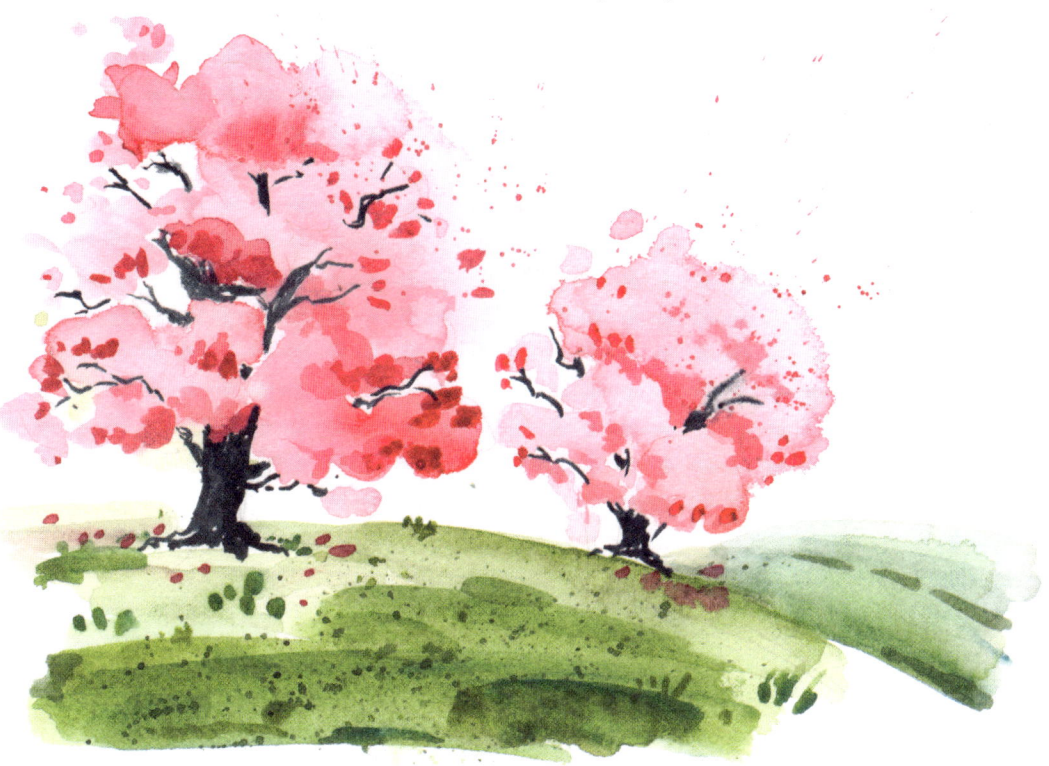

BLOSSOMING CHERRY TREE IN THE WILD

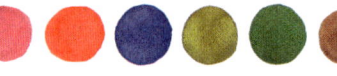

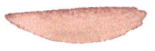

• permanent rose, scarlet lake, ultramarine blue, rich green gold, permanent sap green, burnt umber, indigo, sepia, Naples yellow

1. Start by wetting the portion of the paper that will form the hill and cherry tree. Allow the water to sit for a minute, so that when you paint wet-on-wet you will have more control over the paint spread.

   Mix a very watery pink using permanent rose and a dash of scarlet lake. Use this mixture to paint the leaves on the cherry tree. Use medium-wet ultramarine blue to paint around the cherry tree, and as you work towards the edge of the hill add a very light rich green gold.

As the paint dries, add a slightly less diluted pink to the bottom of the cherry leaves. Use a very light and watery mixture of sap green and ultramarine blue to paint the river. Leave this layer to dry completely.

2. Next, rewet the entire area covering the hill and cherry tree, but avoid the river. Again, allow the water to dry a little. Then, using a medium-wet mix of ultramarine blue, permanent sap green and rich green gold, apply another wet-on-wet wash to the mountain. Focus the darker tones around the cherry tree to create depth, but keep the edges soft, like candy floss.

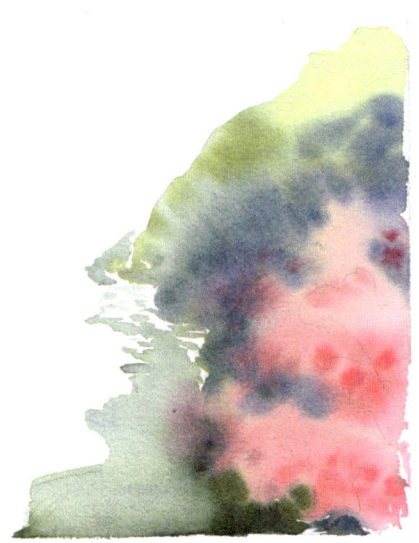

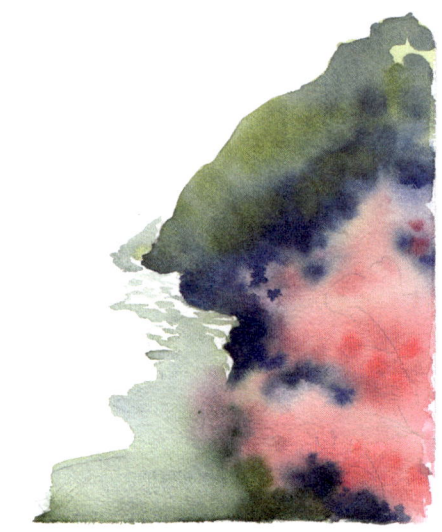

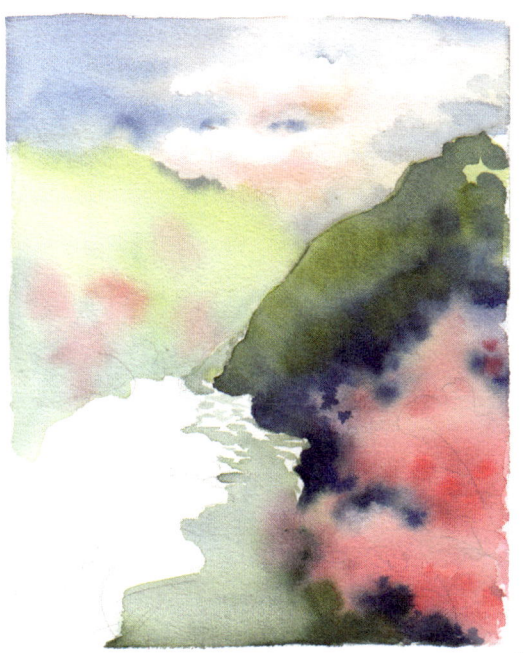 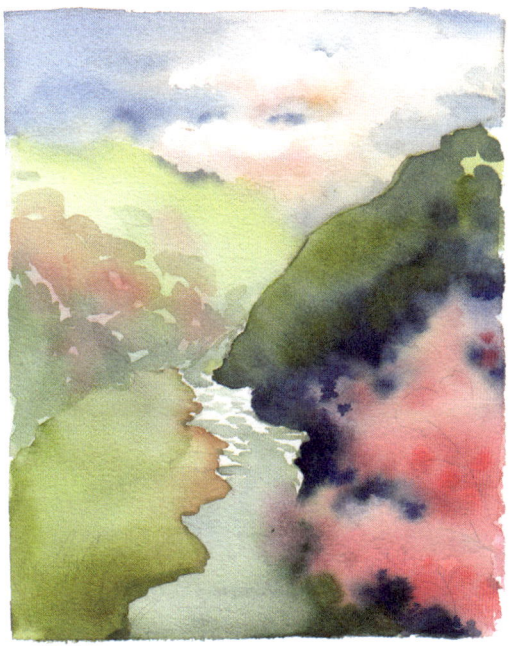

3. Paint the other hill using the same
steps and colours as in step 1, but
use more water to create lighter
shades. Add a few drops of the pink
mixture to indicate cherry blossom.
Paint the sky and a couple of clouds
using a technique from page 90.
Allow this layer to dry.

4. Using a medium-wet rich green gold
with a dash of burnt umber, paint the
remaining area of the shore. Add more
colour in the foreground and more
water towards the back. On the left-
side hill, add brushstroke scribbles in a
semi-circular motion, using a very diluted
permanent sap green, ultramarine
blue and permanent rose allowing the
colours to mix on the paper.

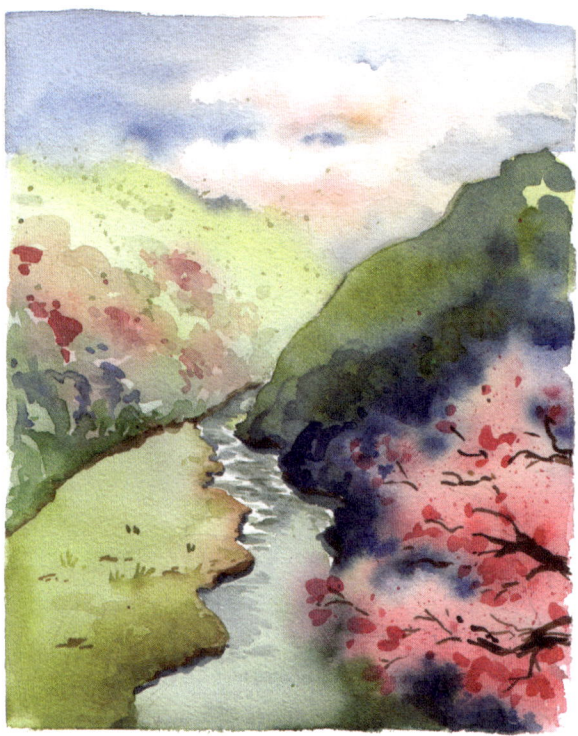

5. For the cherry blossom, mix a thick consistency of permanent rose with a touch of scarlet lake. Use this mixture to dab in separate blooms and petals. With a fine brush and a mixture of burnt umber and sepia, paint branches using just the tip of the brush. Continue with the same dark brown mixture to add shadows along the coastline and across the hillside, enhancing depth and form.

For the hills, shore and river, add scribbly brushstrokes in their original colours to deepen the shadows.

6. Continue to overlay paint to build areas of colour and shadow using thick paint mixtures of the same colours from relevant ares. Use a mixture of ultramarine blue and indigo to paint the grass in the foreground, Let lighter blades of grass from the previous layer show through underneath.

To create highlights on the right-hand hill, use a very thick Naples yellow; thanks to this paint's opacity it will sit beautifully on the darker colour, just like a gouache. For highlights on the river, use a flat brush and undiluted white gouache to create a dry brush effect. Make splatters with both permanent rose and white gouache over the cherry tree.

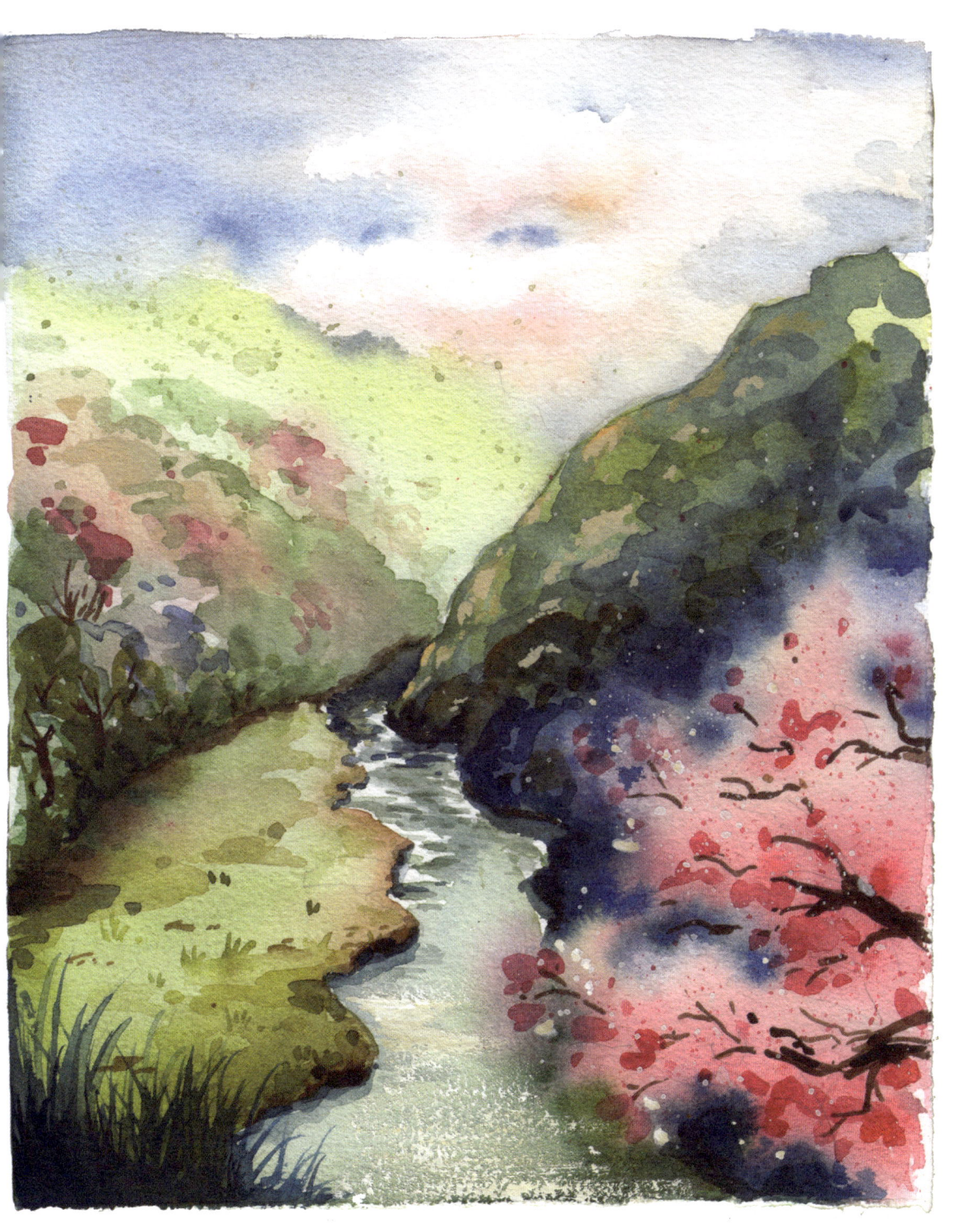

Summer

Summer is the greenest season, when plants are thriving and nature is in its richest state; it's when the sun shines bright, creating contrasting shadows everywhere you look. When observing nature in this light, it's easier to make out the shapes of different objects and bring them to paper.

For me, summer is associated with holidays and the sea, which is why for the following exercise I have chosen a warm and sunny bird's-eye view of the Sicilian coast, allowing us to explore the contrast in scale between foreground objects and background view.

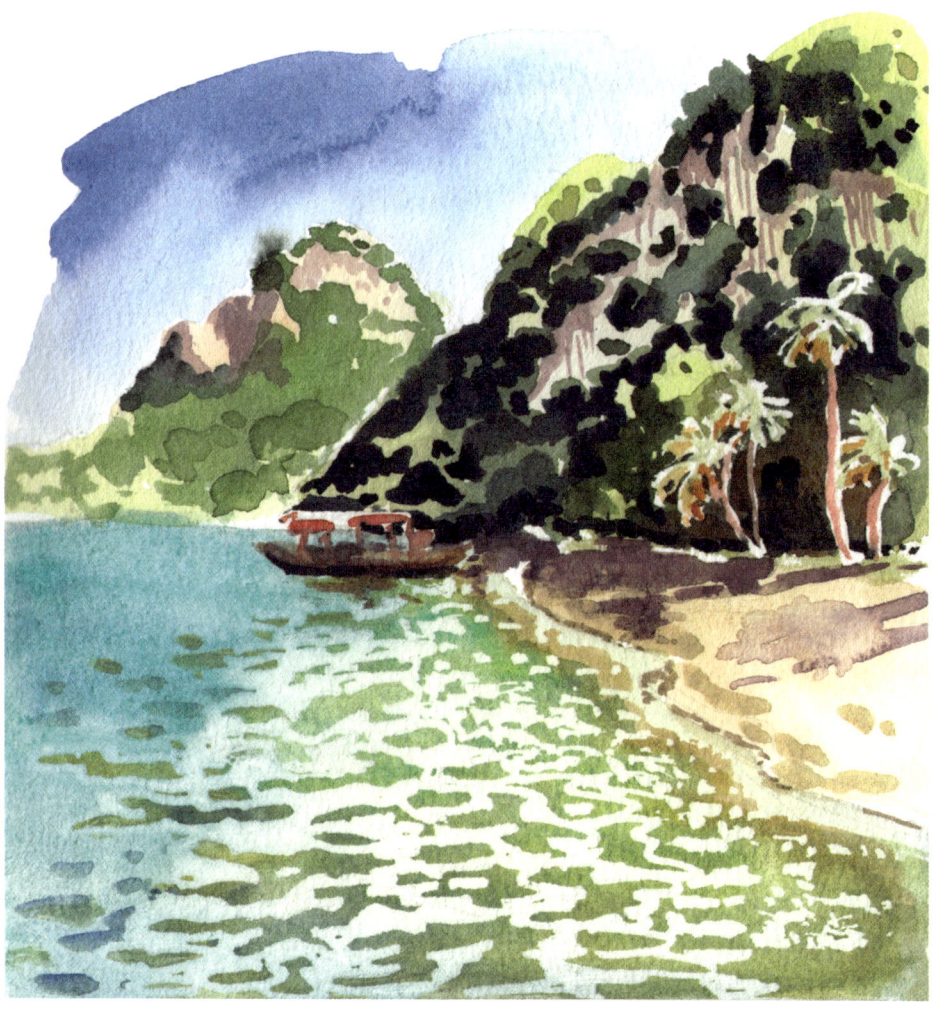

MEDITERRANEAN COASTLINE

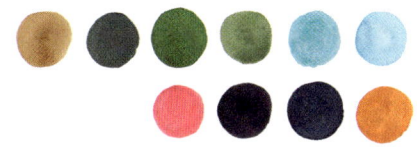

• raw umber, perylene green, permanent sap green, rich green gold, cobalt teal blue, manganese blue hue, permanent rose, neutral tint, indigo, quinacridone deep gold

1. Use masking tape to secure your paper to your work surface. Begin by applying masking fluid to preserve a cactus, a flower and a few abstract shapes in the background. Also, protect a long line along the coast. When the masking fluid is completely dry, apply a wet-on-wet wash, mapping out different areas of the painting (see page 19). Use medium-wet colours of raw umber for the hill, perylene green mixed with permanent sap green for the dark greenery, and rich green gold for lighter greenery.

For the sea, use a thick mixture of cobalt teal blue and manganese blue hue. Use the pulling technique from page 22 to make the sea closest to the shoreline lighter. To paint the building in the foreground, use permanent rose with a dash of sap green.

2. As the paint dries, use a clean, damp brush to lift some of it, shaping the slopes of the hills through soft highlights and contouring.

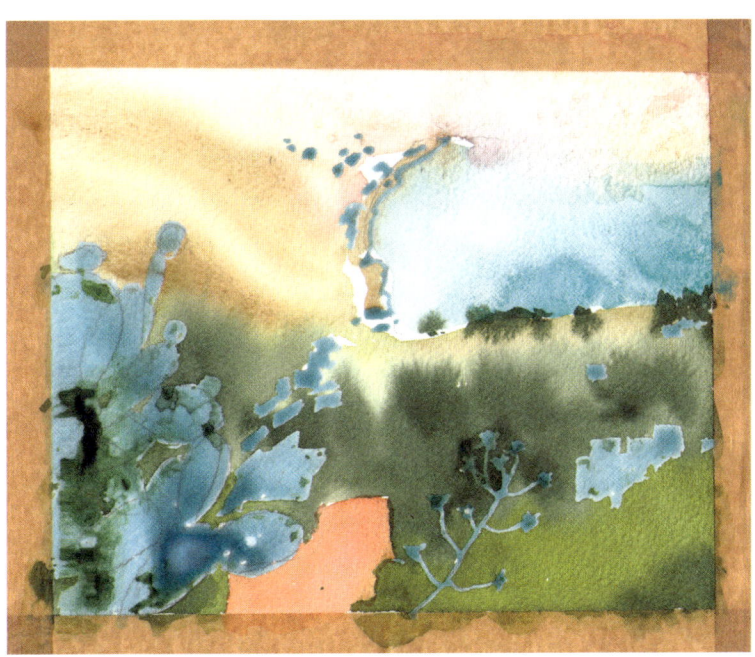

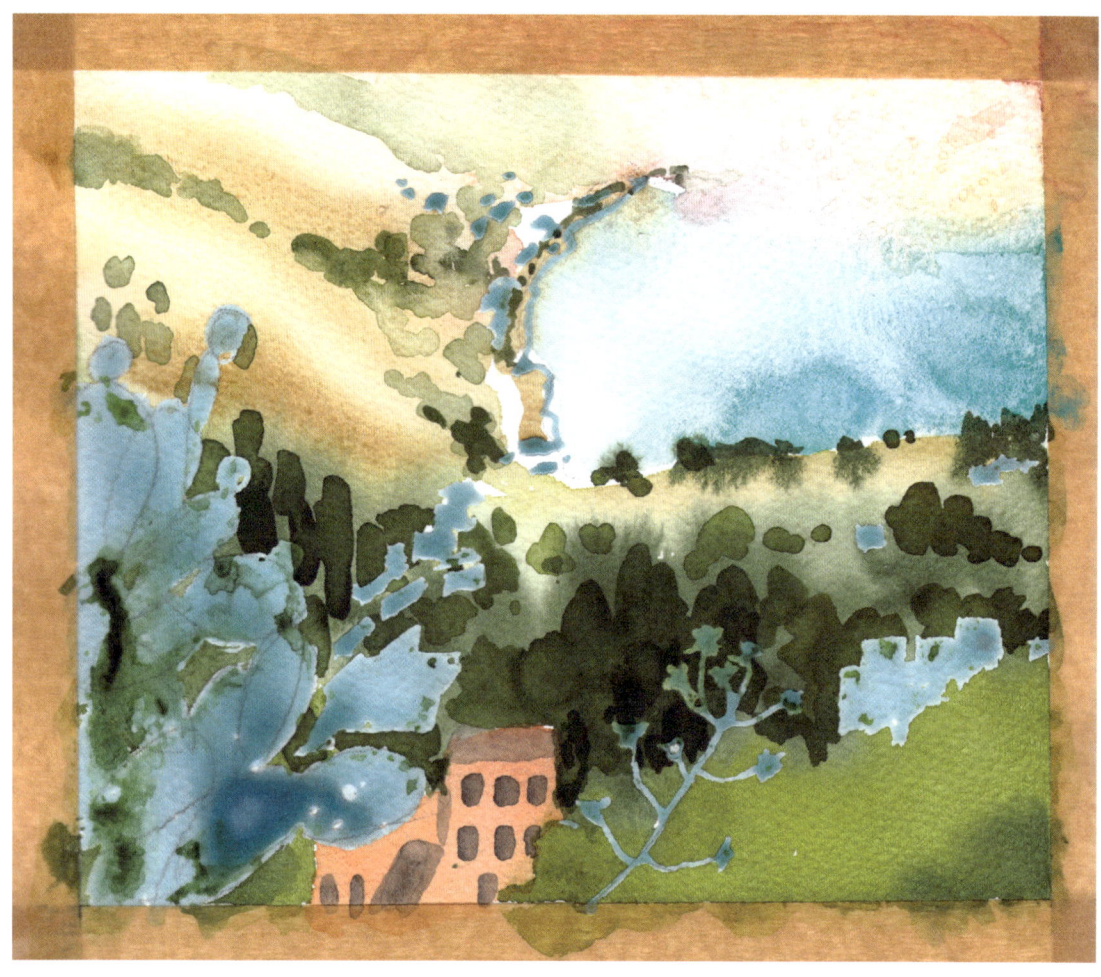

3. Load a round brush with a blunt tip with a medium-wet permanent sap green mixture to paint tree shapes. Arrange the trees in natural-looking clusters; think of them as somewhat elongated blobs. For the trees in the distance, use a very diluted sap green and smaller brushstrokes.

Paint around the green bush in the foreground to preserve its lightness.

Use a diluted neutral tint to suggest the roof and windows of the building. Leave to dry.

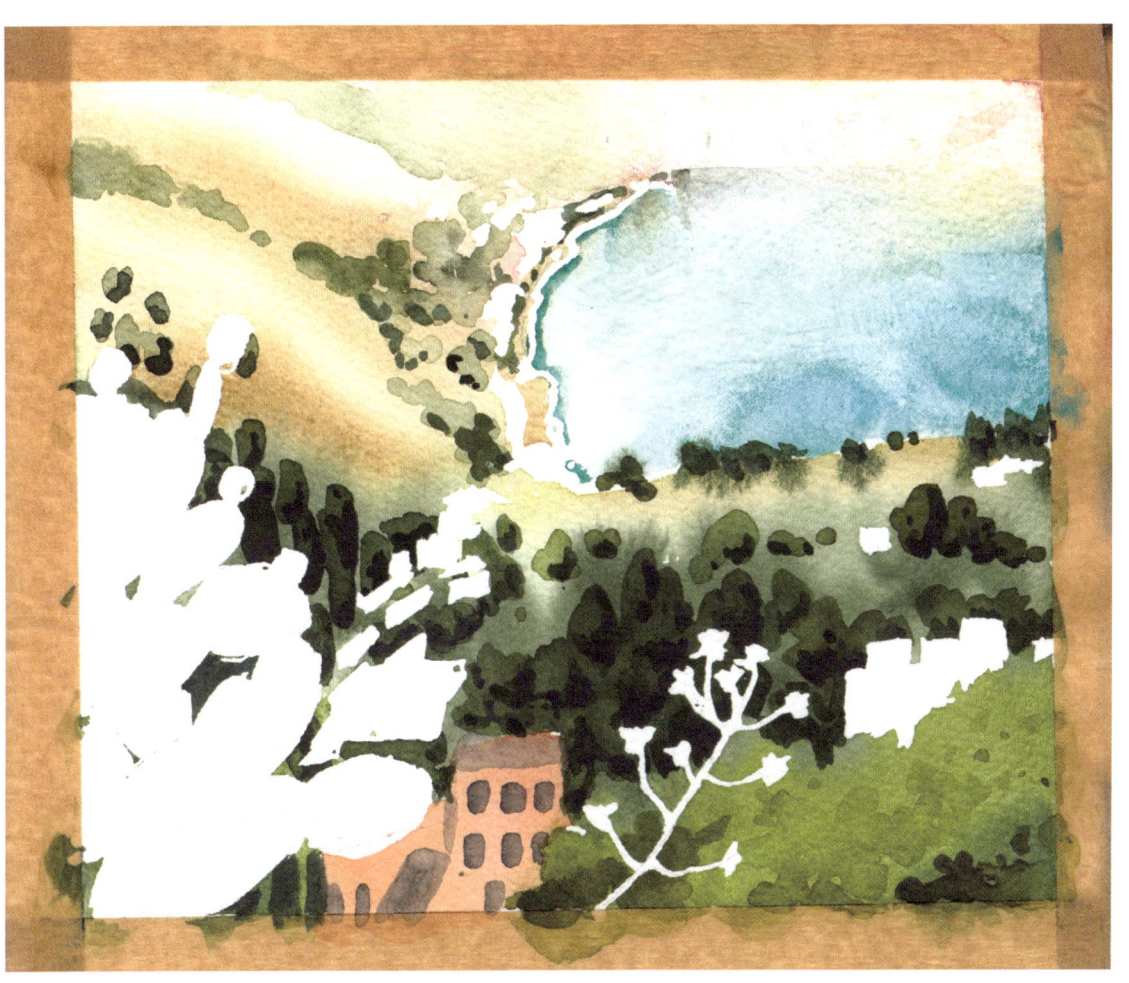

4. Create a thick mixture of permanent
   sap green and indigo and apply it to
   create shadows on the trees. After the
   paint has dried completely, peel off
   the masking fluid.

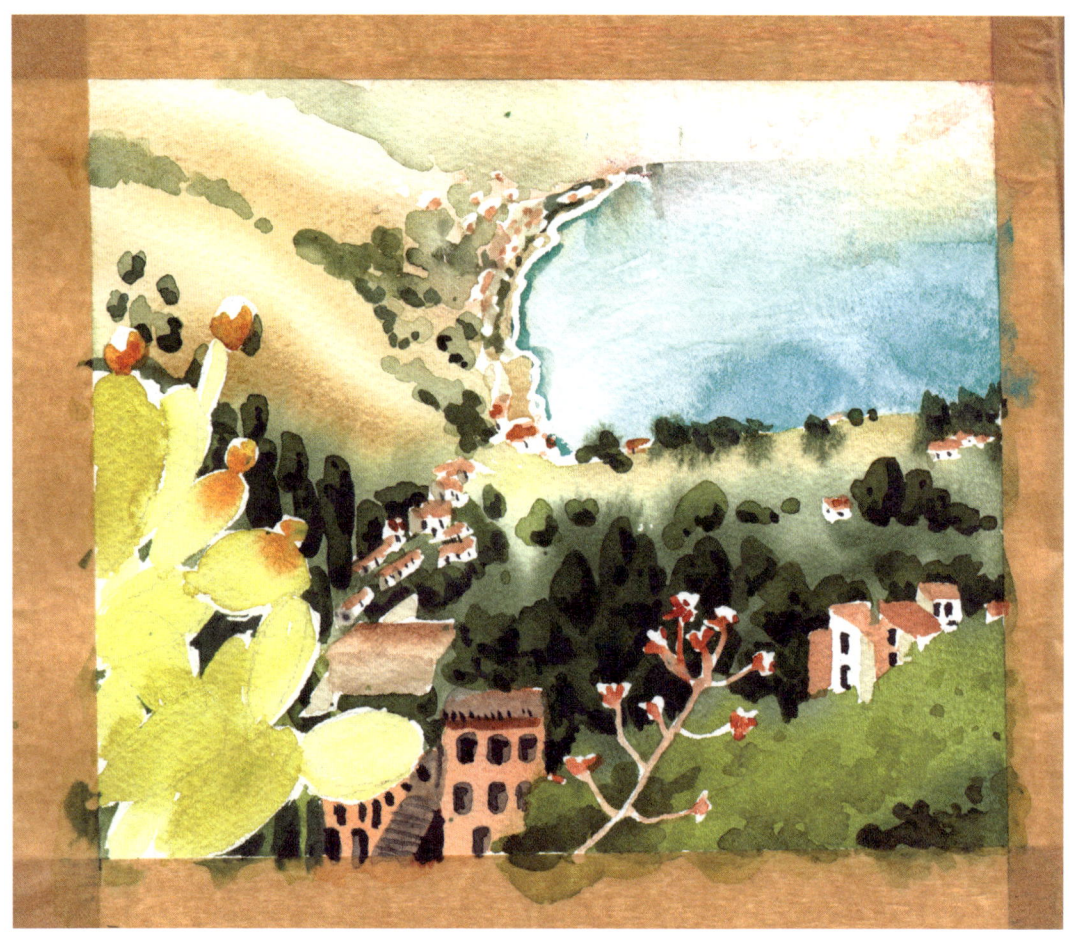

5. Paint a light wash of rich green gold over the cactus shape in the foreground, and use quinacridone deep gold for the cactus flowers. Don't colour in the whole cactus but leave some of the edges white.

6. Use permanent rose with a dash of sap green to paint the plant at the foreground, using more saturated colour on the flowers and lighter on the stem. Use same colour to paint small strokes and dashes to suggest rooftops, and small brushstrokes with neutral tint for windows.

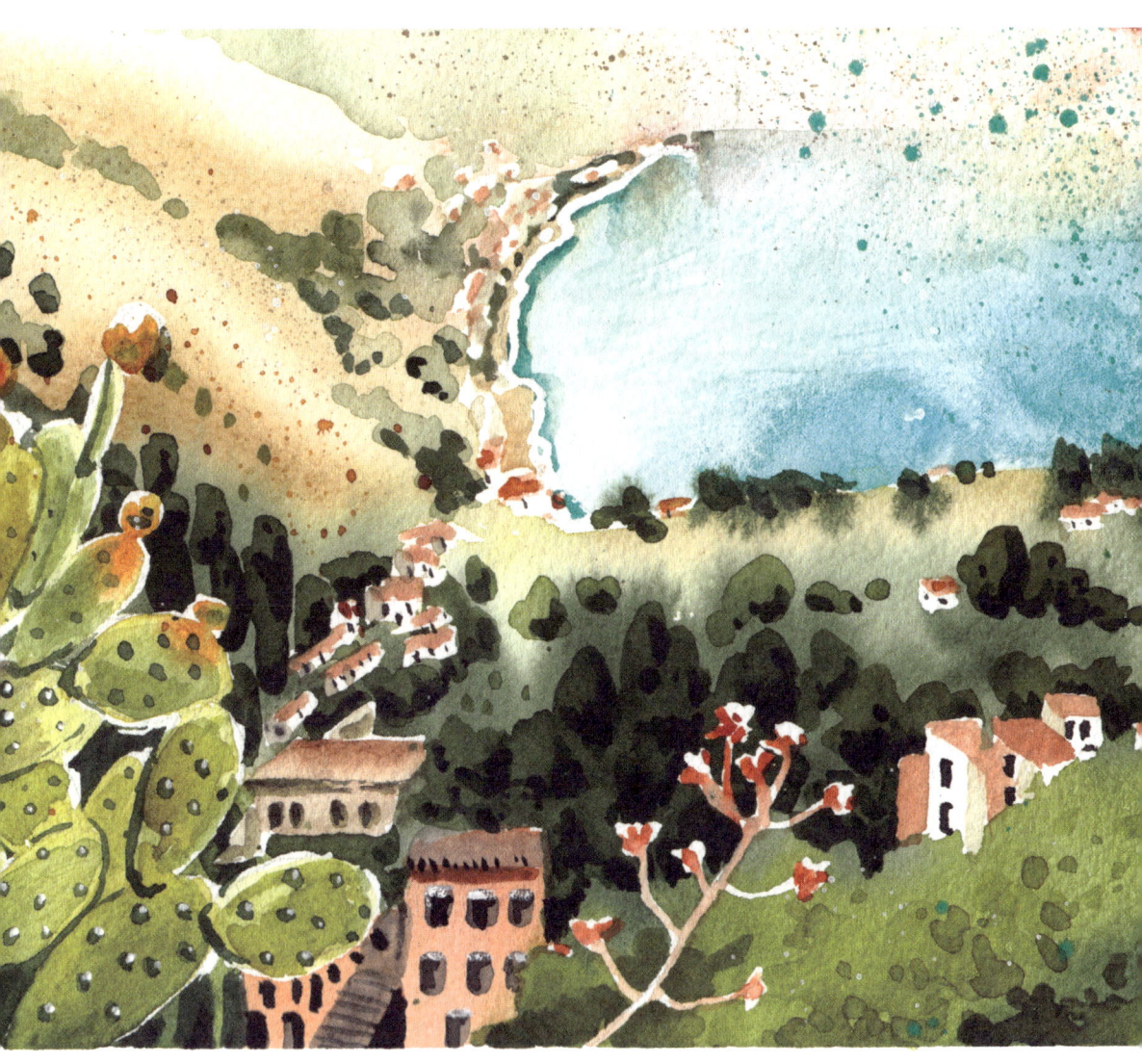

7. Build up the cactus shape by adding more of the original colour to different areas, and add sap green dots with white gouache to suggest cactus pricks. Finally, add splatters of different colours across the painting using a small and medium-size brush.

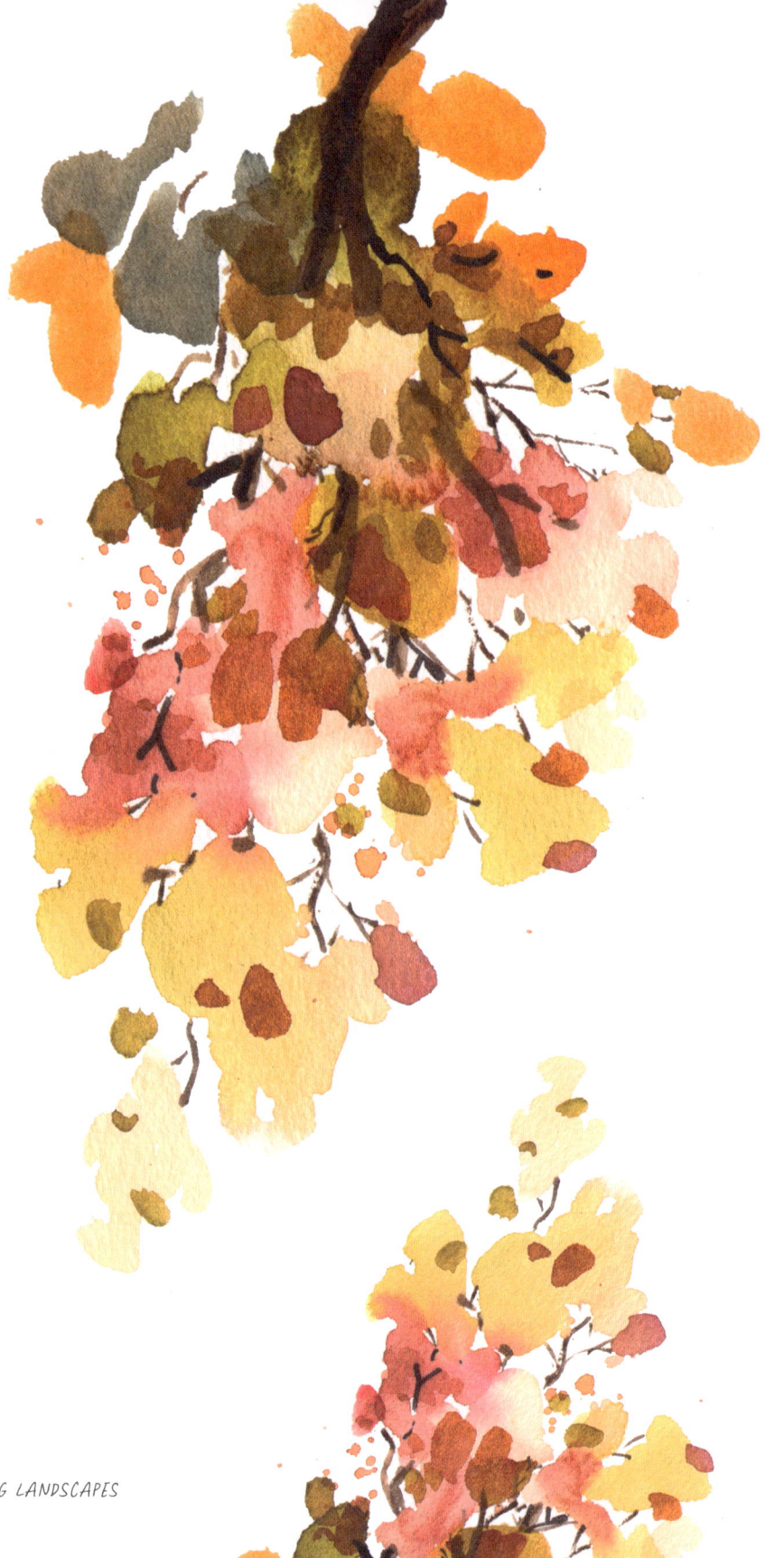

Autumn

Autumn has a warm and rich colour palette, ranging from deep greens to gold, orange and red hues. As the days get shorter and the temperature drops, the time spent walking outside on a warm autumn day feels extra special.

As you walk, you may notice that the colours of the leaves on the trees change in a certain pattern. Sometimes it's from the top down or from the inner canopy to the outer canopy, and there's almost always leaf clusters one side of the tree that change colour first. I find this effect beautiful; when parts of the tree glow with gold and red whilst other areas remain green, it creates a natural contrast that feels alive and dynamic. In the following exercise, we will explore these autumnal hues.

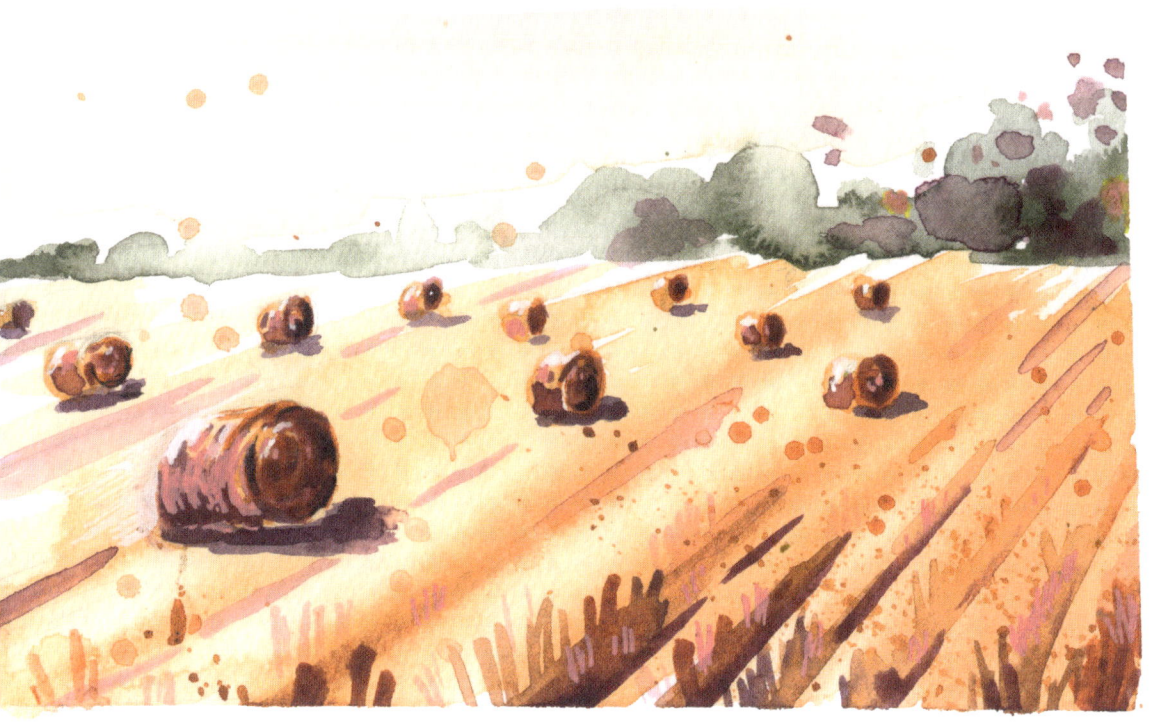

AUTUMN IN CENTRAL PARK

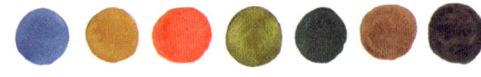

• cobalt blue, quinacridone gold, scarlet lake, green gold, perylene green, burnt umber, sepia

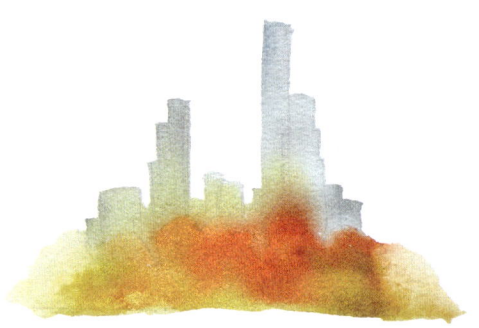

1. Begin by applying a light, watery wash of a mixture of cobalt blue and quinacridone gold across the skyline of the city. Next use separate scarlet lake, quinacridone gold and green gold to loosely shape trees in the distance. Use the colours in uneven proportions, allowing them to flow, mingle and bleed into the skyscrapers.

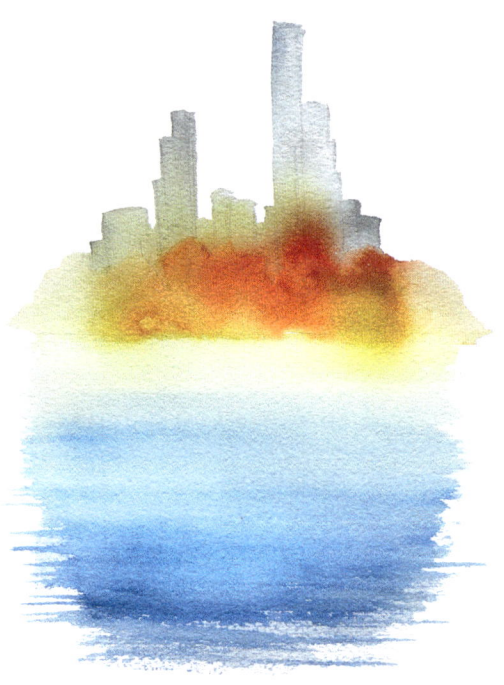

2. Whilst the paint is still wet, take a large flat brush loaded with water and pull down from the trees to create a soft gradient wash. Towards the bottom of the painting, introduce light cobalt blue, and with the same flat brush use a left-to-right motion through the wet area to create soft waves.

3. When the surface of the water is almost dry, paint a reflection of the trees using their original colours. Allow this layer to dry.

4. To paint leaves in the foreground, use a round brush with a blunt tip and make dabbing motions to create dots of various sizes and distances from each other.

Just like in nature, apply colours to the clusters whilst also allowing sections to bleed into each other. Introduce perylene green to the original palette of scarlet lake, quinacridone gold and green gold. To make the painting look loose and careless, splash paint over the still-wet tree area, which will add more texture to the leaves. Let this layer dry.

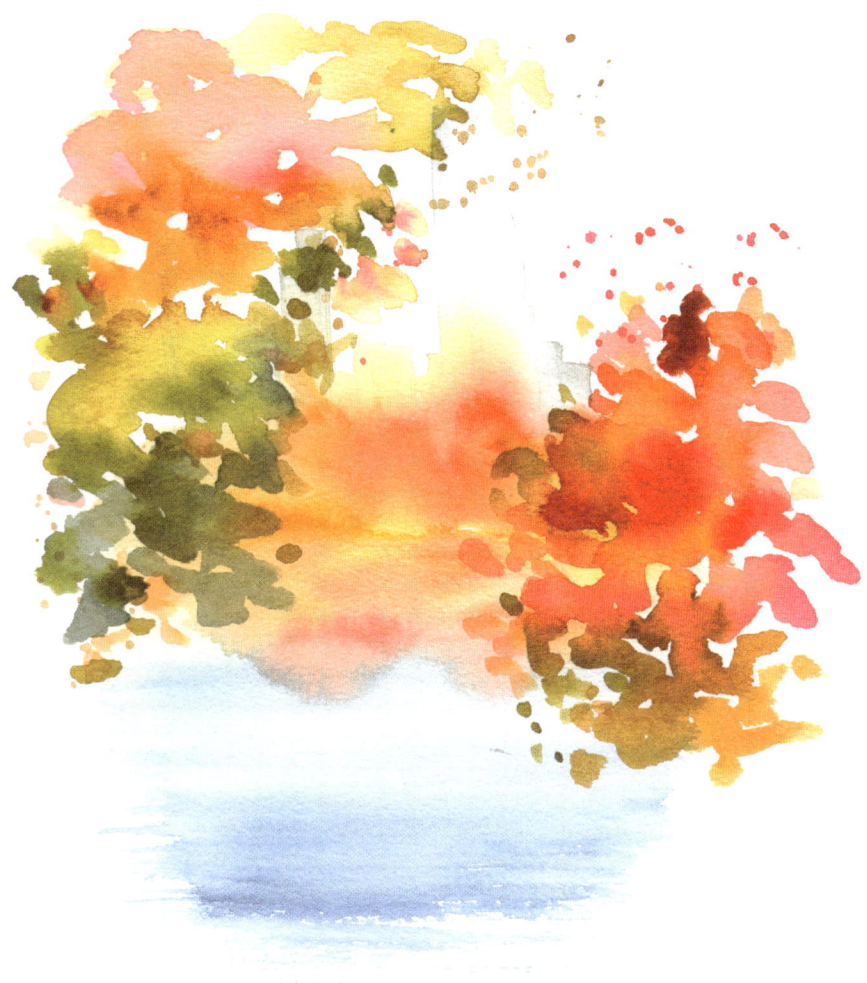

5. Create another layer of leaf clusters, focusing on the bottom areas to define shadows. The trees in the background also need some definition, so use the softening technique to show the edges of individual trees: firstly, outline the shape by drawing a line, then soften it by pulling water away from this line (see page 23).

6. Add another layer to the skyscrapers by applying a few more washes to some of them using the same colours before. Then, using a liner brush, draw vertical and horizontal lines suggesting windows.

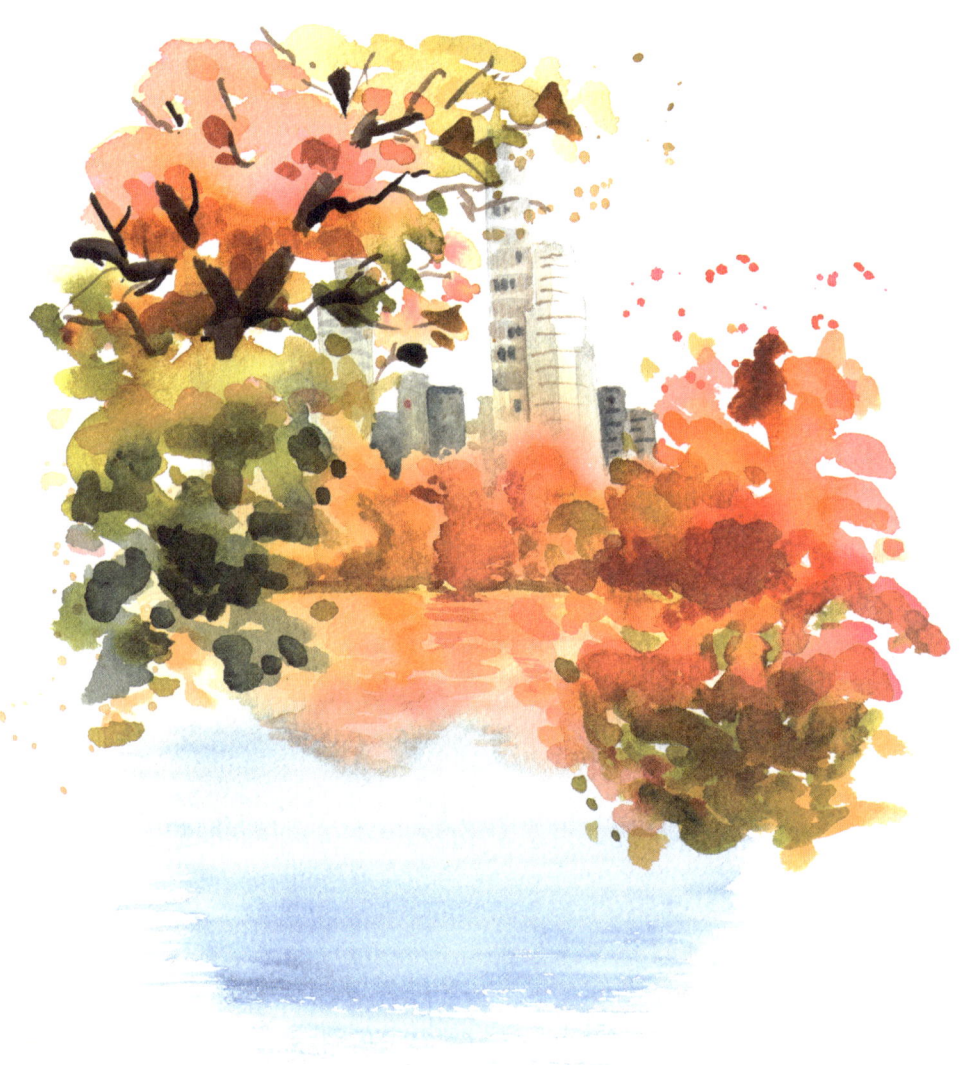

7. With a thick mixture of burnt umber and sepia, start adding tree branches. Paint the branches over the darker sections of the leaves, avoiding the lighter areas, as this is how they would most commonly appear in nature. Whilst you want to keep your painting relaxed, you still need to try to make the anatomy convincing. Dab in a few darker leaves here and there.

8. Finally, paint a loose reflection of the buildings and foreground trees using the objects' original colours. Gently paint overlapping horizontal lines to keep reflections hazy.

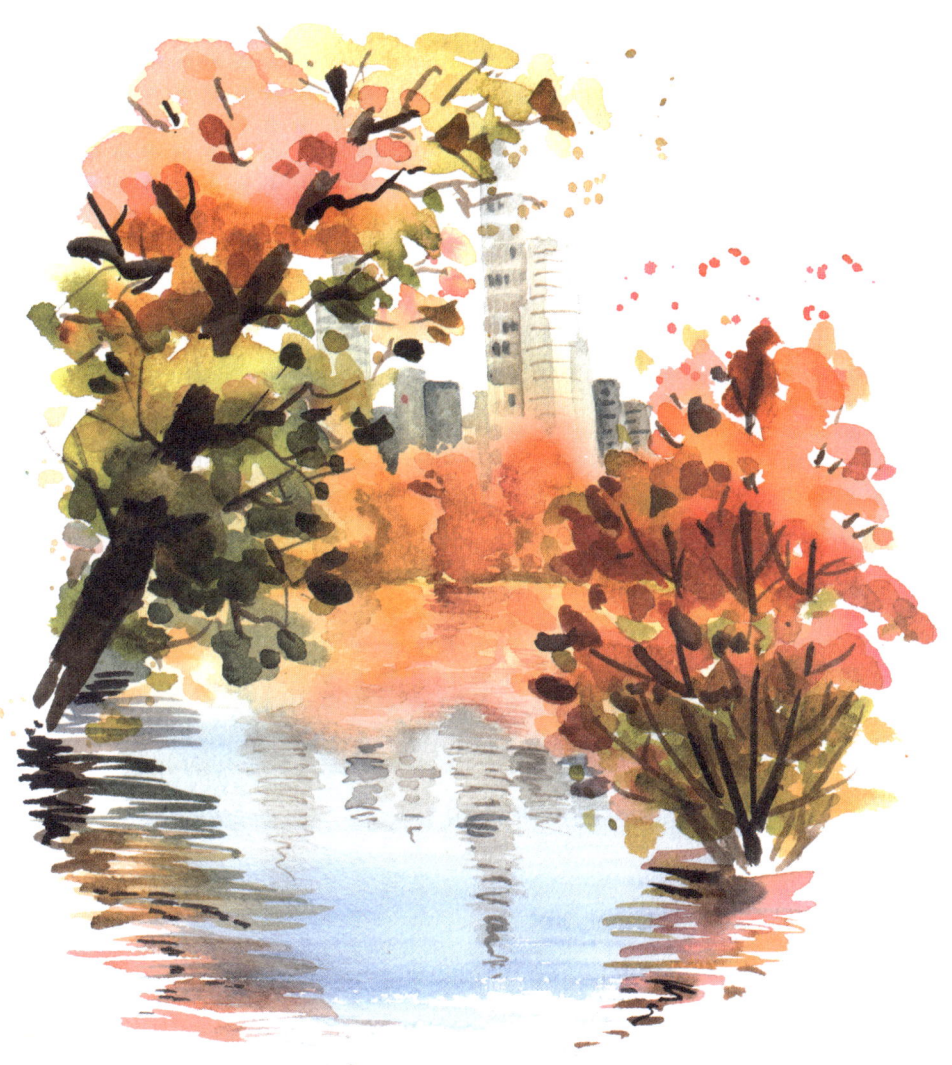

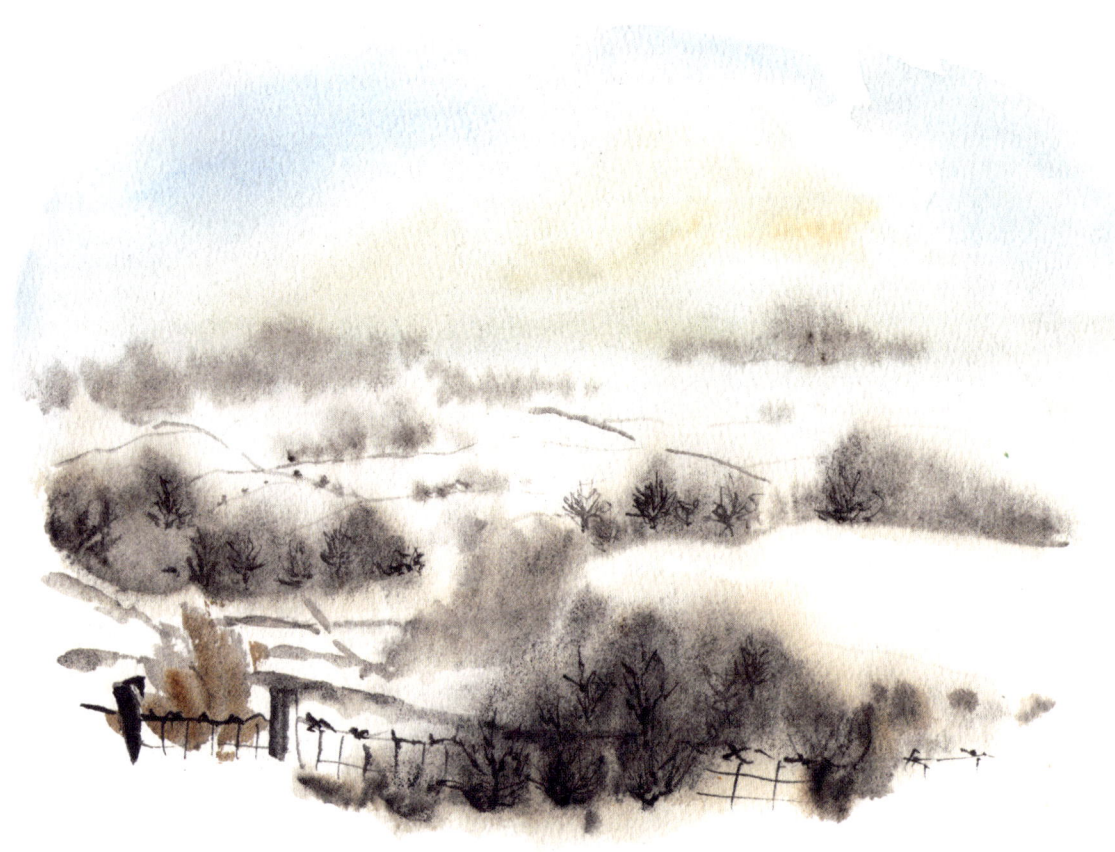

Winter

Growing up in Lithuania, I am used to very white, snowy winters. It is a particularly beautiful sight when skiing or taking a walk in the forest, as the fir trees are covered with a soft blanket of snow. In this climate, all other trees are naked and there is very little greenery.

Another image that now defines winter for me is the UK landscape. The colouring is completely different from the snowy scenes I'm used to. There are lots of evergreen trees, along with those that have shed their leaves. The colour palette ranges from rich, dark greens to earthy browns and muted rusty tones.

For the next exercise I have chosen a more 'traditional' image of winter, so we can explore how to utilize the soft effects of watercolour.

SOFT SNOW

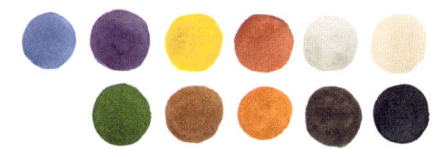

● cobalt blue, winsor violet, winsor yellow, light red, Davy's gray, buff titanium,
permanent sap green, burnt umber, quinacridone deep gold, sepia, indigo

1. Use masking tape to secure your paper to your work surface. Start by wetting the sky area. Onto the wet surface paint radiating lines using wet cobalt blue and winsor violet, leaving spaces between the lines.

To the white parts add a diluted winsor yellow and light red separately. If the paint starts spreading too much, use a damp, clean brush to lift the paint and maintain the radiating shape.

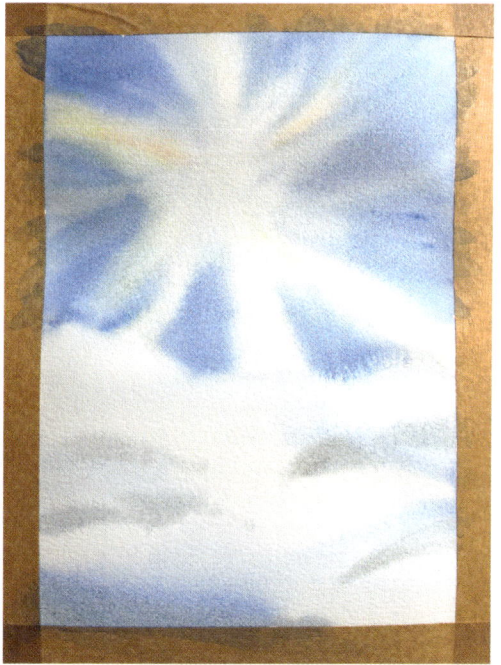

2. Next, wet the ground area and add curved brushstrokes for the hills using a mixture of cobalt blue and Davy's gray.

As the paint begins to spread, use a clean, damp brush to lift it from the lower part of the curve, creating a defined hard edge. Allow this layer to dry.

3. Create a watery mix of Davy's gray, cobalt blue and buff titanium. Use this mixture to paint uneven cone-shaped firs.

Whilst the paint is still damp add a few needles sticking out of the snow on the ends of the branches using a mixture of permanent sap green and burnt umber.

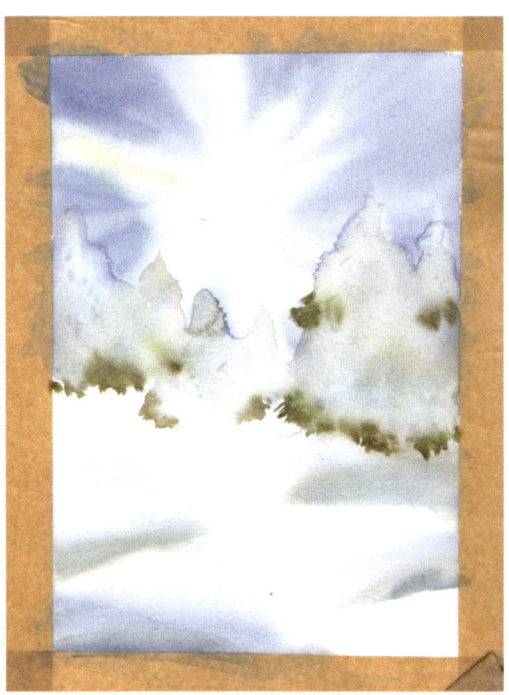
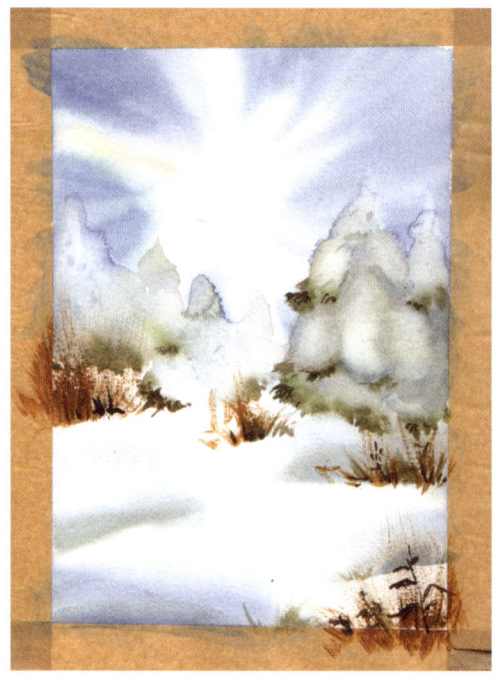

4. To form a blanket of snow, add shadows using darker tones of the original colours, and lift paint from the highlighted parts to show the roundness of the snow blanket.

5. Load a flat brush with burnt umber mixed with a dash of quinacridone deep gold. Gently wipe the brush into a paper towel and, using a swift veritical fanning motion, paint dried-out plants, focusing them behind each snow slope. Add some strokes of sepia for contrast.

6. Once the previous layer is dry, it's time to add a winter tree using burnt umber with a dash of quinacridone deep gold. Start painting it in a light shade first to show some branches lit by the sun. Use a round brush for the trunk and a fine liner brush to arrange branches. Add sepia to the mixture to create dark shadows on the tree.

7. For the final touches, use a light mixture of indigo and Davy's gray to create shadows of each object, placing them with the direction of the sunlight in mind.

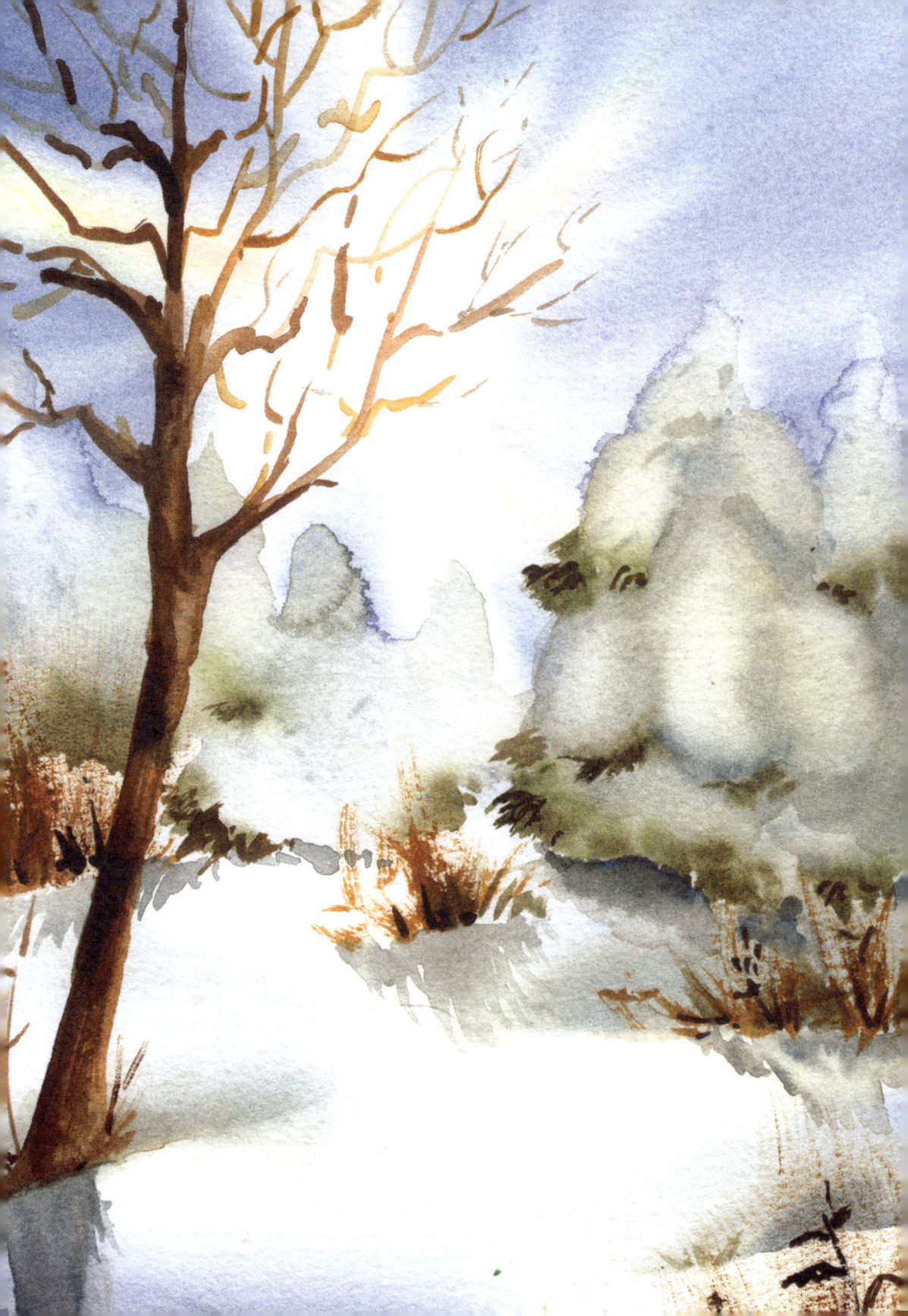

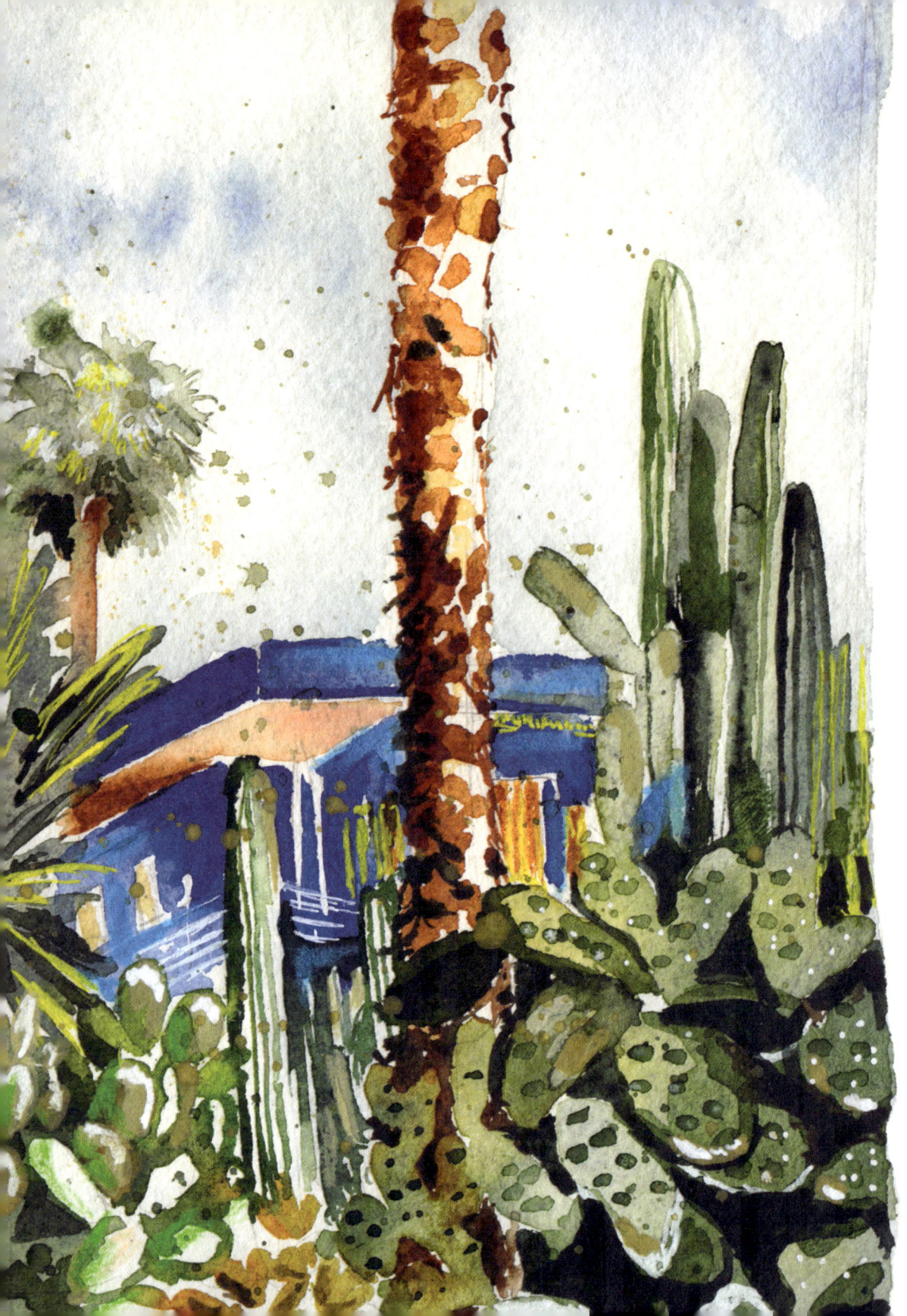

Travel sketches

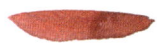

We travel for lots of reasons, to see new places, learn about history or new cultures and build memories, and it's only natural to want to capture those precious moments and breathtaking views. As an artist, transferring these memories onto paper is deeply meaningful, as not only are you recording the moment with your brush, you're also preserving how you felt at that time.

To start with, you could practise replicating images you find on the internet, which will help you to build confidence, but the ultimate goal is to create a connection with the world around you by painting the moments that truly matter to you.

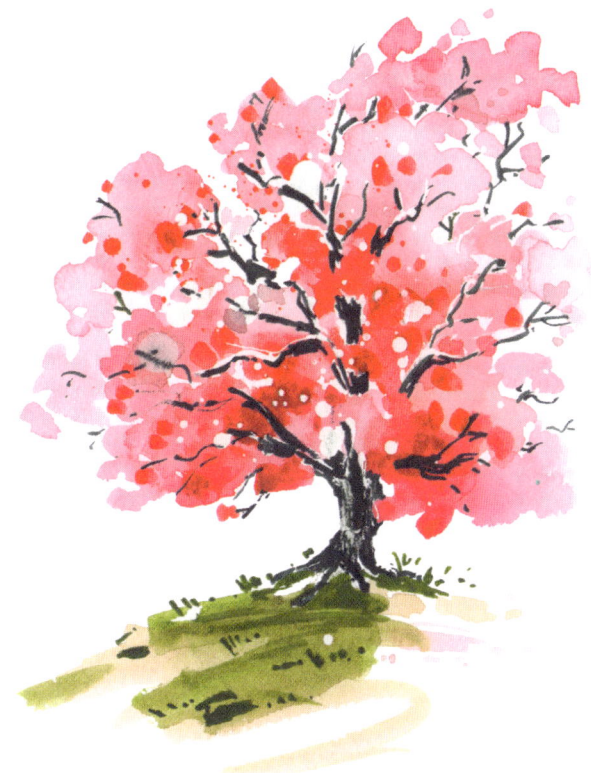

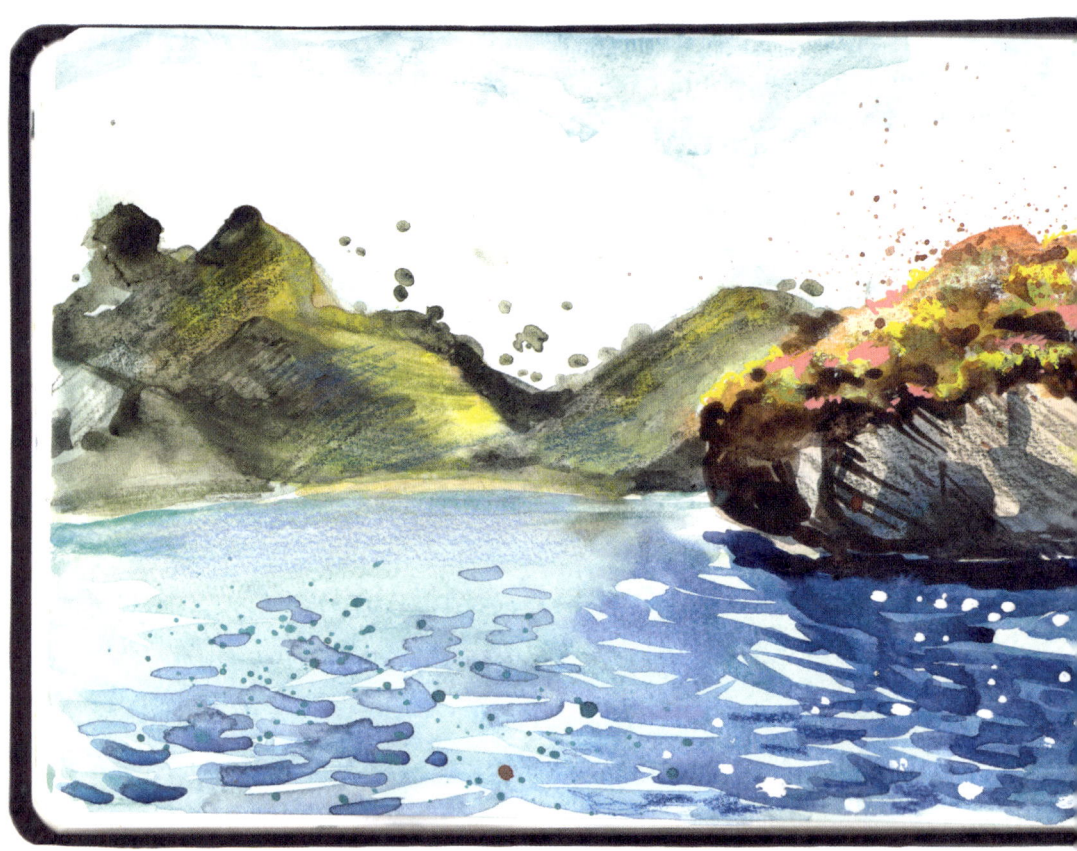

Sketchbooks

Painting in sketchbooks has lots of benefits, but the greatest one is that you create something precious that you will treasure for years to come.

I organize my sketchbooks by travel location, so they become a diary of a particular trip. It's not always possible to paint on location, so I usually take lots of photos and sometimes create small pencil sketches. I always have my sketchbook with me, because you never know when an opportunity will present itself to make a quick sketch of something.

When choosing a sketchbook there are a few things to consider: format, paper weight and paper quality. In general, landscape format works better for landscape painting (the clue is in the name!). I also find that smaller sketchbooks are perfect for teaching yourself to paint in simple shapes.

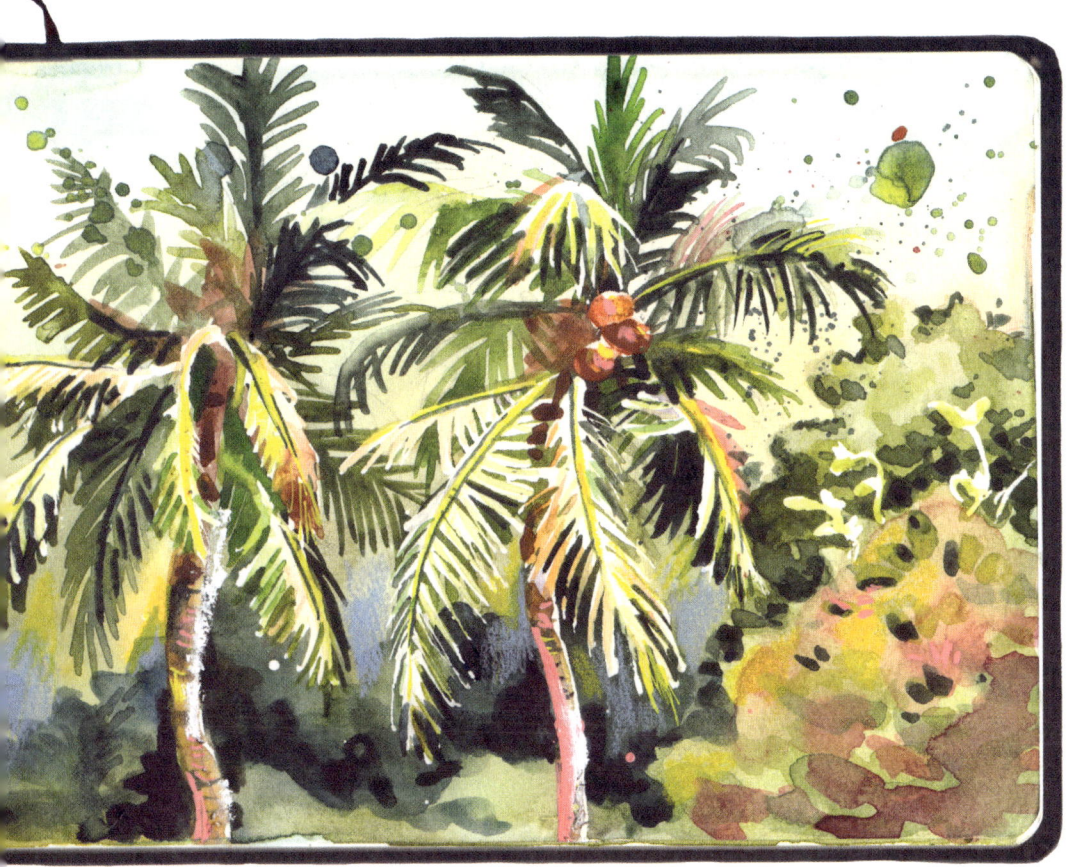

Paper weight is important too. If you are in the habit of laying lots of washes, your sketchbook should be at least 200 gsm (around 74 lb). You can get away with thinner paper if doing mixed media sketches, for example one layer of watercolour wash combined with ink pen.

In terms of paper quality, artist-grade-paper sketchbooks will be more pleasant to work with but are quite expensive.

Student-grade-paper sketchbooks still do the job effectively, and they remove the pressure of painting in an expensive sketchbook, because let's face it, even when you are pretty confident in your painting, you will still do the odd sketch that you aren't happy with. Nothing kills creativity more than the fear of ruining an expensive sketchbook, so I suggest starting out with a student-grade, 100 per cent cotton, acid-free sketchbook, and getting an artist-grade one when you feel more confident.

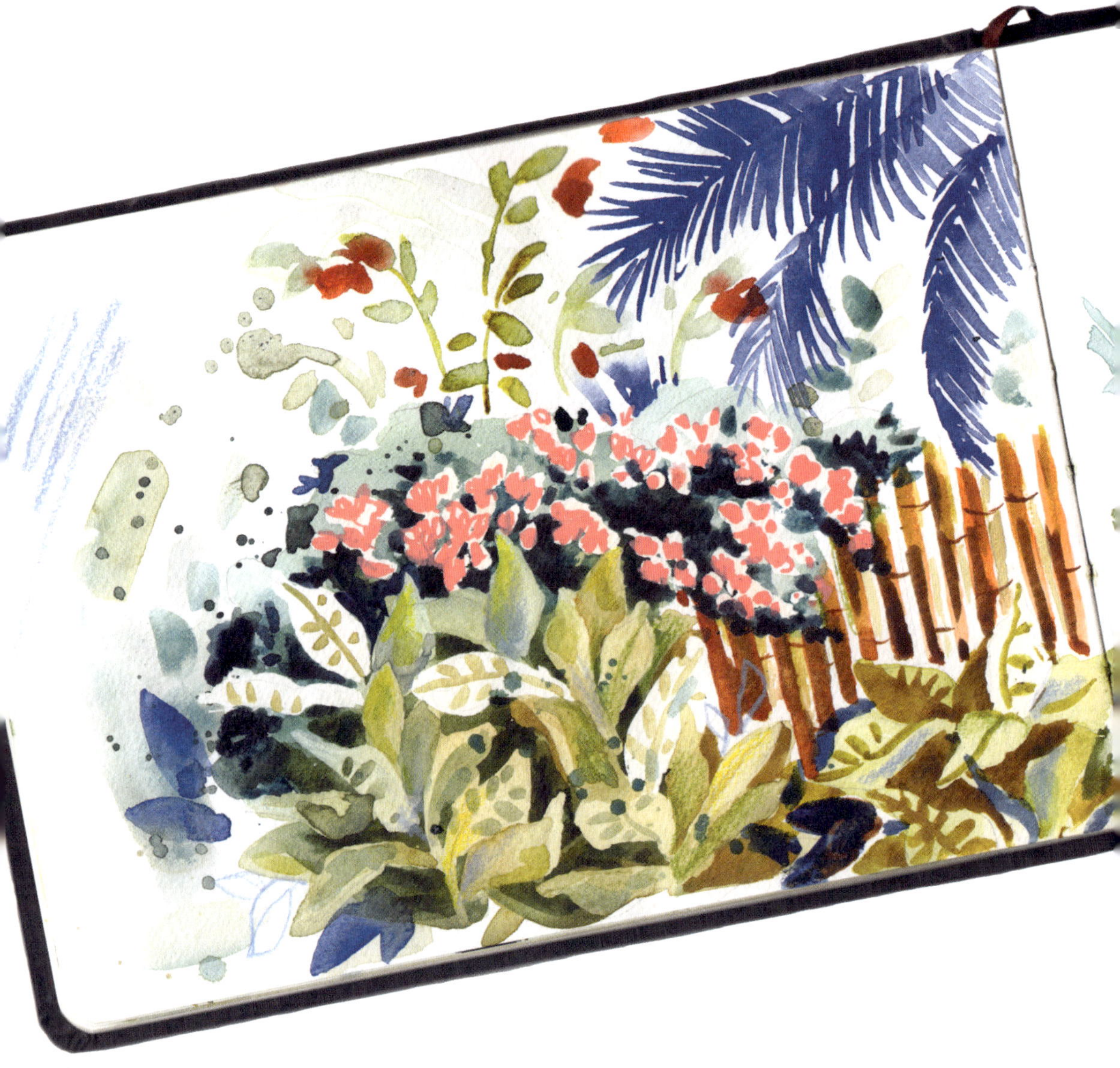

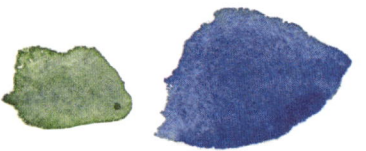

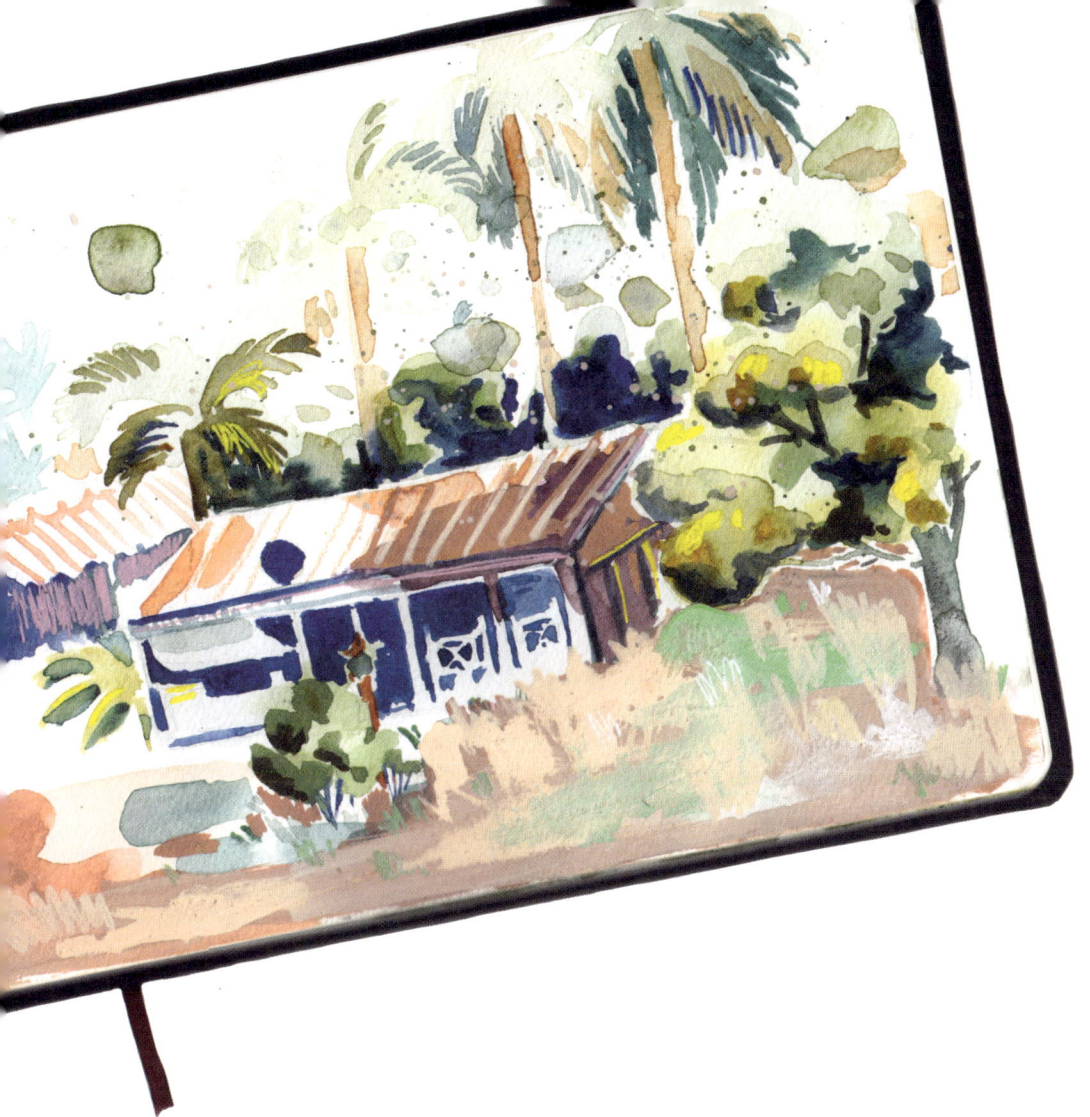

Capture the essence

Sketchbooks are for sketching. And sketching is all about capturing the essence rather than mirroring the reality too closely. You don't have to count the exact number of trees in a space and depict the correct amount, nor do you have to keep them in their original place if they are covering an interesting object that you'd like to paint. Your sketch will still reflect the place, even if a few details are slightly different from the reality.

Mixed media

I used to think of mixed media as an eclectic collage filled with all sorts of paints, pens and textures. In reality, anything you add to your watercolour painting makes it mixed media. You can enhance it with coloured pencils or add a few acrylic pen highlights; it doesn't make it any less of a watercolour painting. In fact, everything you add to your artwork makes it more unique and interesting.

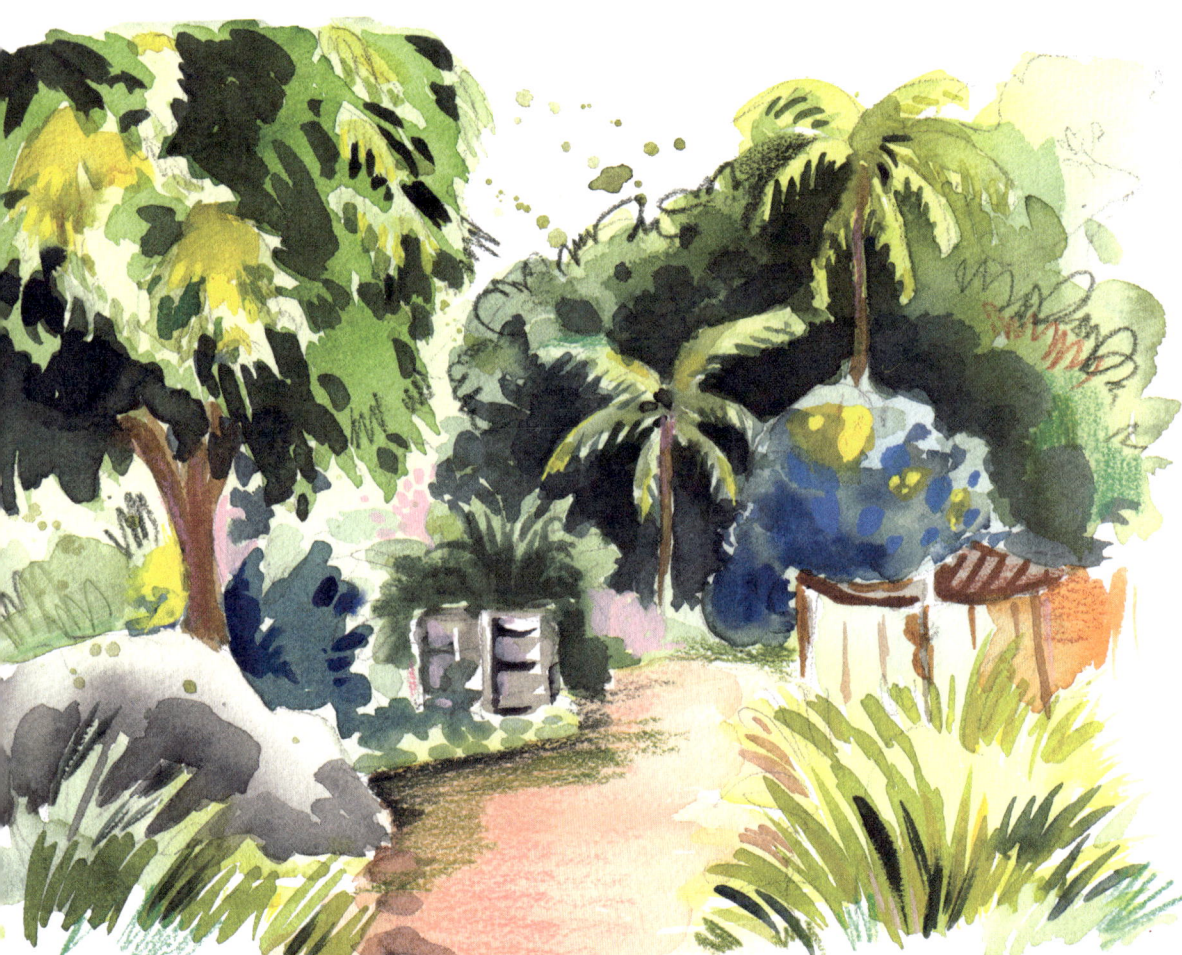

Watercolour and graphite

As well as using graphite pencils to make a sketch before painting with watercolour, you can combine a more detailed pencil rendering with colour washes. In this way, you don't have to worry about making your sketch too light, as the pencil marks become a stylistic choice. You can lay watercolour washes on top of pencil marks or the other way round.

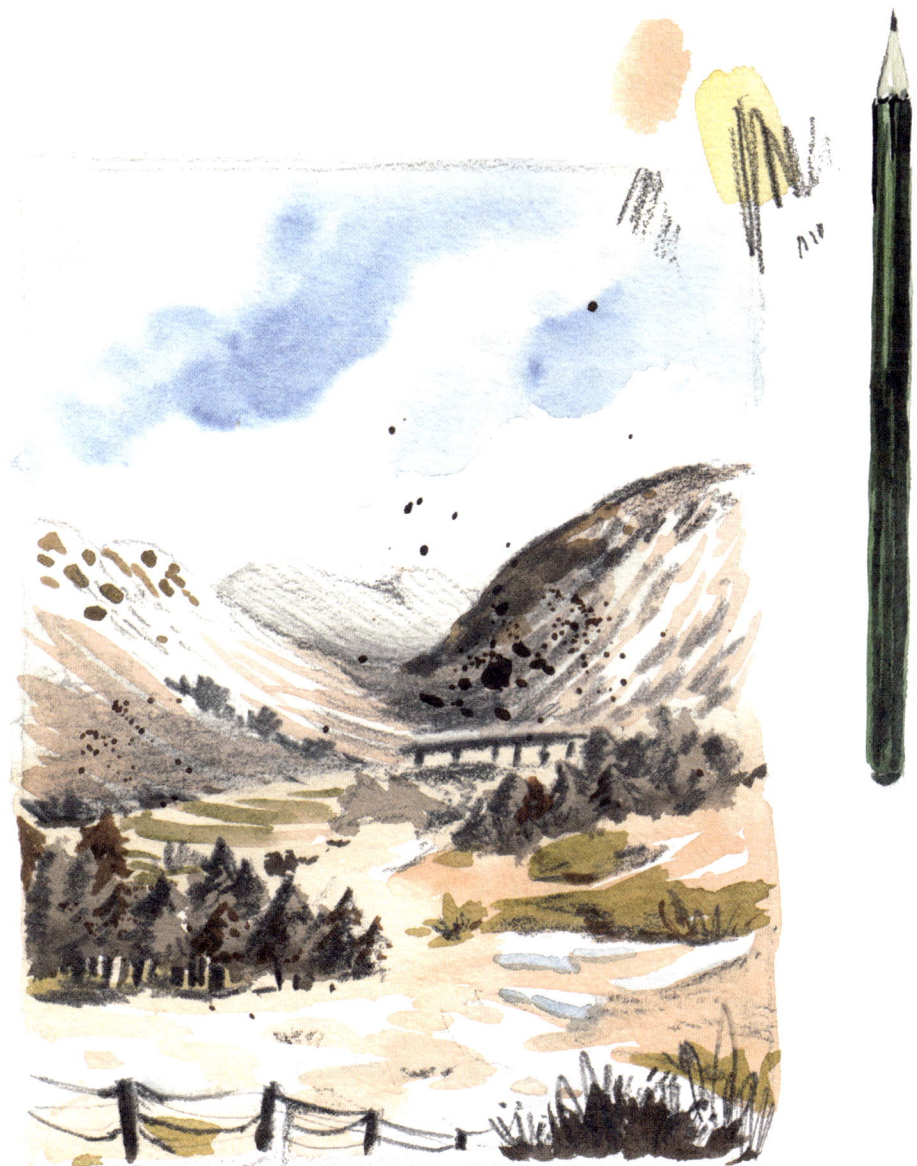

Watercolour and coloured pencils

My favourite trick to enhance watercolour is to use coloured pencils. Watercolour gets lighter and less saturated as it dries, sometimes losing the desired colour shade, but if you draw over it gently with a coloured pencil, you can make it more vibrant without making it too obvious that something else was added. I personally welcome the textures pencils can offer, and enjoy using them as part of a composition.

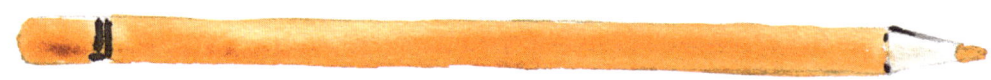

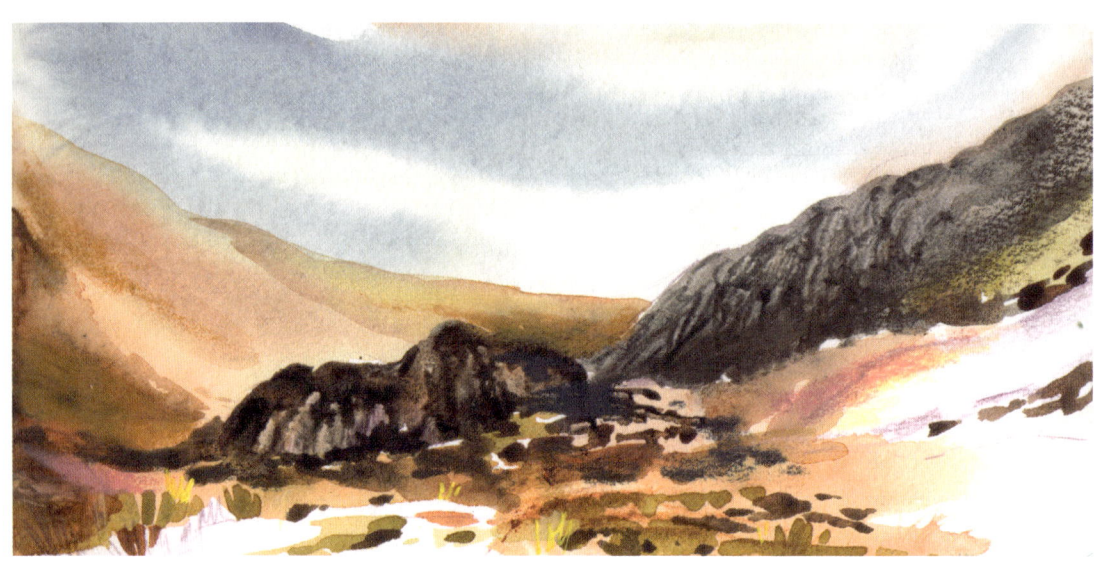

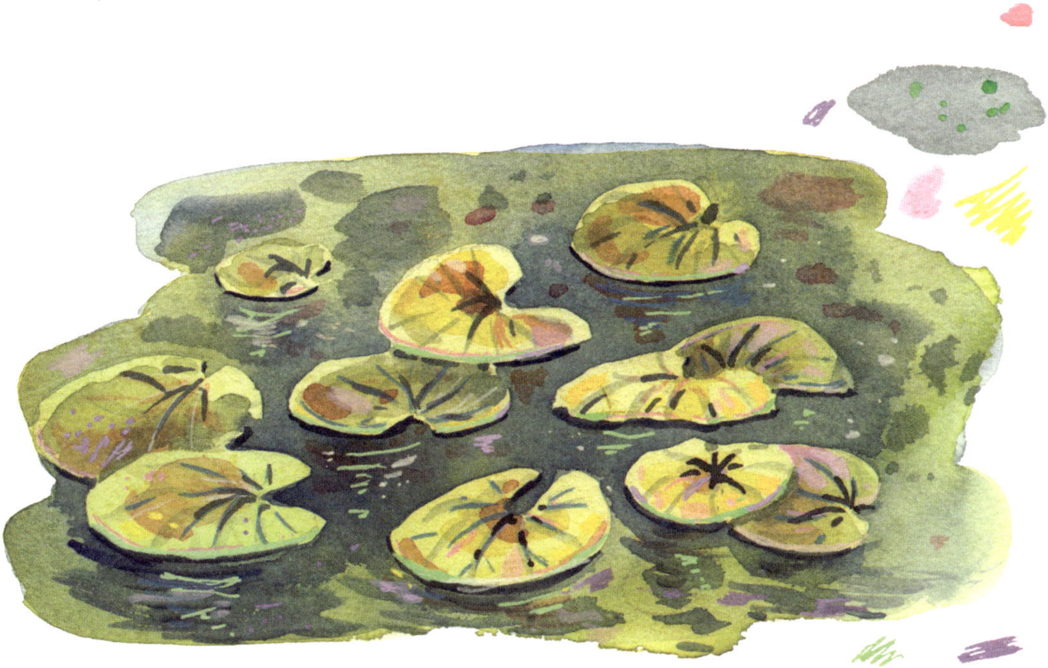

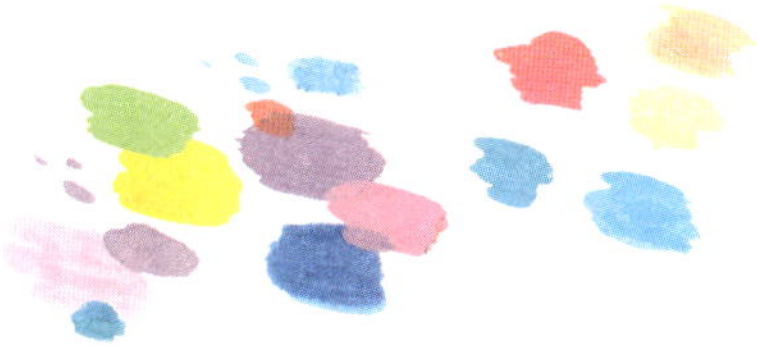

Watercolour and acrylic pens

I use acrylic pens when I want to add colours that are hard to make with any other media. It greatly enriches the colour palette of the painting, and it's also useful to be able to lay light colours on top of dark ones. Acrylic pens are very opaque, and no matter how many layers you create using them, they will keep the same colour and smooth texture.

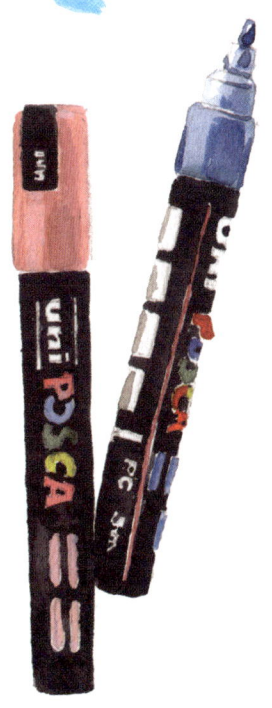

Watercolour and ink

Watercolour and ink is probably the most popular mixed media combination. The balance between the two can affect the style of your piece, whether the ink defines the structure or simply adds subtle detail.

Here are a few ideas to try.

In this example, a Japanese calligraphy pen was used to create an outline of the scenery and a watercolour wash was laid on top.

The ink from the pen was reactivated by the water and started mixing with the watercolour, creating darker tones.

In this sketch, brown ink was used to create shadowy areas on the trees, and the wash in general looks very similar to watercolour. It can perfectly disguise as watercolour while adding more saturated colour to the painting.

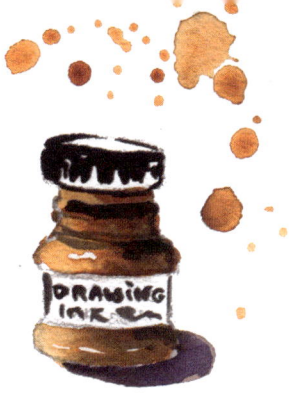

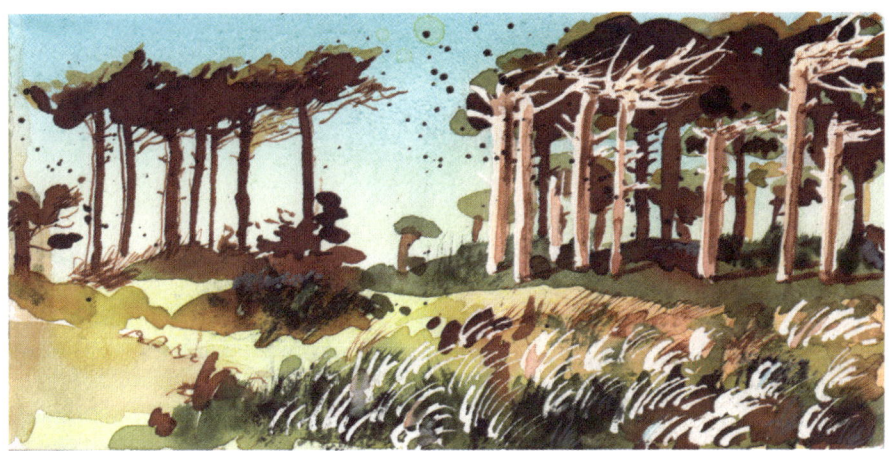

Below, different objects were painted as colour blocks and then a few details added with ink pen.

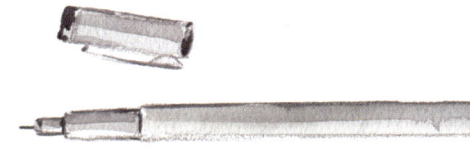

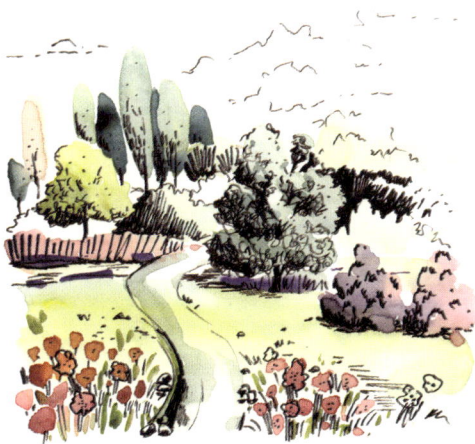

Note:

Every ink pen can be laid on top of a dry watercolour wash, but not every ink pen is waterproof, and if you lay wash over it, the ink can bleed into the water. Pigment liners, or fine liners, are the best to use under watercolour wash if you don't want the colour to run.

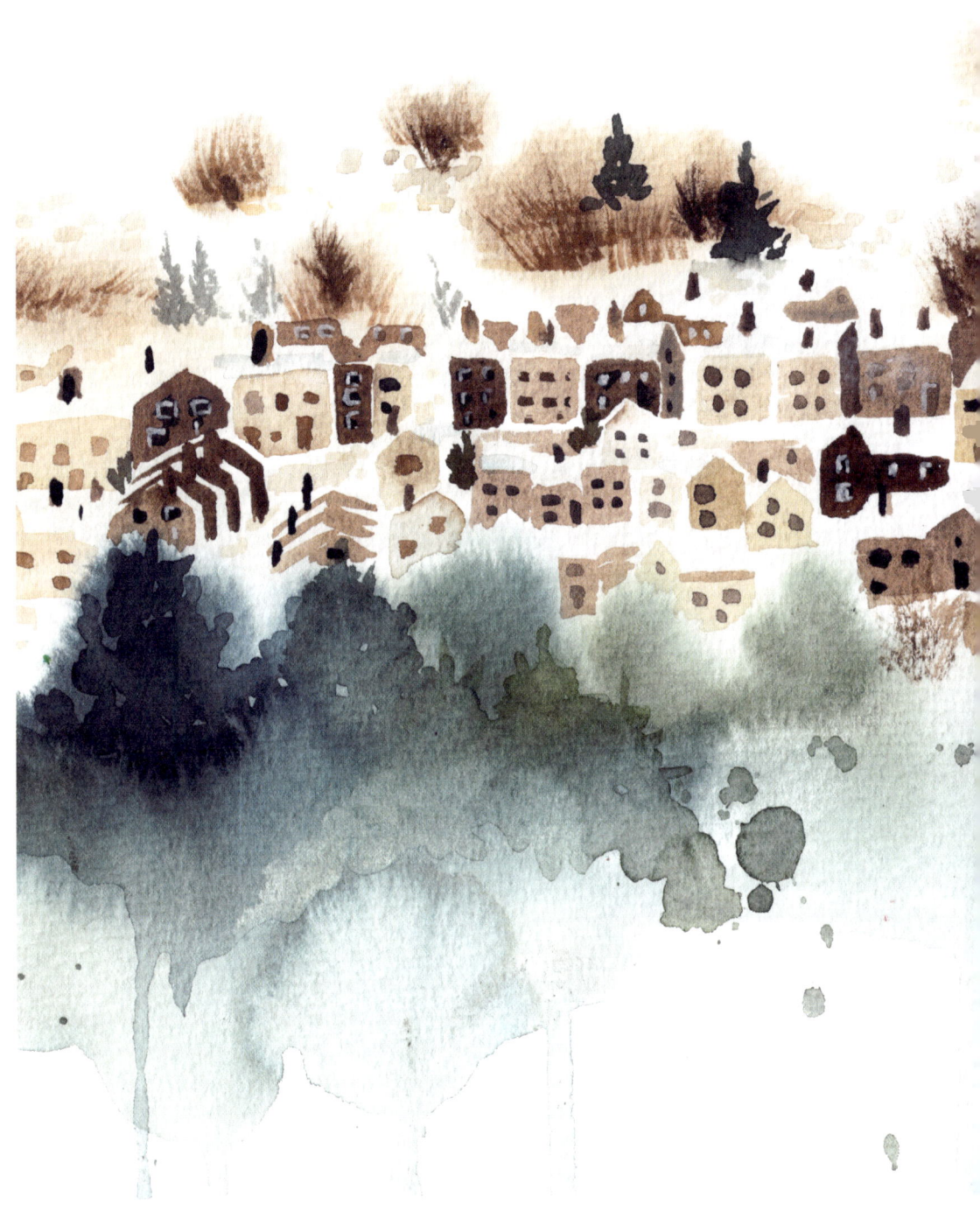

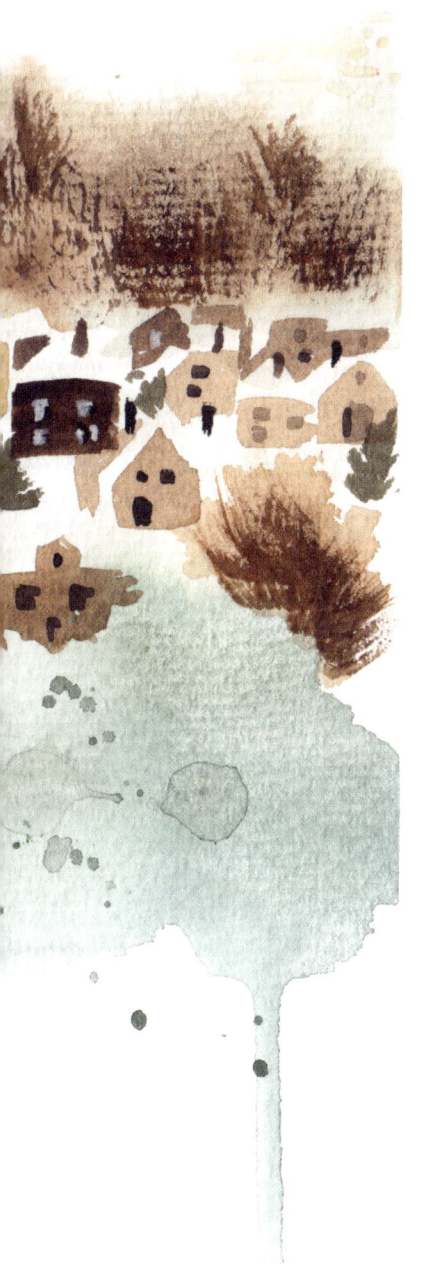

Final thoughts

When is the work finished?

It always feels to me that the work is finished before my last brushstroke. With this in mind, I try to stop before I want to because it is so easy to overwork with watercolours. Slightly unfinished work has more air in it, and more story than the one painted edge to edge and coloured in like a colouring book. Don't try to paint everything in one sitting; take a break, or come back to it the following day – you will be surprised how taking this space from it helps to bring a new perspective, and you will know exactly how to finish your painting.

Learn from the masters

Even with all the beautiful views around you, sometimes you can feel stuck and cannot put paint to paper. In this case, other artists can be a great source of inspiration. They have already solved problems of composition, colour and form, and it's been a lifelong tradition among artists to learn from the masters. Learning is not copying, if done the right way.

In his book *Steal Like an Artist*, Austin Kleon defines 'stealing' as a positive way to be inspired by your influences without copying their work. He promotes the practice of analysing other artists' thought processes and applying the same way of thinking to your work, as opposed to just visually copying the work. Look at paintings in galleries, museums, books and online, and think about what makes these particular works of art so appealing. Maybe it's an unusual colour combination, a skilfully utilized contrast, striking composition or originally placed brushstroke. Analysis of other works leads to a better understanding of your own work.

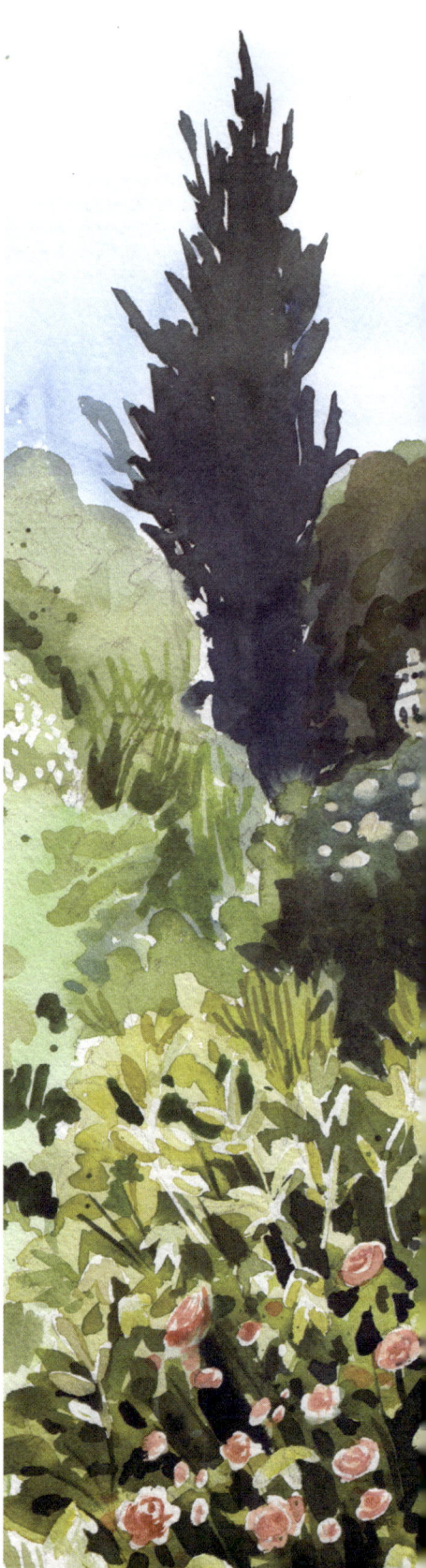

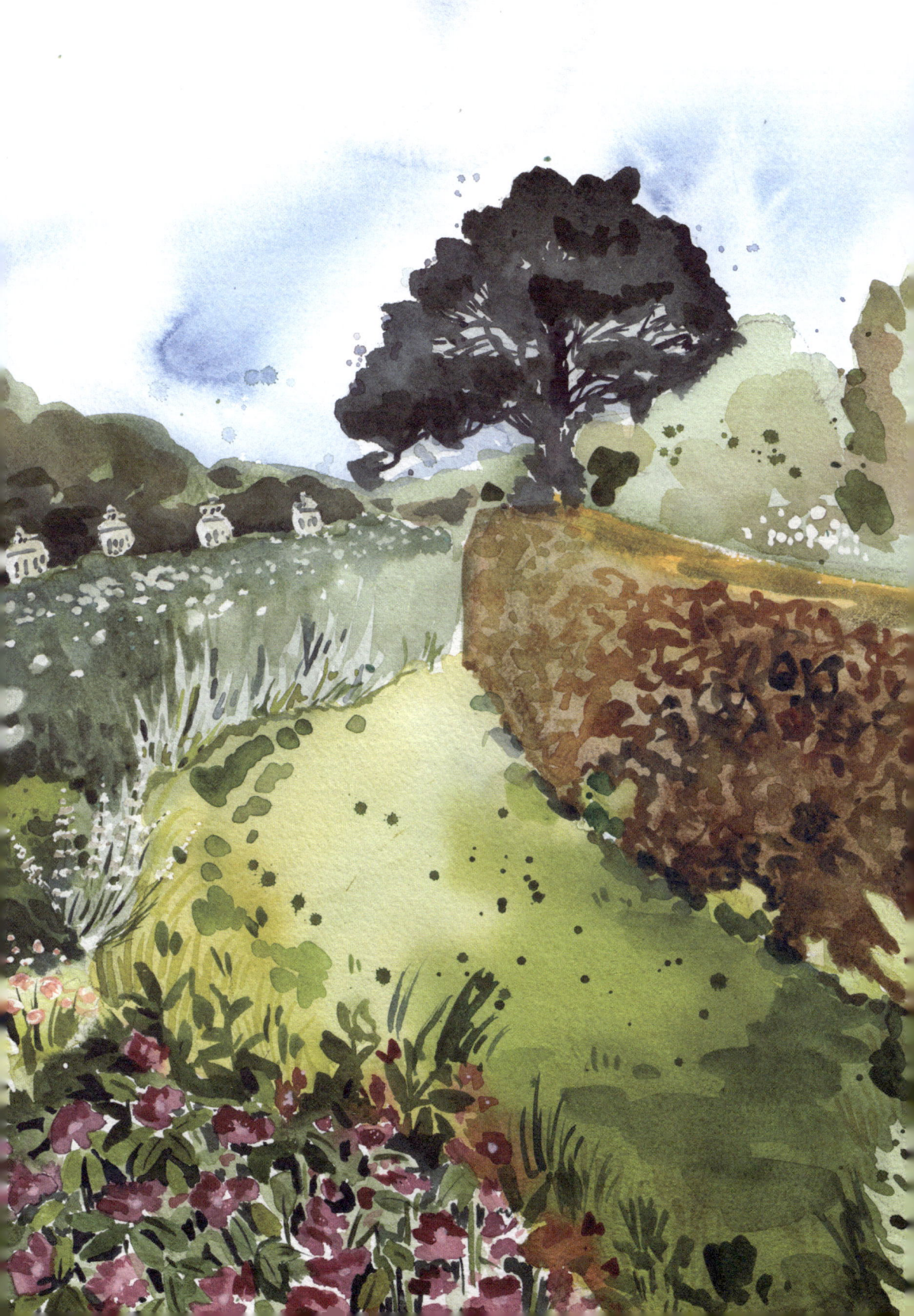

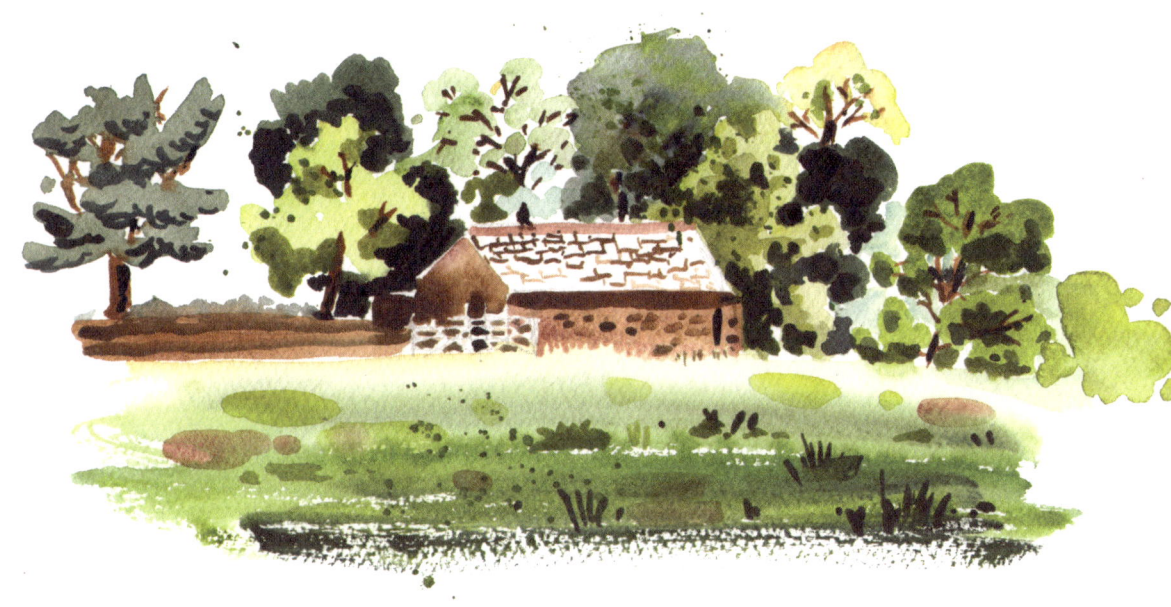

Getting out of a creative funk

When you paint for a while, you will unavoidably encounter creative funk. This not only comes from feeling stuck, but also when life just gets in the way – and it always does. At those times it feels like because you haven't painted in a while, you don't know where to start. Other times it feels as though you are getting nowhere with your work, and the comparison with other artists only serves to convince you that you will never be as good.

I have had enough creative funks now to know how to get out of them. The first step is to be kind to yourself. Remember that you are not painting for the results, but for the love of painting. You will never feel that you know enough or can create to the level you want. There are always things to improve, but this is the beauty of it – if there was an 'end' point, when you were 'finished', there would be no point carrying on. So you have to learn to love the process.

Secondly, start small. I always advise starting with swatches, small sketches, doodles – anything to get you warmed up. Every step counts, and you don't always have to plan to create a big artwork; you could just have a fun play with watercolour washes, which still counts as showing up and will eventually lead to a state of flow.

Ideally, have a dedicated space for your painting, filled with books, paintings and other inspirations and things that make you happy. When you make a space for creativity it will be easier to invite it into your life.

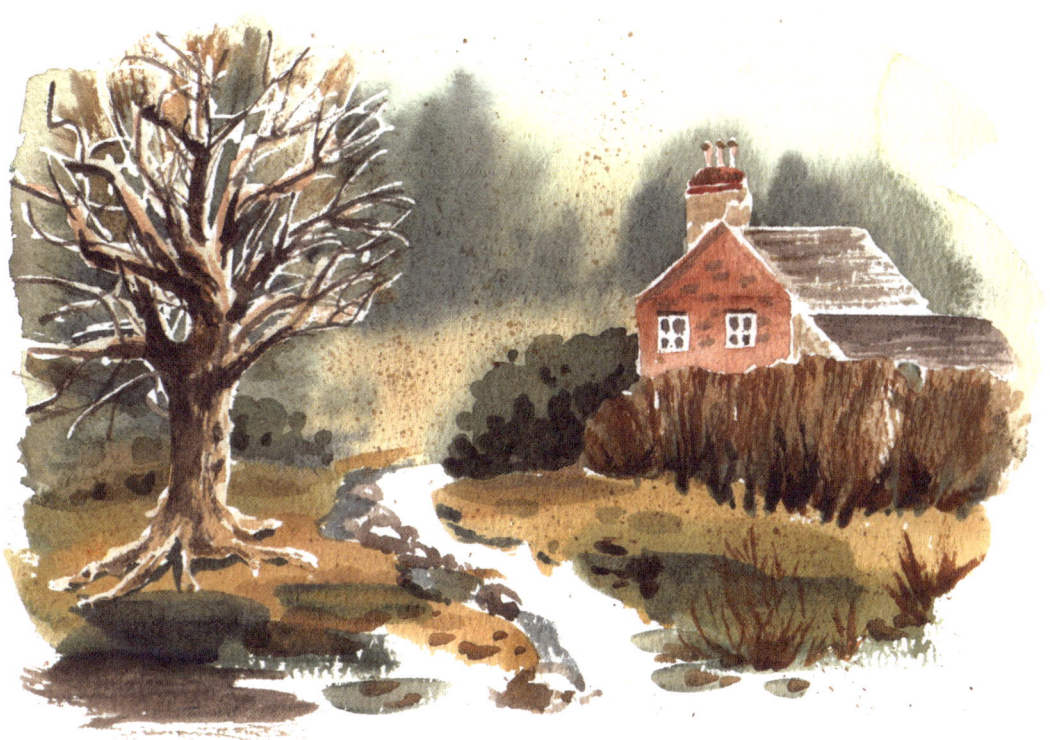

Find a way to just keep going, no matter how you feel, because eventually you will feel great, you just have to trust the process.

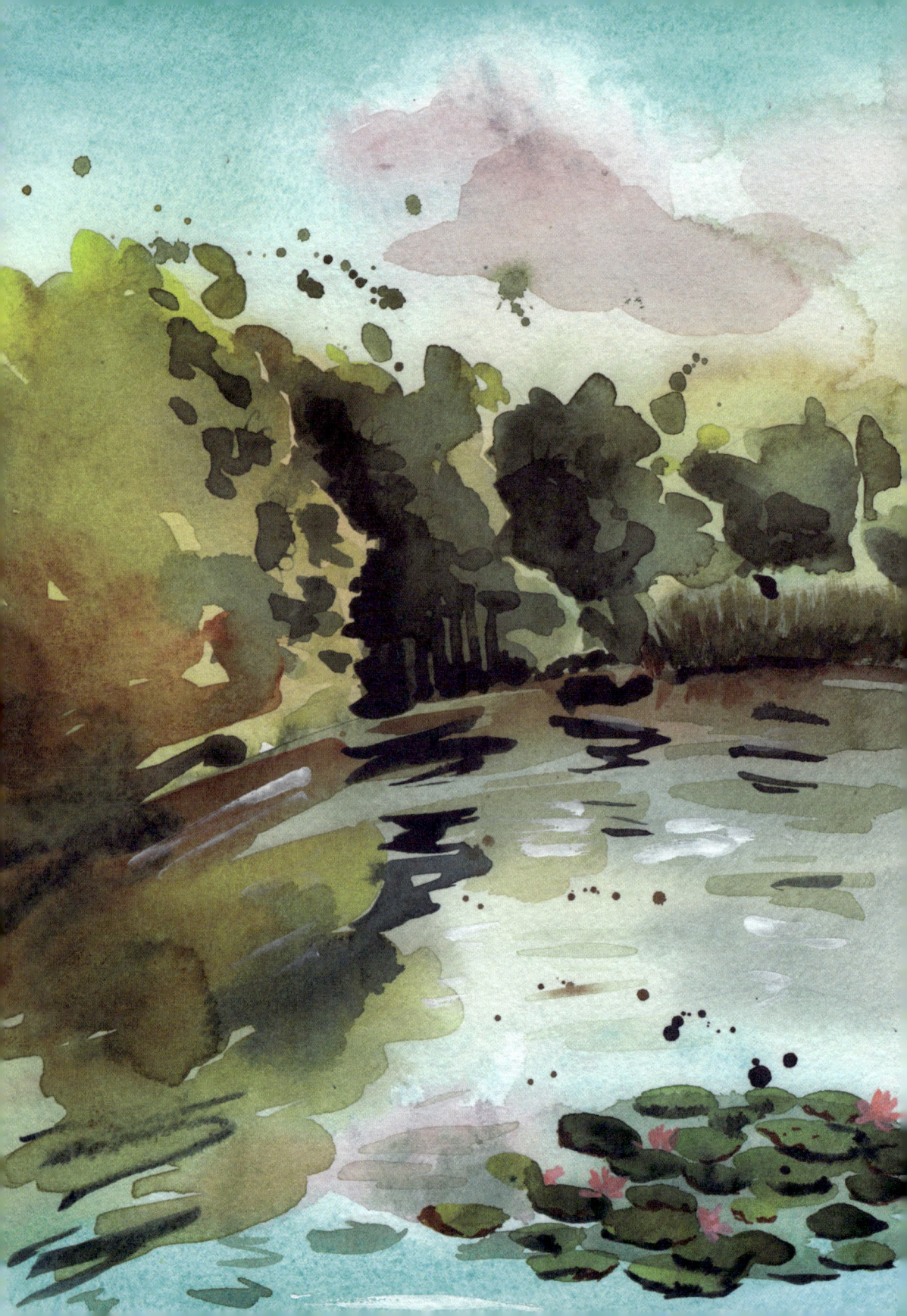

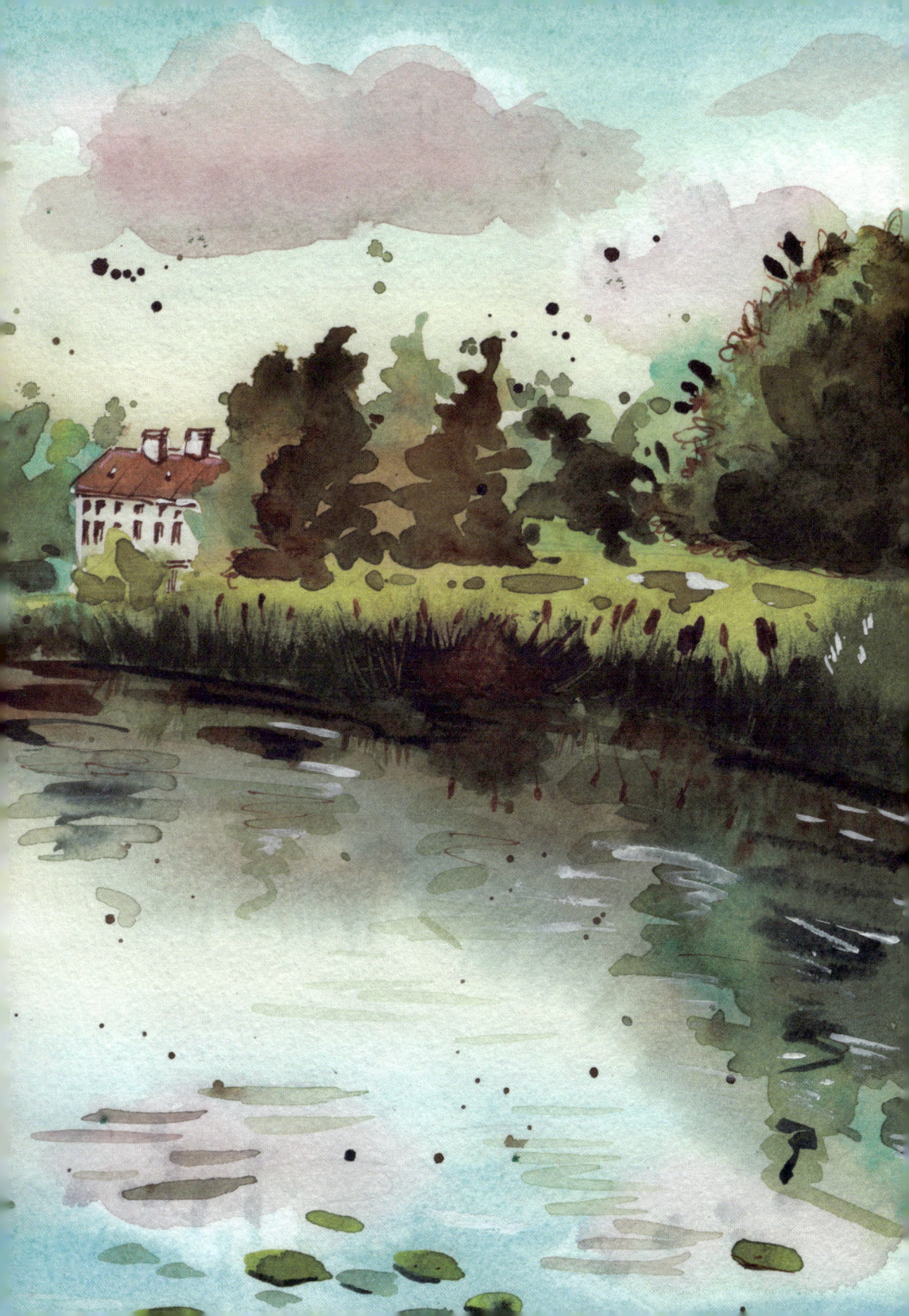

Further reading and resources

To read

Steal Like an Artist by Austin Kleon, Workman, 2012

Keep Going by Austin Kleon, Workman, 2019

Mastering Composition: Techniques and Principles to Dramatically Improve Your Painting by Ian Roberts, North Light Books, 2008

Sketching for the Absolute Beginner by Peter Cronin, Search Press, 2021

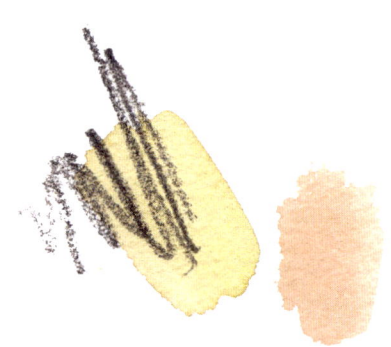

To use

PAPER BRANDS

Arches
Canson: Moulin du Roy
Canson: Heritage
Fabriano: Artistico
Hahnemühle: Cézanne

Handmade paper
Khadi
Panart Global

BRUSHES

My favourite travel brushes are from Fuumuui and are great to use when painting on the go. Use the code INGA20 to get a discount: https://fuumuui.com

SKETCHBOOKS

Khadi handmade paper sketchbook
Etchr Lab perfect sketchbook
Etchr Lab everyday sketchbook

Author acknowledgements

This is one of my favourite parts of the book to write, though I always feel a little nervous trying to find the right words to express just how grateful I am. This book would not have been possible without the incredible support, talent, and dedication of so many people who made a profound impact on both the project and me personally.

First and foremost, my deepest thanks to my favourite team in the world — the amazing people at Leaping Hare Press and Quarto Group. I am eternally grateful for your belief in me and your commitment to bringing meaningful work into the world. This is my third time working with you, and I couldn't be happier to create alongside a team that shares my vision.

Monica Perdoni, Editorial Director at Leaping Hare Press, thank you for being the spark at the beginning of every project. Your inspiration reaches me on both a professional and personal level, and I'm so thankful for your guidance. Charlotte Frost at Quarto Group, your editorial skill and calm leadership turn what could feel overwhelming into a smooth, steady journey from start to finish. Rachel Malig, thank you for your careful copyediting and for shaping the content with such skill and thoughtfulness. Nicki Davis — your design has brought the aesthetic of this book to life in the most beautiful way.

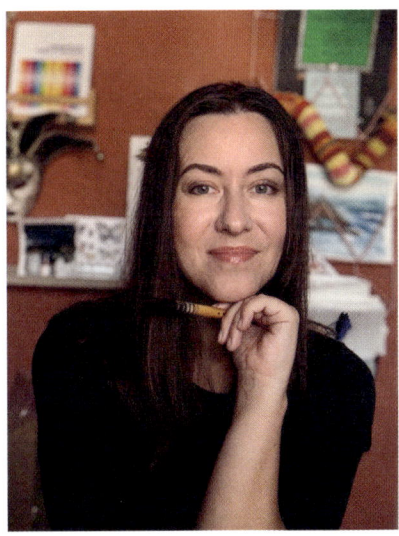

And, of course, to those closest to me, who are part of my every day, and without whom none of this would matter. My husband, Arūnas — my friend, my partner, my support, and my love — thank you for being by my side through everything. My son, Lukas, you're growing up so fast into such a kind, intelligent young man. You inspire me every single day. And of course my parents, Irina and Alfred, thank you for teaching me that I am enough, that results come through doing, and that wherever you land in life is okay, as long as you keep putting an effort.

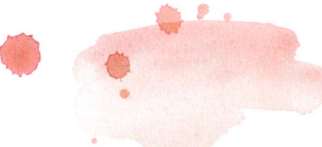

Index

Quarto

First published in 2026 by Leaping Hare Press,
an imprint of The Quarto Group.
One Triptych Place, London, SE1 9SH,
United Kingdom
T (0)20 7700 9000
www.Quarto.com

EEA Representation, WTS Tax d.o.o., Žanova ulica 3, 4000 Kranj, Slovenia
www.wts-tax.si

A catalogue record for this book is available from the British Library.

ISBN 978-1-83600-818-7
Ebook ISBN 978-1-83600-819-4

10 9 8 7 6 5 4 3 2 1

Design by Nicki Davis

Assistant Editor: Izzy Toner
Editorial Director: Monica Perdoni
Senior Editor: Charlotte Frost
Senior Designer: Renata Latipova
Senior Production Controller: Rohana Yusof

Printed in Guangdong, China TT112025

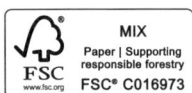